RISE UP TO LIFE

Rise up to Life

A BIOGRAPHY OF HOWARD WALTER FLOREY
WHO GAVE PENICILLIN TO THE WORLD

BY LENNARD BICKEL

WITH A FOREWORD BY
SIR ROBERT MENZIES

ANGUS AND ROBERTSON

First published in 1972 by
ANGUS AND ROBERTSON (U.K.) LTD
2 Fisher Street, London WC1
102 Glover Street, Cremorne, Sydney
107 Elizabeth Street, Melbourne
89 Anson Road, Singapore

© Lennard Bickel 1972

0 207 95454 2

Printed in Great Britain by
Ebenezer Baylis and Son Limited
The Trinity Press
Worcester and London

TO: THE OXFORD TEAM

FOREWORD

HOWARD FLOREY WAS A GREAT MAN AND IT IS HARD TO
find the words to do justice to him. It is, or should be, unnecessary
to describe his vast contributions to medicine and to science;
these are already a part of history. But one can pay tribute to the
qualities which made them possible. He had the essential attributes
of greatness: courage, integrity, tremendous drive and an un-
swerving sense of direction. Lack of any one of these often renders
high intellectual achievements, even genius, ineffectual, but
Florey possessed them to a degree which made the best of his own
great gifts and served to guide and inspire the talented collaborators who surrounded him.

It was Florey's courage which made penicillin therapy an
actuality. Undaunted by his failure to get enough penicillin
produced commercially for a therapeutic trial, he turned a
university department into a factory against every sort of difficulty and in the middle of a world war. He must have known the
consequences of failure, but he also knew the consequences of
success.

His integrity was apparent to everyone who knew him. He was
completely free from cant, humbug and pretentiousness, and, like
a breath of fresh air in a stuffy room, he could dispel the academic
pretences which are so stifling to scientific research. If he did not
know something, he said so, and he was equally ruthless towards
the ignorance of others. When asked his opinion of some cherished

vii

plan or theory, he would give it with complete honesty, usually in words of one syllable, and he was usually right. He wasted little of his own time and none of other people's.

His sense of direction enabled him to follow his chosen path which was truly the advancement of science, despite the endless diversions and distractions which arose from his own successes and from the high offices which he held and despite the fog of bureaucracy which engulfs every great innovator in our modern society.

It is a sad fact that the heroes of one's youth become tarnished when seen through the eyes of advancing age. But the admiration and respect which I felt when I first met Florey more than thirty years ago have increased with every year that has passed, and, like so many others, I am grateful for the privilege of having known him.

SIR ROBERT MENZIES

By kind permission—
first published,
The Lancet, London. 2/3/1968

CONTENTS

THIS BOOK IS THE STORY OF A MAN WHOSE LIFE AND WORK affected the welfare of the whole world. The idea for the book began when a cleaning lady, who also made the tea, at the John Curtin School of Medical Research in Canberra, gave her last two dollars as the first contribution to a memorial fund when she heard that the people to whom she served the tea were planning to honour Lord Florey. 'I knew he was the man who saved my life because he made penicillin work. But he was also very human and warm, and a great man, so I gave him my last two dollars, until next pay day.' Miss Emma Burkervisc was a displaced person from Latvia who spent six years in a camp in Germany after the Second World War. During those years penicillin was used to save her life. On a visit to the John Curtin centre in 1966, Florey spoke to Miss Burkervisc as she stood with her mop and bucket in a corridor.

This book is written for her and others like her around the world who did not know the man to whom they owe their lives. It is not a work of reference, but the story of a man and what he did. There is no bibliography because the literature on penicillin and the resultant antibiotics—other than the first historical papers referred to in the text—is too voluminous to be manageable and is continually expanding.

The accomplishment of this story is owed to the goodwill and kindness of people in three continents, as well as to the co-operation and support of many organizations and individuals; they are so numerous that recognition of every one is impracticable in these pages. The debt to them all is profound; but there are special people whose names must be mentioned in gratitude since, without their goodwill, the story of Howard Florey could not be told.

Acknowledgment is especially due to Lady Margaret Florey, for trust and immense kindness; to Florey's only daughter, Mrs John McMichael and her husband in Edinburgh; his son, Dr Charles D. V. Florey; and to those members of the inner circle of the Oxford team who have not been blessed enough for what they achieved—Dr Norman G. Heatley, for his friendship, advice and unlimited patience; Professor Sir Ernst Chain, of Imperial College, London, for guidance and insight; Professor E. P. Abraham, the author of Florey's memorial in the Proceedings of the Royal Society; Dr Gordon Sanders and those of the staff at the Dunn School who provided intimate pictures of Florey the man and the scientist. Not least is acknowledgment of debt to be made to Florey's long-term friend, Professor Robert Webb, and to the boy of fourteen who became his man for life—James Kent.

Special debts are owed to Lord Adrian and Sir Alan Drury of Cambridge; to Lord Carrington and the late Sir Lawrence Bragg; to Professor Brian Maegraith of Liverpool; especially to Dr C. M. Fletcher of London, along with Dr J. M. Barnes; and to the great kindness of Professor H. H. Harris; Dr P. L. Bazeley; Dr Dennis Bodenham; as well as to the late Professor Sir Harold Raistrick; and to Professor R. J. V. Pulvertaft of Dorset; and Dr E. N. C. Crawford of Magdalen College, Oxford.

Acknowledgment is here made to officers of the Medical Research Council, and help was forthcoming from the staff of the Royal Society, as well as from many librarians—especially Mr M. W. Davies of the Royal Army Medical College, Millbank. The list is extensive and applies to many sources throughout America, Australia and Europe. In Stockholm, the *Nobelstift-elsen*, through Mme Ehren, gave every help. In the United States, officials in charge of the nation's archives, the Army Medical History group, the Surgeon General's office, plus executives and scientists in some of the leading drug houses made valuable contributions.

AUTHOR'S NOTE											xiii

Among the American pioneers of penicillin, the spirit to assist
with this book was unstinted; my thanks go especially to Dr
Robert Coghill, formerly of the Northern Regional Research
Laboratories, at Peoria, Illinois, USA, and to other officers there,
including Dr Dwight Miller for generous help; Dr Wallace
Herrell, who worked in the Mayo Clinic; Dr Gladys Hobby of
the first penicillin team in New York; Dr Max Tishler; Dr
William Gibson of Vancouver; Dr Lewis H. Sarett; Dr Vannevar
Bush; and Mrs John Fulton of New Haven in particular. These
are among the many people who have given generously of time
and memory.

The confused German story, in the appendix of this book,
could not have been unravelled without the efforts of scientists
with the Bayerwerken laboratories at Leverkusen, the help of
Professor Bernhauer, Dr Heinz Öppinger and officials of the
German Federal Republic archives services, specifically Dr Zoske
in Freiburg. The help of the Australian embassy in Bonn was
invaluable.

The list in Australia is no less lengthy and thanks are due to
Florey's niece, Dr Joan Gardner, his sister-in-law Mrs Emmeline
Brebner and his lifelong friend, Mrs Molly Bowen of Adelaide.
I am also indebted to Sir Robert Menzies; the Rt. Hon. John
Gorton; Sir Marcus Oliphant, now Governor of South Australia;
to Professors R. D. Wright of Melbourne; G. M. Badger of
Adelaide; Frank Fenner of the John Curtin School; Bede Morris
of the same institution; G. J. V. Nossal and David Grey of Mel-
bourne; and no less to Sir Macfarlane Burnet; the late Sir Douglas
Copland; Sir John Crawford, Vice-Chancellor of the Australian
National University, as well as the Chancellor, Dr H. C. Coombs.
Sir Roland Wilson and Sir Hugh Ennor must be thanked along
with Mr and Mrs Robert Edwards of Adelaide; Mr Neville
Whiffen of Abbots, Kurnell; especially Mrs Pauline Fanning of
the National Library of Australia and those many librarians and
officers of different organizations and pharmaceutical houses
whose research was crucial. My thanks also go to my own wife,
Pauline, without whose application this work would not have
been completed.

The confidence and support of the Commonwealth Literary

Board, Australia, were also necessary to the pursuit of the research and completion of the work. To all these, I express my appreciation.

LENNARD BICKEL
London, January 1972

THERE HAD BEEN HEAVY RAIN DURING THE NIGHT AND THE February day dawned in mist across the sodden Oxfordshire countryside, slate-grey with the cold of midwinter. When he woke he felt too ill and too depressed to go to the laboratory and so he whiled the morning away.

For sixteen years he had carried a time-bomb in his breast, and after lunch on that last day it exploded. The coronary was massive and left him no chance of recovery. The borrowed time on which he had lived for so long had run out. He sank into coma and in the evening his heart ceased to beat and the lines of pain and long life eased from his face.

The end came to Lord Florey in his rooms at the Provost's Lodgings in Oxford's stately Queen's College, on the opposite side of the world from South Australia where he had been born, beneath the corrugated iron roof of a rough stone cottage—sixty-nine years earlier, the only son of a migrant bootmaker.

Howard Walter Florey died a revered statesman of science, a peer of the British realm, an immediate past-President of the Royal Society, Chancellor of the Australian National University, Nobel Laureate, holder of hundreds of awards, medals, degrees and distinctions, and the man who had bequeathed penicillin to the world.

In the last thirty years of his life, the three decades spanning the middle of this century, he had been the epicentre of a medical revolution—marked by furious drive, imagination and initiative —which had opened a golden age of healing in the midst of the

most violent war in history; and while he had not been directly
motivated by a crusading spirit to relieve human suffering but
rather by a direct scientific challenge to intellect, he had opened
the floodgates to the tide of substances from the astonishing
micro-world from which was drawn the armament of the antibiotic age.

Such was his impact on clinical practice and his contributions to
frontier knowledge in medical science that at the memorial
service in Westminster Abbey Lord Adrian—himself a Nobel
laureate—said of him in his reedy voice,

'*He was one of the great leaders of medical science . . . millions owe
their very lives to him, and to what he did . . . Florey is to be honoured
as were Pasteur and Jenner and Lister.*'

Florey had always been ready to acknowledge the debt owed to
the men of science who had gone before him, and he had always
paid his due to the fortune which had touched his work. Jenner
had avoided untold suffering and disfigurement with his cow-
pox vaccinations without knowing the complex factors of
immunology that were involved, while Lister's aseptic surgery
had lessened some of the barbarism of earlier days when fearsome
operations were performed in morning coats and physicians
attended childbirth with unwashed hands carrying the agents of
puerperal fever. Along with these, the progress which flowed from
Louis Pasteur's stupendous achievements had brought much
advance in the prevention of infectious disease by the age-old
enemies of human health, the micro-organisms.

By the time Howard Florey began his medical research career
in the early 1920s, the agents of the major contagious diseases had
been identified and generally classified; but although medical
science knew the enemy by name and by pathological effect, and
could culture colonies and observe their morphology, the practising clinician was still powerless to combat deep-seated infection and was totally without any systemic substance which would
attack the thriving bacteria and remain passive against human cells.

When Florey started his research, nearly fifty years had passed
since the import of Pasteur's findings had dawned upon medical

consciousness—the first indication that the answer to systemic infection by bacteria was hidden in the world of micro-organisms.

This half-century had also brought heartening advances with vaccines, serums and the diphtheria anti-toxins and a few specifics such as Ehrlich's arsenic treatment of syphilis, quinine against malaria and the blessing of digitalis. Yet there had appeared no answer to the invading organisms which had plagued humanity throughout history. In the second decade of this century, as in all others that had gone before, the medical practitioner still resorted in the face of rioting bacterial infection to false optimism, reassurance in the hope that immunological response would overpower the infection, and to any measures that offered partial relief to the suffering patient. Beyond that they were powerless— and the evidence of their impotence could be seen in any crowded infectious diseases ward in the public hospitals.

For the generation of the day, scarlet fever, meningitis, rheumatic fever, diphtheria, bacterial heart infection, septicaemia and osteomyelitis were words of doom. The fear of infection haunted all operations, minor and major, and attended maternity wards with the spectre of puerperal fever and general sepsis. Pneumonia, in which death claimed one-third of the sufferers, cholera and tuberculosis, known as consumption, were as common as carbuncles and chronic catarrh.

That same generation, understandably, did not consider itself to be living in a medically backward age but it was, in fact, an age of clinical tragedy, for the answers to these dread diseases had been indicated in previous decades. Although the clues had been recorded in the literature for Florey to exhume some twenty years later, medicine stuck to its well-beaten trails. Consequently, millions of children died each year from bacterial invasion; at least one-half of the recorded deaths under the age of six were attributed to infectious diseases. In adult life, the toll was almost as heavy until the first impact of the new sulphonamides and their derivatives was registered in the late 1930s.

Only now can the enormity of that tragedy be realized; for, not only were the incidences of bacterial infection far more numerous than today, they were also far more dangerous, with the causative agents brought to high virulence by continual

2

passaging through living systems. Only now can the lack of
control over infection be clearly seen for the barrier it was to
imaginative and sophisticated surgery. Correction of cardiac
defects and organ transplantation were unheard of and, in plastic
surgery, the first sterile burn wounds were not achieved until the
1940s when Florey handed a salt-spoon amount of muddy-
brown powder to a young Royal Air Force surgeon.

It was, then, a grimly serious situation which Florey's young
mind had to face. The mortality rates from the major infections
ranged from 10% to 100% in the more serious systemic infections, with the only form of treatment being a hazardous and
extremely difficult use of animal antibody preparation, relevant to
only a small minority of cases.

For the more serious illnesses such as pneumonia, septicaemia or
subacute endocarditis, the picture was as black as it had been a
hundred years earlier—before Pasteur—with the possible exception of the supportive therapy of intravenous transfusions. In the
even more widespread venereal diseases—then little discussed in
public as a social issue—infection by the syphilis spirochaete and
the organisms of gonorrhoea received only crude treatment by
long-term injection of arsenic preparations or the primitive
irrigation of the urethra with a fluid antiseptic. Hidden from most
western eyes, in the peoples of the less privileged nations, were
the teeming cases of yaws, a disease caused by a close relative of
the syphilis organism. Yet this was all changed in a few brief
years by Florey's decisions and actions.

In his eulogy in Westminster Abbey, Lord Adrian said,

> Florey inspired the research and made it succeed. His persistence
> and courage made him the central figure of that attack;
> although he was always embarrassed by praise which did not
> include his colleagues, when he came to work with a team he
> could not help but be the leader . . . we have still to adjust our
> ideas to the extent of the revolution in medical treatment that
> Florey brought to success.

His group—the Oxford team—was small by today's standards,

but their achievements were monumental and their names have
gone into medical annals even if they are not recalled by the
public. Florey led them in a quantum leap into new healing
ability, new knowledge and understanding. Together they turned
the doctor's surgery into a place of healing and opened up a rich
world of therapeutic substances. They showed that the mites of
the soil and fungal life possessed chemical manufacturing skills
which human chemists still cannot match. With Florey's leadership they threw back shutters on the behaviour of human tissue
and biological defence mechanisms.

Their monumental leap took chemotherapy far beyond Fleming's dream of an antiseptic for infected wounds to the wholesale
slaughter of bacteria in deep-seated infection and, by sparking the
gold rush of research on a global scale, revolutionized the pattern
of world disease.

Like a wet sponge on a blackboard, penicillin and the subsequent antibiotics wiped away the dread of pneumonia, meningitis, tuberculosis, anthrax, septicaemia, syphilis and the feared
childbed fever.

The triumph of this greatest of the antibiotics came from a
marrying of pathology, physiology and chemistry in precisely
planned experimentation based on the fusion of disciplines; and
it all had its beginning on the day in 1910 when a tousle-headed
lad nick-named 'Floss' ran home from school, his head full of the
fire of resolve, imparted by his chemistry master and announced
that he would devote his life to research. His sister, Hilda Florey,
among the few women medical students of the time, had smiled
and asked him, 'Do you want to be some sort of Pasteur?'

More than fifty years later, sitting in the grounds of the great
university he helped to create in Canberra, Florey recalled that
moment. 'Until then', he said, 'I had never heard the name of
Pasteur.'

DO NOT FEAR TO DEFEND NEW IDEAS, EVEN THE MOST revolutionary. Your own faith is what counts most. Have courage to admit an error as soon as you have proved to yourself that your idea is wrong: and remember always that some ideas that seem dead and buried may at one time or another rise up to life again, more vital than ever before.

Louis Pasteur, in advice to his students

FLUCTUATING
FORTUNES

CHAPTER I

IT WAS MIDWINTER IN EARLY 1922 WHEN HOWARD FLOREY
first came to the city where he was to reveal the therapeutic power
of penicillin and lead the work which changed the pattern of
disease in the world.

Oxford in the murk of a February day was strange to his
Australian eye. Gusts of sleet swept the streets filled with young
people, horse-drawn carts and coughing lorries. Bright lights
gleamed on the dark pavements from shop windows and book-
stores, full of the animated talk and warmth of students. Like all
England the university city was deep in the reaction that came with
the aftermath of the Great War—flappers and Oxford 'bags',
coloured scarves and daring stunts.

This was Oxford, city of life and colour, as Howard Florey
first saw it when he carried his bag from the railway station to his
room at Magdalen, the college where eventually his and other
names would be engraved in stone, commemorating service to the
well-being of humanity. But on this cold February day the tribute
was then three decades away and Florey's only distinction on the
day of his arrival at Oxford was that he had graduated in medicine
two months previously in far-off Adelaide and had been named
the 1921 Rhodes Scholar for South Australia. He had no standing,
no wealth beyond the grant money which would have to see
him through the first years and was a total stranger to his new
setting. He was then twenty-three, with a serious manner and
large expressive eyes beneath a mop of hair which had earlier
earned him the unsuitable nickname of 'Floss'.

Oxford was quite different from the broad, sunlit streets
of Adelaide with its quiet new university, which had still a

self-conscious dedication to the important business of education. But with all its shortcomings and lack of opportunity, it had been home, and he had left it with the deep feeling that he would not go back.

'It may now seem an odd thing to say,' he recalled many years later, just before he died, 'but I think I left Australia feeling it was highly improbable that I would ever return. I left my homeland because there were no opportunities in those fields in which I was interested—things like research in physiology, for example. In those days there were very few openings in the medical schools and the universities; there was no depth to science and places were not very well equipped, and there seemed no background to the research which then coloured my life.'[1]

If he arrived at Oxford with the melancholy of an expatriate who did not expect to see his home again, it was soon to evaporate under the warmth of new companionship, new interest and new encouragement that he found all about him.

Florey had come through an academic pipe-line designed to turn out competent general practitioners trained to the standards of the previous century. But he had emerged the other end with scientific ambition, and once at Oxford he felt increasingly sure of his choice. As he looked around, he grew more certain that he could compete in this tougher arena he had chosen. He could also feel he had some roots in the area for he had come to commence his career in research only seven miles from the small town of Abingdon where his father, Joseph Florey, had been born and had followed the trade of his father, Walter, as the local shoemaker.

The softly rounded hills behind Adelaide stand within the protective arm of the Mount Lofty Ranges which shelter the city from the hot winds blowing off the vast, semi-arid land of near-desert and mallee scrub. From these hills, which change colour with the seasons, the sweep of the great Southern Ocean can be seen over the city where at night the street lights diminish the glow from the stars in the southern night sky.

Nowadays the modern brick-and-tile bungalows march in orderly ranks across the open paddocks and crowd the hillside where, at the turn of the century, the Florey children roamed in search of mushrooms, read their books, chased home the family cow for milking and from where, perched high, they could see their father rattle home from the city in one of Adelaide's first cars.

They lived in a big, pretentious house of yellow stone cut from a nearby sandstone quarry. Joseph Florey had given it a circular staircase and a spacious verandah that encircled the first floor under the wide, corrugated iron roof. He was riding a business boom in a colony that had become part of the federated nation of Australia and the house, the children and the spluttering car were Joseph's symbols of affluence.

The stone walls of the house stood solidly in the sun among the massed roses and the banks of azaleas. With its backdrop of high pines and great gum trees the place had a feeling of permanence for the children that lasted as long as Joseph lived. They had moved to the house from the small, tin-roofed stone cottage in the Adelaide suburb of Malvern when Howard Florey, the youngest child and only son, was a little more than two years old. He was born in the cottage on the 24th September 1898, but it was in the big house his father had called 'Coreega'—an Aboriginal name of unknown meaning to him—that Florey grew up and called home. This was the house he remembered all his life, the place in which he had announced to his sister, Hilda, that he would spend his life in research and where his father spent the last sixteen years of his life.

Born in 1857 in the small Berkshire town of Abingdon, Joseph spent his early years learning his father's trade. But in his late teens he spread his wings and went to London. By 1878, when he had reached his twenty-first birthday, he had drifted into another trade and had changed the pattern of his life.

In a factory at Islington, where he worked as a warehouseman, Joseph met William Ames and his sons and, through them, Ames' daughter, Charlotte. All details of the courting, all reasons which attended their decision to marry, are lost in time. But on an April day in 1878 young Joseph Florey stood facing the altar in the old parish church at Eltham, then on the southern out-skirts of London, and waited for his twenty-three-year-old bride.

By the early 1880s when their daughters—Charlotte, and then Annie—were born, Charlotte had grown pale and was racked with fits of coughing. In time it led the doctor to suggest that there might be a better hope of recovery in a drier and sunnier climate. So, in 1882, they boarded a vessel bound for Australia and faced the long, harrowing journey to a distant land which was still nothing more than a scattered collection of settlements. The long weeks at sea, the discomfort of shipboard life through the tropics, the storms, and then the struggle to make a new home in a continent still little known and largely unexplored, formed no prescription for recovery from the disease of consumption attacking Charlotte.

Joseph worked hard and planned well to win her a good life. He settled into Australian ways quickly, borrowing £400, an impressive sum for those days and using it to set up house and start his own bootmaking business. He found a small cottage—in the Adelaide suburb of Parkside—called Argylle Cottage, in Clyde Lane, and there the ailing wife tried to face the task of making a home for Joseph and her two little girls.

But as a means of saving Charlotte, all the efforts and the upheaval were doomed before the start. The tubercle bacilli then destroying the tissues of her lungs would not be denied by a change of location. She sank steadily, growing paler as the blood came with the incessant coughing, fading away rather than dying. During the last months Joseph took in a housekeeper-nurse to run his home and the woman brought with her a daughter, Bertha Mary Wadham. Mrs Wadham's daughter, a second generation Australian, was practical and efficient, and she eased their grief with constant attention as Charlotte finally slipped away. The quality of calm and capability which Bertha showed appealed to Joseph in his grief and difficulty, and, before long, she accepted his proposal of marriage and became mistress of his household. She bore him three children, expanding his family to five. The first was Hilda, a bright child full of humanity who became one of Australia's earliest woman doctors. Then came Valetta, gifted musically and, after her, Howard Walter, the last child and only boy.

From the memories of those who could still recall Bertha and

Joseph, after their son became well known, it is clear that Bertha was value for money to her husband in the brains and the native intelligence she brought into the family. Certainly she was no beauty, nor was she a social catch. But from the time she came into his life Joseph began to develop into a keen and shrewd businessman who quickly built a prosperous company with factories in Adelaide and Melbourne. The name of his 'famous Chromella brand shoes' spread across the eastern states and he pandered to the ladies with 'new fashions and high-class leather direct from the British Isles'.[2]

The firm earned the money that took them from the stone cottage to the big yellow mansion in the hills, but their wealth never brought Bertha the place in society she sought, for, in the Adelaide of their day, the strata of society were firmly fixed by the rigid laws of the Victorian age. It was not enough just to have money; and if that money came from trade, then it was all the more unacceptable. The well-born among the professions, and the landed gentry with pastoral holdings, formed a tight circle of influence which lingered on in fluctuating importance for many decades after the Florey household broke up.

Bertha's plain looks and her difficulty with grammar were no aid to her social ambitions. Neither was she helped by her quick tongue and sharp features. She did, however, have an imperious dignity when leading her brood of five into Sunday morning service at St Michael's, at which their nearest neighbour, the Canon of Adelaide, Archdeacon Clampert, delivered his weekly sermon.

The local ladies, whose middle-class voices made Bertha's a little out of place, would remark that, although she wore more expensive clothes than they, she was always slightly overdressed. Her satins were too shiny, too close-fitting and the heavy veil she wore was obviously an attempt to soften the lines of her face.

But it was always clear that Bertha was the steel in her family, and it was from her that her son inherited the forthright manner which became his hallmark in academic life. He took more after his father in looks and in steadiness and resolve, but his features were just sharp enough to resemble Bertha's and his tongue

could be as waspish as his mother's when all did not suit her as
mistress of 'Coreega'.

From his earliest days in the Adelaide hills, Howard Florey
gained a friend he would keep for life. Molly Clampert was the
daughter of Archdeacon Clampert, the Canon of Adelaide, whose
wife became Florey's godmother at a belated christening.
Molly was eighteen months older than Florey and assumed the
role of guide and tutor from the time the Floreys moved into
'Coreega', which had a common boundary with the extensive
grounds of the rectory. Molly took Florey to his first lesson at
Miss Thornber's kindergarten, riding with him down the hill in a
horse-drawn tram, admiring his new red velvet suit and his tight
fair curls which Bertha had carefully arranged. Molly remembered
this day when, more than sixty years later, Florey was raised to
the peerage. She recalled that she had nicknamed him 'Dowie' after
a Mormon preacher with long curls who had been visiting
Australia from America. She wrote to Florey then, addressing
him as 'Lord Dowie'.

These were happy days when Florey's father had the money to
send him to good schools, first to Kyre College, later to be named
Scotch College, and then in 1911, when he was thirteen, to the
fashionable St Peter's Collegiate. Five years of study and sport
in the solid and permanent surroundings of this institution, with
its big stone buildings set in wide, spacious grounds, shaped and
moulded him for the rest of his days. It was here that he came
under the influence of the chemistry master, Mr Thompson, the
man the boys called 'Sneaker'.

Mr Thompson emerges from those days before the First
World War as an interesting character who earned his nickname
for his habit of wearing rubber-soled shoes so that he could sidle
quietly up to groups of boys and listen to their conversations. He
brought credit to St Peter's for the role he played in shaping the
mind of a boy along the path that led to a revolution in medicine.
He certainly deserves more credit than the headmaster, who sought
to persuade Howard Florey and his father that, as there was no
future for chemistry research in Australia, 'the boy would do
better to become an engineer'.

But the love of science and the feeling for chemistry which

Mr Thompson had planted in the young Florey sent him home to blurt out to his sister his decision to devote his life to research. These feelings were too strong to be ousted by the opinion of the eminent headmaster.

'I don't know why', Florey said much later, 'I turned to medicine but, at the time, it just seemed a very natural thing for me to do.'

Whatever the techniques used by Thompson to teach science, they certainly struck a deep chord in the boy as the results in his school records show. At the end of his first year he gained a credit and won a special prize for chemistry; he was awarded a scholarship; and took first place in physics and chemistry. He maintained this leading position in each of the five years he was at the college. This was the start of a scholastic reputation which he continued to build, despite illness from bouts of pneumonia. It came from an outstanding ability to absorb facts and to recall them with ease, an ability which later led a British scientific authority to note that 'Florey had been born with a test tube in his mouth'.

Soon Florey was widening his reading and his studies with the same intensity with which he had always pursued sport—tennis, football, cricket and swimming—and later he became a school prefect and an officer in the school cadet corps. This all-round pattern of behaviour proved vital to his chances when he eventually applied for the Rhodes Scholarship.

In his final year at St Peter's he did so well he was awarded a government bursary to help him through his first three years at medical school. He also won another special prize for chemistry. The bursary was not, at the time, essential to him, but before its time expired it had become extremely useful as a bridge to another grant which enabled him to complete his medical studies.

Florey had two good years without much worry or frustration at the medical school at Adelaide University in a small class of twenty-four students. In these years what money had not done for Bertha's social ambitions, it did for Florey with new contacts and friendships among students from a wide section of Australian life. Soon 'Coreega' became a regular venue for evening gatherings and week-end tennis parties at which everyone would

drink wine and argue points about the medical school or about the
Great War that was raging on the other side of the world.

Florey's student friends played tennis much more than any
other sport, and Florey developed both a powerful backhand
and forehand, which eventually won him his 'blue' when he
played for Adelaide University. He played with an utter dedication to winning and would show a ruthless streak which sometimes
offended his friends. He would go on reducing an opponent
coldly and efficiently long after it was apparent he would win
easily, and there were times when he would glare aggressively
across the net at female opponents in mixed doubles and berate a
partner for not pressing home a victory to the last stroke. It was
a streak that at Cambridge, when he went on there from Oxford,
was to earn him enemies and cost him his coveted Cambridge
'blue' for tennis. It was a facet of his nature which he displayed
repeatedly in his career—when he fought for other people,
argued for his rights or battled against the ineptitude of organizations and individuals.

In the medical school, the work, for Florey, was sheer delight.
He engaged biology, anatomy, bacteriology, histology and
physiology with a flair that was a tribute to his old master at St
Peter's and brought a fresh spate of prizes and awards.

The Great War dragged on and slowly contaminated the
enthusiasm of Australia's youth. There was no conscription, but
the students were made to feel that their place was at the Front.
Now and again young men would disappear from the community to re-appear briefly in khaki, and then would be gone.
The war warped judgment and frayed tempers. In the street any
man or youth apparently fit enough to go to war could expect to
be insulted publicly; sometimes he would be handed a white
feather, usually by women who had suffered a loss or old men
who were themselves well beyond soldiering. So widespread was
the fever that people in reserved occupations were given prominent brass badges to indicate that they were too precious to be
sent to the trenches.

Howard Florey was caught in this tide twice and on the first
occasion, when he approached his parents with his intention to
enlist, Bertha was aghast. Both she and Joseph threw every argu-

ment in his way. He was only eighteen, an only son, and his health was too poor from the bouts of pneumonia he had suffered. In the end it was the Government decision to issue badges to medical students that stopped his going off to take his chance in war. A year later he tried again, but was deterred by his father's illness which was to lead to his death.

In the meantime Florey's circle of friends had spread beyond his own class at medical school and began to include people from more junior classes. Among these came Mary Ethel Hayter Reed. She was young and lithe, moved with a swinging walk and talked with assurance and self-confidence. There was no pretence about her although she came from a family which held a prominent place in South Australian society. She played tennis with spring-heeled joy and, with her fair-haired beauty, she soon became a central figure of Florey's group. He found her fresh and appealing and she had the attraction of a will of her own that blended with a readiness to listen to him talk of his hopes and plans. This relationship began shortly before his father fell ill. There was no commitment, no attachment that either recognized and they were never engaged.

Florey was not twenty when his father began to fail under the strain of business troubles. The collapse of Joseph's firm was never freely discussed but details which survived the years suggested that he had been grossly defrauded by a smart accountant he had taken into the business to relieve himself of some of the work load. The accountant had been too smart, and not only removed some of the burden of work from his employer but also relieved him of his capital.

Joseph did not recover from the blow. In September 1918, he travelled to Melbourne to wind up his affairs and never returned. He collapsed and died at the age of sixty-one.

There was very little left. With debts and obligations, surrounded by creditors and competition, the family soon found themselves no longer the owners of 'Coreega'. When all was settled, Joseph's entire estate amounted to little more than £7 000. The firm, the factories, the outlet for the 'famous Chromella brand shoes'—all went, along with 'Coreega' and the years of affluence, and Bertha had to retire to a little brick house on the

3

outskirts of the city, not far from the stone cottage where Florey
had been born.[3]

The family soon broke up, with Hilda going off into medical
practice and Annie leaving for a nursing career overseas. Florey
faced a grim time, knowing his bursary finished at the close of the
next year and that it would have to be replaced with another
scholarship if he was to continue his medical education. He
responded with hard work and long hours of study which made
him the dominating intellect of his class, and he maintained this
position until the final examinations.

This concentration on work made inroads into his leisure, but
on some week-ends he would borrow a ramshackle motor-cycle
and ride the coughing, spitting machine across fifty miles of
rough track to spend a week-end by the sea with his classmate,
Alan Hobbs.* In the tough, final examination at the end of their
five years of study Hobbs failed and had to sit another year before
he started his career in surgery.[4] Florey again headed the class and
found that he not only had his degree in his pocket, but also a
Rhodes scholarship to Oxford.

Earning his passage as a ship's doctor, Florey sailed for England
early in December, at a time when the world was starting to
react to the slaughter and the waste of the war which had finished
three years before. The upheavals, the inflation, the unemploy-
ment and hunger marches, the great strikes, they were all on the
way; and in a small room in a brick tower in a London hospital
a Scottish-born bacteriologist named Alexander Fleming was
catching tear-drops in test tubes to show how a substance he had
named 'lysozyme' could dissolve certain types of harmless
bacteria.

---

* Captured by the Japanese and sent to the infamous Burma railway Hobbs
first heard of the penicillin work in a jungle camp when a sick soldier
gave him a scrap of newspaper to read. The Oxford discovery was reported
in five lines.

CHAPTER 2

LIKE MANY OTHER RHODES SCHOLARS FROM ACROSS THE world, Howard Florey found his early days at Oxford—despite his driving ambition—rather aimless and full of idle and curious wanderings. This listless period of suspension and gradual adjustment from the open and airy society on the other side of the globe to the new environment of the old university city extended into weeks as he sought to make contacts and form new friendships.

The struggle to merge into the Oxford scene and to belong began from the moment Florey reached the gate at Magdalen and the porter called his 'scout'. For the first time in his life he had a personal servant who would clean his shoes, bring meals to his room and make his bed; it was the 'scout' who would guide him through the first difficult days and the strangeness of the new and to Florey peculiar customs and traditions. Magdalen— among the most gracious of colleges with its fifteenth-century cloisters and chapel, its cream-panelled rooms and dinner in the old Hall at night with beer in tankards—at first left him ill at ease, though later he came to love and enjoy the surroundings.

But there in 1922 Florey found a tough-minded central group, oblivious to strangers, whose determined zest for gaiety and life came from the time they had spent as teenagers in the mud of Flanders. A few months before, at the bottom of his application for the Rhodes scholarship, Florey had sought to explain away his absence from the trenches. By trying to do so he showed some sense of guilt that he had not succeeded in his plan to go to France to fight the Germans.

Consequently, being among so many young men who had fought made a sense of belonging even harder to achieve. But as

the evenings went by he made a nodding acquaintance here and
there, though generally he drank his beer or wine alone. It was all
overcome in time and by events, but it set him a little apart and
sharpened the difference he felt from most people around him—
a difference that became more and more noticeable as the months
and years went by.

The first relief from loneliness came when he met a fellow
Rhodes student at Magdalen, John Fulton of the United States.
Fulton was round, jolly and outgoing in his manner, so that
friendship came easily to him, which in turn brought him confidence. He began an association with Florey in those first few
weeks that developed into comradeship and a mutual respect. It
was a relationship that lasted the rest of their lives and eventually
had bearing on the first steps towards industrial penicillin production.

Soon after establishing this first friendship Florey made contact,
through the Rhodes organization, with another South Australian
who was already a familiar name in the university, having rowed
in the annual boat race against Cambridge in 1920. This was Hugh
Cairns,* the 1919 Rhodes scholar from South Australia, two years
ahead of Florey and with a wealth of experience behind him.

What ended Florey's period of isolation more than anything
was the summons he received in March to an interview at
Magdalen with the great physiologist, Sir Charles Sherrington.
The opportunity to work under Sherrington in the Magdalen
laboratory where physiology was on the frontier of human
knowledge left Florey agog with excitement, and by the time he
presented himself at Sherrington's door he was already burning
to be taken into the great man's orbit. But his ardent ambition
was also mixed with the same awe and feeling of intimidation that
would fill so many of his own students when he, too, came to hold
position and power backed by an enviable world reputation.
He went to a meeting that was to be the most important event in

* By 1921 Cairns was already working in the Radcliffe Infirmary in Oxford,
and was on his way to a top position as one of the great neurosurgeons.
He subsequently became senior consultant on brain and nerve surgery to
the British Army in the Second World War, and was knighted for services
which included pioneering penicillin therapy in war wounds with Florey in
North Africa and Sicily.

his early career feeling eager and apprehensive, equipped only
with his own vigour and capacity. But the man waiting was to
endow him with a quality of scientific method and intellectual
approach that would bring about the flowering of his vision and
the broadening of the horizons. Florey's own courage, drive and
ambition did the rest.

Sir Charles Sherrington was like an inquisitive bird in a white
coat. To conduct his interviews and sound out his prospective
recruits he used his laboratory as though it was a cage of long
familiarity, hopping quickly from one vantage point to another,
his mind always racing ahead of the questions and the expected
answers. He would pause a moment to snap out a question and
then pose with his face held to one side, his grey head tilted back,
the watchful, gimlet eyes staring down an elevated nose. Then he
would be off to a new position, restless, quick, with unblinking
stare of appraisal, always giving the impression he knew exactly
where the questioning would go and when it would come to an
end.

Sherrington was the first really great man Florey had met. The
first impression, enduring for more than thirty years, was still
fresh in Florey's mind when the great physiologist died in 1952
at the age of ninety-four—his mind as clear as a bell.

The questioning over, Florey found that suddenly the bird-like
mannerisms were gone and Sherrington was brushing his thin,
white moustache, his eyes full of warmth and humour. He talked
with feeling, showing a love of words, colour and life. Then,
having put Florey at his ease, Sherrington told him he had decided
to admit him to his department. The decision meant more than
that Florey was to come under Sherrington's tuition and influence.
At times he would be made to feel he was almost a member of
Sherrington's family, with visits to his home and dinner seated in
chairs that had been used by Darwin and Lister, Ehrlich, Rutherford and many other great men of science.

This first meeting between Florey and Sherrington was, in
effect, the first step by them towards the age of antibiotics (a word
that was not coined until 1941 by Waksman in USA), but neither
the greying genius nor the unknown twenty-three-year-old

Rhodes scholar from Australia could know then where their exchanges were to lead.

Young Florey just knew that this man had been a professor since 1891 and that he had laid the foundations of modern understanding of the functions of the brain and spinal cord, monumental labours that were to earn Sherrington the title, among North American medical historians, of the 'Columbus of the human nervous system'.[1]

At the time of their meeting in Oxford, Sherrington was already a legend in medical science; and as President of the Royal Society and the British Association, he was a man with influence and power across the whole structure of British science. Unseen then, but emerging clearly in later years, Sherrington's own development as a scientist and his lines of interest affected all that Florey was to do. Even a cholera study in Spain in 1885, when Sherrington met the great Nobel prize-winning histologist, Ramon Y Cajal, was to lead to an event in Florey's own career.

Along with Sherrington's quality of character that was to help build and shape Florey, was a supreme mastery of the techniques of experimental use of living creatures. Sherrington's skill was at such a level, by Lord Adrian's claim, that no other laboratory in the world could match the standard he set. Lord Adrian's tribute to Sherrington, in later years, included the phrase, 'But it is seldom that such a brilliant experimental skill is combined with such an appreciation of the wider bearings. He studied the spinal reflexes and through them came to the picture of man reflecting on his nature.' Sherrington used this skill to advance his understanding of the physiology of man, but not in a speculative approach to the problems of this subject, nor in pursuit of theory with little foundation. His method was to use the experiment to show a fact and elucidate a situation.

From the beginning of his tuition of the young Australian he dinned this approach into his brain, repeating again and again, as he did to his other students, his concept of an intellectual approach to experiments,

'Always remember, Florey,' he would say, 'the more intelligent the question you ask of Mother Nature, the more intelligible will be her reply.'

Sherrington took the role of Florey's mentor and scientific guide, consciously nurturing curiosity and easing him into research from where he could follow his own interests. He went beyond the teaching of method and scientific approach and the experimental use of knowledge, as it then stood, to the role almost of a father and counsellor. He saw in Florey a young man driven by ambition, by his own capability, and by the dire need to get somewhere before the time and the money of his Rhodes scholarship ran out. And he felt, with Florey, that there was little time to lose.

Florey turned his back on the distractions of university life from the day he started to work under Sherrington. Avoiding the supper parties, the cheese and wine gatherings, the evening discussions, he gave way to his appetite for knowledge. With Sherrington's guidance he plunged deeper and deeper into the literature of world physiology, setting a habit of avidly reading papers on new work that he was to retain all his working life. The flair he had developed back at St Peter's in Adelaide, of storing away vital facts, was his great strength, and as he worked so he strengthened his power of recall.

Sherrington also directed his interest to the bloodstream and the behaviour of tissue, in health and in disease. Together they looked deeply at the role in life of different components of the blood, especially the action of the lymphocytes and leucocytes in the body's defence system against infectious disease—an aspect which Sherrington himself had studied a decade before Florey was born. He encouraged, too, Florey's growing interest in the processes of inflammation and the way in which different cells reacted to the invasion of foreign organic matter. And always, when Sherrington saw the strain of work showing on the young man's face, there would be an invitation to the house, sometimes for a drink and a talk, sometimes for a dinner cooked by Sherrington's wife, Ethel Mary.

Florey long remembered these kindnesses and the help they were to him in his earliest struggles. In later life he followed Sherrington's example, but he could never equal Sherrington's flair for hospitality. Florey could be a genial and engaging companion, but he was never able to produce the same depth of warm sympathy, nor the great fund of stories of bygone days, as Sherrington.

The old man would talk endlessly of the past and his meetings with the famous. He could recapture in detail his visit to Russia in the troubled and dangerous days before the Revolution and recount his dinner with the famous Pavlov in Leningrad. He could talk of Paul Ehrlich and Darwin and Lister, with deep understanding of the problems of the times, and with a fluency of language and a love of colour and life that he imparted to Florey but which the latter could not match.

These attributes brought Sherrington the reward of affection and admiration from many of his students. Florey maintained all his life that he had been lucky to 'fall in with Sherrington' and, even in the great leap that was to come with the opening of anti-biotic therapy, held him to be among the greatest physiologists of all time. He was thrilled at the opportunity he was given and resolved not to neglect his chance. He told his friends back in Australia, 'The atmosphere is so different here. They take an interest in you, and if you show any promise they give you encouragement.'[2]

So he began a year of toil and study, avaricious for new knowledge and for the data he needed to pursue the honours and research degrees at which he aimed. Through the delightful days of his first spring in England Florey worked with concentration and resolve, hardly lifting his head to notice the sheen of coming summer spreading its pale green through the trees of the deer park and over Addison's Walk. Summer came, and went, as he built steadily on the basic operating skills and the knowledge he had gained in Adelaide, and, as he worked that year, he was exactly two decades away from the day when he would proudly write to Sherrington, then in retirement, of astonishing results and the 'almost miraculous effects of a most potent weapon against common forms of sepsis'.

In these early months, as he prepared for his first Oxford examinations, Florey competed with a strong and ambitious group of students, spending all his spare hours familiarizing himself with the techniques, equipment and installations, the processes and methods, for delving into the microscopic aspects of the small blood vessels, always forcing his mind into new concepts and his hands to an elegance of experimental ability.

Often, in the working years that followed his time under Sherrington's guidance, associates would remark that Florey's greatness as an experimenter lay in a combination of manual dexterity and imagination, together with a fine judgment that picked out the significant observations. He could, they said, select the most fruitful procedures with uncanny precision, with what seemed an instinctive ability to prefer the simple situation that would answer plainly—one way or the other. He was, in fact, following Sherrington's tenet; he asked intelligent questions of nature for a purpose and generally obtained intelligible answers.

It became so much a part of his intellectual approach to science that Florey was often credited with an insight that could cut through dead wood and red tape and save time; and in the years when his own students were going out to fill key places in research across the world he would sometimes walk through the laboratories and stop and ask here and there, 'Tell me, as simply as you can . . . what is the question you are asking in this experiment?'

When the time came for examinations he sailed through with flying colours, capturing a First in the competitive Honours School of Physiology and obtaining his M.A.; and the way he did this clearly marked him down, in the eyes of his tutors, as set for a distinguished academic career. Florey was elated, and Sherrington was satisfied; and from there the young Australian moved further into developing research work, his self-confidence quietly blooming as he saw that he could match his ability against the best in the school. He carried the hope that there would be a post, some appointment where he could go on to take his Ph.D. and find support for his own special interest yet to be chosen. With such results there appeared form and shape to the ambition which had smouldered in him since his chemistry master first fired his imagination in 1910.

Towards the end of that year, his second at Oxford, he heard of a fellowship at Magdalen which was to be thrown open to competition, and with the termination of the Rhodes grant coming uncomfortably close he made several enquiries. The thought of a fellowship at college unrolled the prospect in his quick mind of future security and status, access to laboratory space and support for research. It was all there. In 1924, to be an Oxford don was the apogee of success, a peak once attained that relieved the future of much stress and worry.

Florey was then twenty-five years old, and two years out of medical school, but he knew that Sherrington had become a fellow of Caius in Cambridge at twenty-three and he felt it was not beyond him to rise so high so early in his career. He began sounding opinion on his prospects. But he was doomed to disappointment as the gathered minds of Magdalen involved in such selection matters appeared to be against him, considering him not yet ready for elevation to fellowship.

He was thus advised not to make an application and in the event it was his fellow Rhodes Scholar from the United States, John Fulton, who was admitted to college fellowship at Magdalen long before Florey.

It soon became apparent in his circle that confirmation of his lack of prospects as a candidate for fellowship slammed a door in Florey's face. Sir Rudolph Peters afterwards noted that he seemed over-conscious of his financial position, while others believed he took the setback badly and was keenly disappointed not to have his financial future settled beyond further worry. In his disappointment of the hopes which had flooded his mind, some of Bertha's steel hardened his attitude to Oxford and his immediate surroundings; his reputation as an abrasive character and a man with a rasping tongue, easily upset, began to widen.

His concern and pique became obvious to Sherrington as well as to the other members of the school; and this led Sherrington, with the humanity that characterized him, to raise the matter of change with Florey.

Telling of this exchange many years later, Florey recalled the day when Sherrington came to him in the laboratory and, after a few casual pleasantries, put his head back and, looking down his nose, had asked, 'Tell me, Florey. Do you think you might be interested in taking up experimental pathology?'

In an age when the hiving-off of scientific disciplines from former watertight compartments was a rare occurrence, the term caught Florey unawares and he looked at Sherrington in puzzlement. Sherrington talked for a while about new roots of science pushing out in different directions, creating a prospect for investigations that could become separate areas of specialization. The time was ripe, he told Florey, for someone with a good grounding in physiology to start experimental work in pathology and to explore the new fields and problems opening in that field. If Florey was interested there was an opening at Cambridge.

They stood eye to eye for a moment, and then Florey reminded Sherrington that he had financial difficulties. Sherrington nodded understandingly and said that there was a paid studentship at Caius College and that he had been asked to recommend someone. He had, in fact, already written to Professor Dean and had entered Florey's name. Then, with a pat on the shoulder he was gone.[3]

During the last summer he was to spend in Sherrington's department in Oxford, Florey took an opportunity that came his way to savour adventure and exploration in the Arctic.[4] Accepting an offer to act as medical officer to the University Exploration Club expedition to North East Land near Spitzbergen, he sailed across the North Sea in a tiny convoy of two small ships, one of which carried a small seaplane.

The small force was led by George Binney—later Sir George—and it comprised scientists, ecologists, physicists and specialist surveyors, including Helmer Hanssen who had sledged to the South Pole with Amundsen just before the Great War in the classic race against Robert Falcon Scott.

They reached a remote spot called Liefdefjorden on 9th July 1924, and set three sledging parties ashore to engage in traverses over unknown territory, to make micro-studies of icecaps and crystals, and to map the terrain.

Binney, and the pilot, A. G. B. Ellis, flew sorties from the coast and when they crashed their aircraft into the ice Florey tended their injuries which, fortunately for them all, were not serious. In its way it was an historic expedition, which uncovered new data about unexplored territory, but made its main claim to fame as the first Arctic expedition to make use of an aircraft. For Binney and the others it was a very serious business, but in after years Florey called his northern adventure 'a joke'; he laughed sometimes over the recollection that his major achievement was curing a skin infection with sulphur ointment.

However, Binney presented him with the mounted boss of the wrecked wooden airplane propellor and Florey kept this hanging for many years in his rooms at university.

They were all back safely in Oxford by September, but Florey was soon off to Cambridge where he was admitted to Caius College as a research student and awarded the John Lucas Walker scholarship in the Department of Pathology under Professor H. R. Dean —the man who was to head a penicillin trials committee under government auspices in 1943. Dean was an observant and outstanding pathologist. When Sherrington had written to him recommending Florey for the studentship at the college, to which he himself had been elected Fellow in 1880, Dean did not hesitate to back that recommendation. Florey was brought into the Cambridge fold without delay and into a circle of colleagues and associates that were to have a profound effect on his life's work.

It was the first of many posts that Florey would be offered in his career. Soon afterwards, a senior academic from Adelaide called on him at Caius and, informing him that Adelaide had advertised a post for a lectureship in physiology, said that this had been done in the hope and expectation that Florey would apply. Florey took the remark as a rebuke. Flushing with anger, he asked his visitor, 'Then why the hell didn't you ask me? Why didn't you offer me the job?'

His caller was taken aback and replied loftily that this was not a practice followed by the university in South Australia.

'More's the bloody pity,' Florey replied, and then showed the man out.[5]

Thirty years later Australia was to make several bids to induce this famous son to return, but for various reasons they were all to be in vain.

CHAPTER 3

IN BAGGY, WELL-WORN CLOTHES, HIS STEEL-RIMMED glasses perched on a nose overhung by a flapping forelock of hair, precious papers and books crammed into his bag, Howard Florey went to Cambridge, a figure utterly dissimilar to the Rhodes scholar who had arrived at Oxford early in 1922.

Gone for good was the sun-tanned young man with the quiet, studious manner. Three winters in Britain and nearly thirty months of unremitting study and financial worry had left him pale, a burning ambition in his luminous eyes and a veneer of reserve over an explosive personality. He was resident in the ancient college of Gonville and Caius and the gentle system enfolded the twenty-six-year-old research student with its traditional style. He lived in a comparatively closed community, but he showed an intensity of approach that set him apart and that either made him enemies or friends. There were no half-way people in Florey's circle. His positive nature, his direct speech and blunt expressions, exposed and sharply defined his character and personal attitudes—and just as sharply exposed was his driving ambition to succeed. Within a month or two of gaining independence of action and choice of research subject, Florey was off on the trail that within eleven years was to take him back to the prestigious Chair of Pathology at Oxford.

Later, mellowed, he said of Cambridge, 'They were very good to me. They gave me a free hand and managed to put up with me very well. I enjoyed my years there.'

This understatement, so typical of Florey's manner of speech, covered a period when he blossomed out as a scientist of perception and courage, striding confidently into a field of work so new

that, fifty years later, it can still stand alongside contemporary
science.* Four brilliant papers in that first torrid year of work set
Florey an unshakeable reputation with his chief, Professor Dean,
and widened his circle of contact.

Among his early friends, and also a research collaborator, was
Sir Alan Drury, later a Director of the famed Lister Institute and a
power in the Medical Research Council. Like many others, he
too felt uneasy in his first brushes with Florey.

> His drive and ambition were manifest almost from the day
> he arrived. A great fire seemed to burn within him, and his
> many-sided character was never concealed. We could all see
> the power in him and wondered whether he would ever find
> the right outlets for his greatness. This was the beginning of
> a remarkable career and he was very determined to succeed.
> He could be ruthless and selfish; on the other hand, he could
> show kindliness, a warm humanity and, at times, sentiment and
> a sense of humour. He displayed utter integrity and he was
> scathing of humbug and pretence. His attitude was always—
> 'You must take me as you find me'. But, to cope with him at
> times, you had to do battle, to raise your voice as high as his
> and never let him shout you down. You had to raise your pitch
> to his but if you insisted on your right he was always, in the
> end, very fair. I must say that, at times, he went out of his way
> to cut people down to size with some very destructive criticism.
> But I must also say that in the years I knew him he did not once
> utter a word of praise about himself.[1]

While the tolerant way of life at Cambridge suited Florey, he
blatantly made use of his Australian characteristics in a campaign
to attain his ends. He confessed to this briefly, later, saying, 'I
could always get away with being audacious and do the out-
rageous thing and still be tolerated. They made allowances for
the rough colonials and some people came to expect that sort of
behaviour. It was always a good line of attack.' But if there was

---

* Work on the behaviour of brain cells under pathogenic attack is still
used in reference to the studies of the action of malarial parasites in cerebral
tissue.

guile and planning in his public face, the laboratory was also able to see the real ability that lay behind it and, within a little more than a year, Professor Dean was calling to the Medical Research Council in London for money to 'keep this brilliant young pathologist here at Cambridge; we badly need him'.

With his intense style, Florey applied himself to using physiological approaches to problems of pathology, and in this way brought about a flowering of the ideas and interests which he had gained from Sherrington. There was no boundary to his interest and his early papers were wide-ranging, going so far at one time as to examine the effect of medical X-rays on healthy tissue. Mainly, however, he centred his interest on the smaller blood vessels and on the nature of the cells and their functions.

Life in the college brought Florey opportunities for social activity and for sport, but he took few of these seriously. He sometimes provoked anger by his offhand manner and unwillingness to co-operate, and this cost him many friendships. Some days he would be seen alone, wandering along that pleasant half-mile known as 'The Backs', with a cigarette dangling from his lips, head down, deep in thought. Other days he would be in violent action on the tennis court, playing always as though his life depended on the outcome of the game. One player with whom he formed a lifelong friendship was Robert Webb, a gentle-mannered, American medical graduate who saw and admired the qualities beneath Florey's assumed colonial roughness. One side of Florey's reserve that Robert Webb noted from the start was that Florey never called anyone outside his family by their christian name.

Webb said, 'I don't know whether he took this stand before he came to Cambridge, but he certainly adopted it from the start there. I, and many others, always called him "Floss", but he never—in more than forty years—called me anything but "Webb". He never used a first name, and why he took this stand I never knew. It was always surnames with him, with no exceptions.'

Florey felt comfortable with Webb and appreciated the kindness both Webb and his wife showed him. Webb's graduation at Johns Hopkins in 1916 had been followed by a lecture from a visiting official of the British Ministry of Health, who appealed

for young doctors to go to France to work with the army.
Webb responded, and spent the rest of the war working in
casualty stations, first with the British Medical Corps and then
with the American Army when they entered the war in 1917.
When Florey went to Cambridge, Webb was doing an honours
course in physiology and pathology.

They often played tennis together and, like others, Webb
found Florey a very good player—not Wimbledon class, but well
up to earning his 'blue'. Only Florey's unpopularity and—according to Webb—his unwillingness to mix with the group which ran
the tennis tournament, cost him this accolade.

We played in a knock-out competition and the winner was
to be selected for the university team. He got into the semi-
finals and won, but the date for the final was postponed so
many times, to avoid giving Florey his chance, that people
came to know that this little group did not want Florey to earn
his 'blue'. In fact, he never did. It was never really important
to him, but it illustrated how he could rub people up the
wrong way. I saw him differently. I think he saw just the facts
and felt himself different from people around him. He knew
he could work for what he wanted to achieve and go on
longer than others. I think he always knew that he would do
something big.[2]

At Cambridge, Florey began by exploiting the opportunities
offered in the then unconventional task of using physiological
experiment to find answers to some of the problems facing
workers in pathological research. It led him to interests beyond
the boundary of one discipline and brought close contact with
others who were to help shape events in penicillin research. His
approach to many things was regarded as unconventional;
however, his ability was quickly recognized and soon widely
respected. New ideas were always acceptable to him, but he
centred his main interest in the behaviour of cells and their different
roles and the following year a thesis based on this earned him his
Ph.D.

But before he gained his doctorate, the bachelor life he was

leading at Cambridge started to pall, and he began to write back
home to Ethel with plans of returning to marry, and for them to
combine their skills and future, and seek what opportunities
there were available. Ethel was at the end of six years of study at
the medical school and facing a year as resident in the Adelaide
Children's Hospital. They had reached no agreement, nor conclusion when his nostalgia for home and his impatience for
advance were swept aside by a Rockefeller Foundation travel
grant and a personal allowance from the Medical Research
Council won for him by Professor Dean. Without delay he
sailed to the United States, having chosen to work with the well-
known pharmacologist, Dr A. Newton Richards, at Pennsylvania
State College. It was a fateful choice and led to an association of
great consequence which was to return to life and health tens of
thousands of soldiers of the Allied nations in the European and
Pacific theatres of the Second World War.

Florey established himself with the scientists about him during
his year in the United States so well that Newton Richards eventually came to describe him as 'that rough colonial genius'.
While he was working with Richards—and with other leaders in
science, including A. J. Carlson and Robert Chambers—Florey
heard from Dean. On his return to England Florey would be
offered the Freedom Research Fellowship at the London Hospital,
and he should regard this as a stop-gap measure for a lectureship at
Cambridge and a college fellowship—if he wanted to go back.

With a future of some standing and security now shaping in
front of him, Florey again wrote to Ethel to discuss marriage.
This time he did not mention returning to Australia but suggested
that she should come to London and get married there. He felt
the press of developments about him and suspected that to absent
himself from the scene for too long could react against his chances
of advancement.

The Floreys were married in Trinity Church, Paddington, a
few blocks from the London hospital where Alexander Fleming
worked in his small room above Praed Street. It was the 19th
October 1926, and they stood outside in the churchyard afterwards, arms linked, with the autumn wind blowing leaves about

them while pictures were taken with Florey's box camera. The first two members of the penicillin team were together.

The wedding was a simple affair. Florey wore a lounge suit—his only concession to the occasion being a white buttonhole—and Ethel was in a two-piece costume with white gloves. But it had a touch of home for them. Sir Trent de Crespigny, the Dean of the Adelaide medical school, by chance in London, gave the bride away, and a fellow graduate of the Adelaide school, Neil Melrose Wigg, was best man. It was all over quite soon and there was no honeymoon—Florey had to finish his time as Freedom Research Scholar at the London Hospital before he could return to his new post at Cambridge.

When they had met again, for the first time in five years, Florey was shocked by the change in Ethel and later told friends of his concern. She came to London no longer the glowing, spring-heeled girl of twenty-one he had known on the tennis courts in Adelaide; she was thinner, seemingly taller, very pale and self-controlled. The only woman in her class to get through medical school, she seemed to have acquired a quiet inner strength. She told him that six years of effort, and a gruelling year in the Adelaide Children's Hospital as resident, had been made more arduous by a trouble in her throat that had proved to be a tubercular gland. This had been removed by surgery which was apparently successful, though members of her family conjectured that this may have been the first step in the physical troubles which came on her later.

Installed in a rented house off Hills Road in Cambridge, Florey, worried about his wife's condition, asked his American friend, Robert Webb, to find the cause of Ethel's poor health. Webb was thorough; after a series of pathological tests diagnosed anaemia, set about a successful course of treatment. Restored to vitality, Ethel took her place in the social life of the faculty, earning friends with her charm and intelligence. At the same time, she began demanding a place in postgraduate work for herself, which Florey tried to meet but which caused trouble between them.

Ethel found that her husband had little time other than for his work, and it was only when the Webbs insisted on their borrow-

ing their Austin Seven that Florey was coerced into a belated
honeymoon and they spent a mere ten days running round the
byways of Cornwall.

Florey's own transport was the bicycle. On this he rode every
day to his laboratory and to his tasks as Huddersfield Lecturer in
Special Pathology, teaching physiology and researching in the
experimental problems of pathology. The post brought him
coveted status—a corporate fellowship of Gonville and Caius
College—and with it he reached a situation which his old chief,
Sherrington, had achieved the previous century.

Soon after his return to Cambridge, Florey gained another
helper in his work when he recruited a fourteen-year-old boy,
James Kent, whom he found sweeping out the laboratory he was
to occupy. James Kent was a working-class boy. When he left
elementary school in the spring of 1927, the grip of unemploy-
ment was on the land but he was fortunate to have a sister who
worked in an employment bureau which was notified of a
vacancy in the Pathology Department at the university for a boy
to train as a laboratory technician.

When Florey walked into his laboratory that morning in 1927,
in a sports coat with patches of leather at the elbows, his cycle
clips still on his trousers and his hair falling across his spectacled
face, he could not have looked like destiny to the boy. Florey's
greeting was friendly and when Kent told him who he was he
looked at the stubby little boy, liked the steadiness of his eyes and
asked him if he liked working with animals. Kent had been warned
by the staff to watch out for Florey. 'He'll work you to death if
he can get away with it.' But Kent had no apprehension. He said
long afterwards, 'We seemed to like each other from the start.'

Florey's decision to keep Kent in his laboratory was not a whim
but the result of the inconvenience he had suffered from the rigid
system of shuffling the technical staff from laboratory to laboratory, to give a broad experience to their careers. This system
was imposed by the supervisor of technical assistants, Mr W. A.
Mitchell, with—Kent remembers—the aplomb and autocracy of
a Whitehall general. Thus, Florey's desire to train Kent from the
start to his own special experimental life clashed head-on with

the system and with Mitchell. This was the first of many rows
Florey had with Mitchell, and only by taking the matter to high
University authority did he have his way.

Having taken Kent under his wing, however, Florey accepted
responsibility for him for the rest of his life; during forty years of
companionship, of endless hours working together, there was
always complete understanding. Florey was always master and
Kent was his man.

The free hand he was given at Cambridge did not lead Florey
into a narrow path of research; on the contrary, he pursued a
wide field of investigation. But once having set his central interest on the behaviour of tissue in health and disease, it seemed to
be inevitable that he should ask where the answers to infectious
illness lay.

Florey started his career at a time when advances in medical
research had not yet found their way into the black bags of the
general practitioner—some still used a horse-and-buggy on their
rounds. Yet they, and the scientists in Florey's field, were faced
with a grim situation; the wards in public hospitals given over to
septic cases provided frightful evidence of the inadequacy of
medical practice. Generally, septicaemia was a death warrant, and
one in three cases of pneumonia ended in the coffin. Meningitis,
diphtheria, scarlet fever, rheumatic fever, were all dreaded words.
With the war over, there was little worry about gas gangrene,
but there were the venereal diseases, gonorrhoea—and the destroyer of vascular and brain tissue, the syphilis spirochaete.

In Canada, Banting and Best had given new heart to medical
science with the lessons learned from their therapeutic correction
to sugar balance and the relief which insulin brought to diabetics.
In his search for the one-shot panacea against infectious disease—
the cure-all which became known as the 'magic bullet of healing'
—the great Paul Ehrlich had produced the arsenical known as
Salvarsan as a specific for the treatment of syphilis; the compound,
his famous 606th experiment, which was toxic to the agent of
syphilis—and also toxic to man. It made a grim treatment lasting
well over a year of trial and endurance for both patients and the
administering physicians.

But Ehrlich's grim specific did little to widen the concept of chemotherapy. The idea that there could exist undetected substances with a chemical form structured to interrupt the growth processes of bacteria, but leaving the form of cells in the living system untouched, gained hardly any ground. This was the chemical lock and key theory which had rowelled Ehrlich's mind like a spur. It drew strength from the discovery by a Danish worker, Hans Christian Gram, that there were variations in the structure of the cell walls which held the bacterial life organisms together. Gram showed that some bacteria could be coloured with one type of stain which would not be accepted by other bacteria; some were formed so that the dyestuff molecules could attach themselves to the cell wall, others would not retain this colouring but would accept another stain. Thus the major strains of organisms—which Pasteur had shown were responsible for the important diseases which had plagued mankind throughout history—could be divided into two recognized groupings known as Gram-positive, which accepted his special staining, and Gram-negative, which did not.

The Gram-positive organisms caused such diseases as childbed fever, most forms of severe systemic or local infections, general sepsis, including bone and heart infections, osteomyelitis and endocarditis, anthrax, diphtheria, tetanus, pneumonia, tuberculosis and many others.

Among the Gram-negative diseases were typhoid, plague, cholera, food poisonings, gonorrhoea and a range of fevers including spotted fever and undulant fever.

There were good reasons for the support being given at this time for Ehrlich's ideas of a chemical lock and key attack on infectious disease. Medicine had quinine as a specific; and, within the body's own defences, European scientists had detected and studied the role of nature's own magic bullet, the antibody which attacked invading organisms and destroyed their ability to multiply. The very function of the specific cells, the role of the lymphatic system, and the action of the leucocytes detected in the inflammation processes which Florey studied in the 1920s, led inevitably to the thought of how the invading bacterium was destroyed. There were no watch-dogs with teeth to tear the intruder to pieces, only a chemical molecular structure that stopped the life processes in the bacterial colonies.

In his microscopic studies Florey, with his collaborators, saw these agents of the bloodstream at work, defending and clearing away the debris of the bacterial destruction. Indeed, when he entered medical science, in a world full of so much unchecked suffering, these very agents of the body's immune response were being enlisted in forms of antisera for use in some desperate cases. These were attempts to influence the outcome of already established diseases in human beings by adding antibody forces produced most often in the bodies of horses. This was a scientific approach with severe drawbacks: the antibodies were very specific and acted only on the strain of bacteria infecting the patient; the isolation of bacteria, identification and then production of the antisera took much time; and, since this step would only be taken for people gravely ill, it was all too often too late for improvement. There was also the risk that hypersensitive reaction would make the treatment a dangerous step.

Thus, although medical science knew of nature's magic bullet, and there were specifics—and much research—there was very little that could go into the doctor's black bag. Such was the state of the practitioner's art that some older physicians still accepted the dictum of the great healer-teacher, Sir William Ostler, written as late as 1909: that blood-letting could help some cases of pneumonia. By today's standards incredible tactics were still being used against infection, and without the risky antisera there was little more that could be done, apart from the practices that had already been employed for as long as two centuries.

Medical research was poised on an historical plateau in the 1920s, with books still being published advocating the use of legendary remedies and some recommending herbal preparations in home nursing that came very close to quackery. In the mid-1920s a book, produced by an experienced practitioner who claimed consultation with North American medical associations, seriously recommended the rubbing of bacon fat on the skin as a treatment for scarlet fever. For diphtheria, it said, gargles of creosote and hot water laced with pepper and vinegar would be helpful. The written recommendation of a Dr T. J. Ritter was,

'Sometimes a little sulphur powder blown into the throat through a goose quill is an excellent remedy for diphtheria.' Camphor, hot poultices of linseed meal, the juice of wild cherries, arsenic solutions, sarsaparilla, May apple, blood root and yellow root, turpentine and Glauber salts, liquorice and orange peel—all were hopefully offered to aid the innocuous bottles of unpleasant substances with the high-sounding names that were dispensed from the black bags.

Against sepsis such practices were futile and untouched by advances that had been made in research; the miracles of healing had yet to follow the marvels of discovery.

When Florey went to Cambridge other great scientists were already on the scene: Sir Frederick Gowland Hopkins, the father of British biochemistry, was one; and among his circle were future Nobel winners whose work would have great impact on human health. Of these, Albert Szent-Gyorgyi, from Hungary, was producing the first crystals of his newly discovered vitamin C, and he worked with Florey in a joint project. There were bacteriologists also in the forefront of the advances being made in the vital science of biochemistry, and they, along with Dean's pathological approach to physiology, gave Florey's outlook a protean quality. This in turn eventually led to his philosophy that any advance in medical practice was most likely to emerge from rigorous and imaginative experimentation in joint studies covering the basic medical sciences.

It was this philosophy that led to penicillin; but in the late 1920s as he argued and debated the problems facing them all—the biochemists, the bacteriologists, the physiologists and practising doctors—he heard for the first time of Fleming and the curious case of lysozyme—a naturally occurring substance which was so named because it behaved like an enzyme and had the ability to dissolve—or lyse—the structure of certain bacteria.

The story was told of how Fleming, in 1922, working on bacterial cultures while suffering from a heavy cold, had sneezed over an exposed plate. Fleming, with his flair for observation, noticed patches where the bacterial colonies did not later develop.

His curiosity led him to take a test tube, cloudy with a suspension
of bacteria, and drop in some nasal mucus, producing an effect
that made him pronounce, 'It went as clear as gin.'

Fleming's original work in 1922 had been followed by wider
studies that showed lysozyme to exist in teardrops, in some tissue,
and in the white of chicken eggs.

Thus, the study of lysozyme emerged as a new star in the
search for the substance that would melt away bacteria. It provided the seed for Florey's life interest in antibacterial phenomena
and, with the lesson of the antibodies before his eyes, he was soon
asking questions on the chemical action of this naturally occurring
substance. He was intrigued and sought collaboration to understand the action of lysing of the bacteria and the role of mucus.
The study advanced so that by 1928 he published his first paper,
with Alan Drury, on mucus secretion of the colon; and the following year, again with Drury, and this time with Ethel too, he
wrote a paper on the reaction in the mucus of the dog to fright.

By this time he was eager to pin down the mystery in the action
of lysozyme and in 1929, in collaboration with N. E. Goldsworthy,
reported in the British Journal of Experimental Pathology, on the
antibacterial function in mucus, a paper which carried an appendix
illustrating a culture of bacteria which had been inhibited by a
growth of antagonistic organisms. This was a coincidental
addendum which appeared in the same year as Fleming's text
on the inhibition of a bacterial colony by a mould afterwards
correctly identified as *Penicillium notatum*.[3]

Fifteen years after the event reported in his first penicillin
paper Fleming said himself that it was difficult to remember what
thought processes were involved in what he did; and that to
understand his actions it was necessary to go back into his career as
a bacteriologist.

Fleming's life story, since told with many adornments, is
very well known; but the essential preparation of his mind and
of the vital training that led to the observation he made was
best told in 1944, when he wrote,

As one of the pupils of Sir Almroth Wright (head of the

inoculation department of St Mary's Hospital, London) I had
naturally been deeply interested during the whole of my career
in the destruction of bacteria by leucocytes. During the 1914–
1918 war I spent much time investigating problems in connection with septic wounds, and I was then impressed with the
antibacterial power of the leucocytes contained in the pus
which exuded from the septic wounds. It was clear from these
investigations that the chemical antiseptics in common use
were more destructive on the leucocytes than they were on the
bacteria.

This interest in antiseptics and leucocytes continued in post-
war years, and, in 1924, I was able, by a simple method, to
demonstrate clearly the anti-leucocytic power of antiseptics
and to indicate that if the anti-leucocytic action of an antiseptic was greater than its anti-bacterial action, such antiseptic
was unlikely to be successful in the treatment of a septic wound.

He told how he described lysozyme—and how he came to
the matter of the mould-contaminated plate in 1928 after his
summer holiday. Despite the many conjectures on the treatment
of this culture plate in after years—and as recently as 1970 a
former colleague of Fleming went to great lengths to deduce
whether or not Fleming had incubated the plate—he stated
clearly in 1944 that the culture plate had been deliberately left to
mature at room temperature without any incubation.

Under these circumstances Fleming was not at all surprised to
find the culture contaminated by mould some weeks later. 'It is
certain that every bacteriologist has . . . many times had culture
plates contaminated with moulds. It is also probable that many
have noted similar changes to those that I noted . . . but, in the
absence of any special interest in naturally occurring anti-bacterial
substances, these had been discarded.'⁴

Indeed, it was long afterwards revealed that this had already
happened to Fleming's plate. Fortunately, however, the habit
of keeping a bucket of lysol in most bacteriology laboratories
for the cleansing of disused plates did not apply to the inoculation department at St Mary's where only shallow trays containing lysol were provided. The Penicillium-contaminated plate

was still sitting on top of a pile of discarded plates, untouched
by the acid, when a former colleague called into the laboratory
and Fleming, at random, took the Penicillium-contaminated
plate to illustrate some of the work he had been doing.

On this second occasion Fleming noted, '. . . the staphylococcal
colonies for some considerable distances round the mould were
obviously undergoing lysis (dissolving). What had originally
been a well-grown staphylococcal colony was now a faint
shadow of its former self.'

Thus, Fleming's mind, prepared by his long interest and training, registered the event clearly when the incident occurred. As
the Oxford team were to state in their 1949 monograph, 'It may
have been a stroke of good fortune that the spore of *P. notatum*
fell on Fleming's plate and attracted his attention by lysing some
staphylococci, but the merit of his work lies in the fact that he
recognized the changes produced by the fungus, initiated investigation of its properties, and preserved it so that it was later
available to others.'

This was the meeting of the mind with the event for which it
had been prepared, and a mind which had followed a similar
path of interest to that of Florey with whose name, Fleming
once said, his own would always be linked.

Even more to Fleming's credit, however, was his action in
culturing the mould and making a series of tests on the properties
of the medium on which it grew—a medium which afterwards
became known as 'broth', or, in Fleming's laboratory, 'mould
juice'. At first his mould strain had been identified by a mycologist
in the same building as *Penicillium rubrum*; but since Fleming
knew it was a Penicillium mould and wanted a more suitable
name for the mould juice he 'coined the word penicillin'. Though
this afterwards became the title of the active molecules in the
medium, Fleming made it clear in his first paper that *he* was
referring to the filtrate of the mould juice.

From this point on, Fleming's work took on some astonishing
lapses as a scientific endeavour, for, having shown that the filtrate
of broth had a powerful effect on cultures of the agents of
common sepsis, staphylococcus, pneumococcus, gonococcus and
others, and having shown that it did not damage human leuco-

cytes, he injected the penicillin-laden broth into a *healthy* animal. Having done that he pronounced it did not harm the animal, was not toxic, did not damage human leucocytes and was more powerful against bacteria than carbolic acid. He unaccountably did not take the next obvious step of testing the substance by injection into animals which had been diseased experimentally.*

That he could have done so was shown by Professor J. V. Duhig and Dr David Grey in Brisbane, Australia, when, in 1943, they saved the life of a forty-two-year-old woman dying of septicaemia, with a series of injections of crude 'mould juice' identical to that used by Fleming in his healthy animals.[5]

Because of Fleming's omission to inject crude 'mould juice' into diseased animals he failed to discover the power of penicillin to deal with deep-seated infection. Its true therapeutic value and its potency in systemic use, by injection, were not discovered until Florey and Chain began their project in Oxford in 1939.

In the years that followed his rise to fame, Fleming was confronted many times with this long and inexplicable gap between his discovery and its eventual application and he made some astonishing statements on the lack of chemical co-operation. On one occasion, in the presence of a former Cambridge colleague of Florey, he said, 'I would have produced penicillin in 1929 if I had had the luck to have had a tame refugee chemist at my right hand. I had to stop where I did.' Only later did it emerge that he *had* enjoyed chemical help in his first years of penicillin interest and that a concentrated extract *had* been prepared for him.

This came about through the extraordinary devotion and dedication, under depressing circumstances, of two young workers at St Mary's, Ridley and Craddock. From all this, and what emerged in after years, it became virtually certain that Fleming looked on his Penicillium mould as a producer of antiseptic for infected wounds—wounds such as he had studied in France during the First War—and that, having tried it on a few surface infections and finding its production a bothersome and difficult technique, he lost interest.

He put this lapse on record himself in his Nobel Lecture in

---

* He did however use the mould juice as a topical surface application on one or two patients at St Mary's and also on a colleague.

1945, saying, 'My only merit is that I did not neglect the observation, and that I pursued it as a bacteriologist. The first practical use was to differentiate between different bacteria. We tried to concentrate penicillin but found, as others did later, that it was easily destroyed, and so, to all intents and purposes, we failed. Had I been an active clinician I would doubtless have used it more extensively.' Fleming was a trained surgeon and his extract was used on a number of external infections, on which he reported in a brief paper in November 1932, the year in which the prominent biochemist, Professor Harold Raistrick, and a team of colleagues at the London School of Hygiene and Tropical Medicine, had published their work on unsuccessful attempts to extract a concentrate of active penicillin from the mould juice. With hindsight it became apparent that Raistrick's failure sounded the knell over Fleming's active interest in penicillin, for he was not to write another paper on it, nor mention it in his many lectures, until the work at Oxford revealed the potential of the drug in 1940. Then, Fleming said, 'We had been using it in the laboratory for over ten years as a method of differential cultures. It was used in a few cases as a local antiseptic, but, although it gave reasonably good results, the trouble of making it seemed not worth while.'[6]

In those after years Fleming repeated many times that he had not had chemical aid, though in fact Raistrick's powerful group had taken up the work only a mile or so away from where Fleming was installed in his tiny laboratory. Raistrick afterwards said that he took the step because of his own interest in such substances, and not through any request or urging from Fleming. In fact, he said, Fleming did not ever visit him to see the work, but made contact, infrequently, by telephone.

The Fleming paper which came under consideration at Oxford in 1929 was the text of a lecture delivered to the London Medical Research Club at the end of 1928, a meeting at which Sir Henry Dale was chairman, and it was also in that year that, noting Fleming's penicillin report, Florey took up with Dr E. G. D. Murray* the question of direct work on the extraction of the

* Reader in Bacteriology and afterwards Professor of Bacteriology. Later, he became Professor of Bacteriology at the University of Montreal, Canada.

active substance, but Murray declined to collaborate. Sir Alan Drury said, 'He was quite right to say that he could not tackle it, as he was no biochemist, and he would certainly have told Florey that such work required a biochemically trained man.'[7]
It was during this crucial year in the development of his interest that Florey worked with the brilliant biochemist, Dr Szent-Gyorgyi, when, together with Ethel, the three produced a paper on methods for testing the presence of the adrenal cortex hormone. It was natural that Florey should also press this gifted man for his help—and for his ideas—on the antibacterial nature in Fleming's two substances. But Szent-Gyorgyi was not to be inveigled into the task, though he did discuss it with Florey and helped to direct his thinking on the subject. Florey testified to this before a scientific concourse assembled in Stockholm in December 1945 to hear the Nobel lectures, when he said,

Particularly during the last thirty years or so, biochemistry as we know it has been acquiring new techniques—often of great delicacy—suitable for dealing with many substances which occur naturally. I have never forgotten the remark made by Szent-Gyorgyi, Nobel prize winner in 1929, when I had the good fortune to work with him at Cambridge. He said that biochemical methods were then sufficiently good to enable any naturally occurring substance to be extracted, provided there was a quick test for it.

Florey's final years at Cambridge were marked by enthusiasms and by the seizure of every chance to reach the minds of the men who were leaders in his field of interest across Europe. He travelled, at times uncomfortably because of lack of money, to symposia and conferences, and to work briefly in Strasbourg with Professor Bouin and in Copenhagen with Professor Krogh. He also arranged through Sherrington to spend some time in Madrid working with the Spanish histologist, Ramon Y Cajal, who had won the Nobel Prize for physiology and medicine in 1906 for his pioneer work on antibodies.
Florey's urgent need to study with Cajal arose from a report that the great man had discovered new facts about the staining

of cells and opening new prospects of understanding of the
bacterial structure. The Australian's impatience knew no bounds
until he could make the arrangements.

Not the reason, but the manner of his going, evoked some
critical remarks from the social circle of the faculty, for, with only
a day or two's notice—and with Ethel in the later stages of her
first pregnancy—he insisted in his usual dominant manner that
she should go with him. He was criticized as an inconsiderate
bully; but they both seemed to enjoy the sun and the country.

The visit was successful—with it began his love of Spain—
despite a fiery outburst when, held up by incessant excuses for not
producing experimental animals for his work, Florey stormed
out of Cajal's institute and commenced to pack his bags.*

They eventually had to hurry back to Cambridge for the birth
of their first child, and their relationship together when they
returned gave little foundation for the criticism that had marked
their departure. They enjoyed themselves and when the child, a
girl, was born they called her Paquita Joanna, and had a lot of fun
using their few Spanish words to work out her name.

Paquita was left with no memories of the days at Cambridge,
for when she was one year old, Florey was offered his first pro-
fessorial chair. His decision to accept the post of Joseph Hunter
Professor of Pathology at the University of Sheffield surprised
some of his friends. Dean had suggested that it was time for him
to move upwards, but Drury and others were puzzled by Florey's
decision. Drury commented,

> It was quite obvious to some of us that he was going to be a
> great man in science and I asked him, 'Why turn your back on
> the promise you have here, in these comfortable surroundings,
> to take up routine duties as a Professor?' He had always seemed
> to me to have a very conscious occupation with money and
> security and he told me that money was the reason. 'I get into
> a chair as a young man, and if I get into the bracket of a pro-

---

* Florey retold the incident many times afterwards, saying that Cajal sent
him a present seeking forgiveness; the gift was a bottle of stain which had
been used by Ehrlich in his salvarsan experiments. Its eventual fate, in the
light of Florey's lack of historical appreciation, was never uncovered.

fessorial salary now, then my superannuation contributions will be worth all that much more when I retire. I shall also have a wider control over what I can do in research.' I think that, although he was always full of courage, lack of financial security, which had been with him for so long, worried him very much.[8]

CHAPTER 4

THE MOVE FROM CAMBRIDGE TO HIS FIRST CHAIR GAVE
Florey little relief from the problem of money; from the start it
was touch-and-go whether he would even be able to honour his
responsibility to his young laboratory assistant, James Kent.

His introduction to Sheffield University and the interview
which preceded his appointment as Professor of Pathology, were
not without their abrasive moments, and incidents quickly
added to his reputation for blunt and direct speech which the
more gentle writers of his obituaries were to term 'disconcerting'.
The story told of the interview was that when one sedate member
of the University committee suggested that Florey should join
the British Medical Association as a prerequisite to appointment
he exploded into indignation and told them if the job meant
'joining with that pack of bloody trade unionists', they knew what
to do with their job. He neither denied nor confirmed the story,
but it fitted in with the derogatory remarks he made in later years
on the medical profession in general.

When scientific eminence had laid the restraining hand of
discretion on him, he recalled, 'I was a little bit brutal to them
about what I wanted in the job but, in the end, they told me,
"We don't care much what you do, or what you start, so long as
you get those laboratories into a mess—they have been tidy far
too long." That suited me to a T and for the next four years I
pursued the role of the cell in inflammation, and the pattern of
infectious disease and its effect on tissue.'[1]

He also pressed on with the puzzle of the chemical action of
lysozyme and was quick to seek collaboration on this project.

He had the assistance of Kent in the laboratory, a young man who now knew his ways and requirements and who knew that, although Florey did only one experiment each day, preparations had to be made down to the last detail.

When Florey knew he was going to Sheffield he asked Kent if he would like to go with him, though he warned this might prove difficult. Sheffield already had a laboratory technician, a man with four children, and Florey would not see him dismissed to make way for Kent. 'They have no money at Sheffield. About ten shillings a week is all they can offer, so I'll have to see whether there is any more money elsewhere,' he said to Kent before he left. He pestered the Medical Research Council from the time he took up his chair early in 1932 until, three months later, they agreed to award him 'fifty shillings a week'—but only for one year, with no guarantee of renewal. 'If you come, you will have to take your chance,' he told Kent. But in the end Florey got the renewal and Kent saw out nearly four years in Sheffield in lodgings.

By the end of his first year at Sheffield Florey's name had appeared on more than thirty papers published in the different scientific journals and he had met Edward Mellanby, a Professor of Pharmacology. Mellanby, like his counterpart at Pennsylvania, A. Newton Richards, was also to be drawn into the penicillin epic. He was a northerner from Hartlepool, fourteen years older than Florey and already a member of the Medical Research Council, and soon after obtaining the fifty shillings a week to keep Kent by his side, Florey was questioning Mellanby on the prospect of money to pursue his special interest in lysozyme.

One day, after talking with Mellanby, Florey went back to his laboratory, sat at the bench in front of an old typewriter, and picked out an untidy letter to Sir Walter Fletcher, Secretary of the Medical Research Council,

I have had a talk with Mellanby, who assures me that the MRC has no money for further grants. Nevertheless, I am writing you in the fond hope that something will turn up. As you know, I worked with Dr Marjorie Stephenson at Cambridge on the chemistry of the action of lysozyme and have continued that interest here. As lysozyme is a widely distributed enzyme, I think it has some universally biological significance. It, therefore, seems to me, though not necessarily in the antibacterial sense, to be worthy of further investigation. If you could take an interest in this, I could expand on the problem.[2]

Florey then raised, for the first time with the Research Council, his conviction that collaboration with the discipline of biochemistry would be vital.

'I am quite unable to carry on work on this without the aid of a biochemist, and, for these services, I would like to make an application for an MRC grant to this effect.'

Replying, Fletcher asked whether there was no one ready to collaborate in Sheffield and said that if Florey sent a specific application it would be considered—along with all the rest. Florey sent in his application. Lysozyme, he wrote, could dissolve bacteria—his work had shown it to be distributed through nature in a capricious manner—it was in man and not in the cat, and . . . 'I am anxious to get a biochemist to work on the substrate of this material and I want an analysis of the products which act on bacteria.'[3]

Fletcher kept the correspondence alive, not yet sending the final rejection, and asked whether Florey had anyone in view and how much would it all cost. With a shadowing of events to come, and illustrating the long-term planning in which he was engaged, Florey replied, 'I have no one person in mind, but I have thought of the biochemical laboratories in Cambridge where they are doing fine work and have some very good people, interested in enzymes. The cost, I imagine, would be between £400 and £500 a year.'

He forcefully expressed his view that advance would come from bringing biochemists, biologists and pathologists together, but Fletcher, although professing sympathy with the concept, again could do no more than suggest there might 'be someone to work with you at Sheffield. Is there really no one there?'

Towards the end of 1932, Florey had two pleasant surprises; the Medical Research Council granted him the fifty shillings a week he sought for Kent's wages as well as a small sum of money for his own work—£140. Late in November that year he also heard that Sherrington, along with Adrian of Cambridge, had been awarded a Nobel Prize.

Also important to his years at Sheffield—though he did not realize this at the time—was the presence on his staff of Dr C. G. Paine, a former student at St Mary's who had known Fleming. During his last months at Sheffield Florey learned from Paine that he had used crude penicillin filtrates for surface treatments in his clinical work at the Royal Infirmary in Sheffield, and in the discussion—according to Paine—referred to Fleming's original paper on the mould. Paine had earlier sought a culture of *P. notatum* from Fleming, which had been readily supplied, and carried out a series of applications in the hospital which he later expressed as 'uniformly disappointing' and so were never written into the formal literature. Later the mould underwent mutation and ceased to produce any penicillin. Not until Florey recalled this conversation in after years and sought a note from Paine did he recourse to his notes to report the first cases of external application apart from the few surface applications made by Fleming at St Mary's, during 1929.[4]

Dr Paine reported to Florey that his first cases had included treatment of staphyloccocal infection of the skin surface, and eye infections in two newborn babies from gonococcal organisms and two other babies whose eyes were infected by staphylococci. The treatment was successful in three of the four cases; but since the filtrate was crude and the activity low, Paine drew no conclusions. In hindsight, the case which provided a clear indication of the latent power in penicillin came when Paine was asked to treat a local colliery manager. His right eye had been penetrated by a piece of stone which could not be removed by surgery because of inflammation and infection caused by organisms identified as pneumococci. Glaucoma threatened the man's sight, but when Paine washed his eye with crude penicillin culture, he was able to record within forty-eight hours that the swabs were sterile. 'The foreign body was removed and Mr Nutt (ophthalmic surgeon) told me subsequently that the man had recovered 6/6th vision in his right eye.'

Throughout his years at Sheffield, Florey extended his work on mucus and secretions with intense vigour. He also broke away to look at processes involved in birth control and worked on developing a treatment for tetanus. The results of all this work, done with collaborators, eventually appeared in *Lancet*.

During his second year at Sheffield the pattern of events started to shape a new future for him. In 1933 Sir Walter Fletcher retired and Professor Edward Mellanby was appointed the new Executive Secretary of the Medical Research Council. Florey now had a friend at court—albeit a friend whose influence was financially limited.

It was in fact 1935 before Florey could win a grant from his former colleague at Sheffield, this time to support his work on the action of the lymphatic system. By then Mellanby exerted an influence beyond the limited funds he dispensed and when the Scandinavian pathologist, Professor George Dreyer, died in Oxford he threw the strength of his personality behind a move to get Florey into the chair as the new Sir William Dunn Professor of Pathology.

The negotiations were conducted quietly, but it was Mellanby's influence that guided them. It was his conviction that pathology had moved into a new age of experimental approach and he thought Florey was the man to lead this trend.

Florey could not resist the prospect of returning to Oxford. Indeed, after four years in the smoke and industrial setting of Sheffield, he would probably have settled for a less prestigious post. The offer from Oxford came like the realization of a dream, bringing a certainty of position and power and influence and with it all, the subtle attraction of the prodigal returning in triumph, thirteen work-ridden years after he had arrived as an unknown and unnoticed Rhodes scholar from the colonies. When he was approached to determine whether he was interested, he could not at first believe his luck; and then he glowed with enthusiasm and delight. If his vanity was touched by the distinction the appointment would bring him, it was less evident than the sheer pleasure he showed at the prospect of fashioning a group to tackle the work he felt had to be done in experimental pathology.

Florey's appointment was noted by several leading scientists as 'a milestone in the history of pathology in Britain, because, for the first time, a man trained in experimental physiology—looking at pathology with the physiologist's eye—came into a position of influence on the subject'.[5]

It was like coming home again; he knew the colleges and would enter Lincoln as a fellow; he loved the streets he had wandered as a young Rhodes scholar, and the old stone buildings he had haunted in the days before Sherrington took him in hand; but the laboratories where he was to work were new to him. Professor George Dreyer had fought a long battle for the magnificent site in the Parks in Oxford, and to Florey the red-brick mansion of science he erected had the new look of a Christmas present.

But Florey found it was an echoing vault, half-empty of people and almost devoid of purpose and objectives. When he walked up the short, divided staircase of white stone, through the oaken front doors, and into the foyer with its circular viewpoint up and below, it had the somnolence of a mausoleum. Among the members of the staff he inherited were people who had been close to Dreyer—and Dreyer was an entirely different character from Florey. Dreyer had been outgoing and immediately recognizable as a scholar of note without any taint of ambition; his successor had a different reputation and, as one of the staff taken over at that time remarked, 'One eminent man in the bacteriology group described him as a "bushranger of research" and feared his rough anger and he, and others, who had held a special place with Dreyer, walked round Florey like bantams sizing up their adversary at the start of a cock fight.'

Professor Sir Rudolph Peters, one of the men who had been among Florey's examiners in the Final Honours School of Physiology in 1923, noted, from Oxford, that Florey's appointment to the Sir William Dunn chair 'evidently allayed much of his anxieties about his future'. He added, 'Though there were occasional reports of active arguments, these were unusual.'[6]

These arguments were the growing pains of a new force in medical science emerging at Oxford and Florey, prizing the spacious new building that was his legacy from Dreyer, set about his task of creating a more lively atmosphere. He needed the right men, and he needed money—and of the two, money was the more difficult to get in the middle of a decade of economic depression.

For the first time he made the rounds of the money dispensers: the Nuffield group, the Medical Research Council, the Empire Cancer Council and, finally, the Rockefeller Foundation. He settled down quickly and came face to face with the fact that not only were his problems of finance as acute in the splendid new Dunn building as they had been in Sheffield, but they were also on a much larger scale. Money was by far the more pressing problem if he was to organize the kind of team he had envisaged since his early days at Cambridge.

He summed up his experience in this way, 'Once you get a start in a place like Oxford, you don't really have trouble getting the right people round you.'

When he felt he had the prospect of enough money for at least a start, he began the work of building his team. In bacteriology he had inherited Professor A. D. Gardner, Dr Roy Vollum and Dr Jean Orr-Ewing, and there were also Dr Gordon Sanders and several Australian and American postgraduate students. But there was a big gap in the lines of forces he wanted to employ against the remaining barriers hiding the chemical nature of lysozyme.

His first action was to travel to Cambridge and consult the father of British biochemistry, Professor Sir Frederick Gowland Hopkins. Florey told Hopkins he wanted a good, keen mind to head his biochemical section, someone specifically interested in enzymes. Hopkins proposed that Florey should talk to a German-born biochemist, twenty-nine-year-old Ernst Boris Chain, who had left Berlin where he had worked on enzyme problems, when the Hitler pogrom against the Jews had become too threatening.

Florey asked for an immediate meeting and, soon after, in Hopkins' office, the two men who would share a Nobel Prize with Fleming, faced each other for the first time: Ernst Boris Chain, with hair and moustache reminiscent of Einstein, and challenging eyes, appraising the man he later described as 'that young, vigorous, direct Australian'.

Chain, who had almost become a professional concert pianist,

and whose Russian-born father had died in Berlin, listened carefully to Florey's proposals for a biochemical programme in
Oxford and heard for the first time of lysozyme and its action
against certain bacteria. Then he accepted the offer to join
Florey's staff at Oxford, embarking on a journey to scientific
fame and a relationship with his professor which ranged from
warmth and tolerance and kindness in adversity to days of bitter
argument and quarrelling until—in Chain's own words, '. . . the
very walls of Florey's office would shudder with our shouting',
and eventually they spoke no more to each other and com-
municated only in writing.

All that was ahead of them when they met on this day late in
1935 and Florey explained to the biochemist where his interest in
lysozyme lay and that this project would be one among many
including such things as snake venoms and problems relating to
cancer. And Chain, impressed then with Florey's direct and forthright manner, found an immediate rapport which he welcomed
even more when events in his native Germany made life in
England difficult for him. Long afterwards when telling of this
he stated, 'Florey gave me a unique chance to build up a biochemical section at the Dunn School. He simply told me to
start and to take my own decisions—but he did suggest to me
that I should start work on lysozyme.' In this atmosphere Chain
made his arrangements to leave the Cambridge laboratories and
to join Florey in Oxford as soon as the transfer could be arranged.

During the first months of their association the news reached
Florey and Chain from Europe of a major advance in chemotherapy. For the first time clinical medicine had the promise of a
non-specific compound that would act against bacterial infection
and, as had been the case with Paul Ehrlich and salvarsan against
syphilis, it had sprung from activity in one of the synthetic dyes
produced by the German chemical industry.

This new advance looked to be a veritable revolution. It was
credited to Gerhard Domagk, the Director of the Institute of
Experimental Pathology at Elberfeldt in the huge research complex
of I. G. Farben industries. Domagk had led a team in a 'shotgun'
approach, which put all new dye products, synthetic and

organic, through the antibacterial screen. One of these was a
brilliant red azo dye named prontosil. Although Domagk had
found—as early as 1932—that this dye protected mice experimentally infected with streptococci, the world was not told of his
work until an almost unnoticed paper was published in February
1935.

It was not a convincing paper, nor particularly thrilling. It
showed this same dye which in the mouse system dealt with
bacteria did not do so when used against bacteria in cultures.
The paper naturally came to Florey's attention, since the experiment occurred in the laboratory in Germany given over to experimental pathology. But it caused no real stir until his friends,
Professor and Madame Trefouels and their colleagues at the Pasteur
Institute in Paris, the following year, split the azo dye compound
into two molecular rings, one of which was the dye—which was
clinically useless—the other a bacteria killer, a colourless substance
that had been known for many years—sulphanilamide.

The Trefouels' work sent a quiver of excitement through the
ranks of the believers in chemotherapy. Ehrlich's work with dye
was now followed by Domagk's therapeutic. But this, unlike
salvarsan which was a specific, promised action against a broad
front of infectious diseases.

The sulphonamide derivatives were to dominate the medical
scene for the next five years with almost every effort focused on
honing the molecular structure to strike a wider range of bacterial enemies. They caused a frantic, global scramble. In hundreds
of laboratories, in universities, research centres and in the great
drug houses, the search for Ehrlich's magic bullet became a great
race, with wealth and fame waiting for the winner. Thousands
of slightly different compounds were fashioned and tested in
chemical jugglings that often went beyond the understanding
of the operators. It came close to being a vast game of molecular
roulette which slowly began to produce one, then two, then three
or four sulphonamides, to give medicine its first effective tools
against infection on a fairly broad front.

It was a revolution which turned more and more minds to the
support of the chemical lock and key theory. It took Fleming's
attention at St Mary's. He had been a leading practitioner in

treating syphilis with salvarsan, and the sulphonamide revolution caught his imagination.*

The sheer luck in Domagk's discovery led Ernst Chain to say later, 'It seems a sobering thought, frequently not realized by those who are not familiar with the field, that a discovery of the magnitude of the sulphonamides was made entirely fortuitously, without any logical plan of approach.'[7]

Chain noted that the effective action of the dye was an illusion that was short-lived. It was dispelled a few months later by the Trefouels' work which showed that the antibacterial activity '. . . had nothing to do with its dye nature, but resided in its colourless component which was liberated by enzymic cleavage in the animal body from the prontosil molecule.' Had this particular dye resisted that cleaving enzyme, then the chemotherapeutic nature of sulphanilamide 'could have escaped detection for many decades'.

The concept was put forward by some workers, particularly by some of Fleming's colleagues, that, without the sulphonamides to show the way, penicillin would not have emerged from its obscurity and that the whole development of the multi-billion dollar antibiotic industry would not have occurred when it did.

This is an assumption which took no account of the fact that, from 1929 onwards, when Fleming published his paper on the Penicillium mould, Florey had been on the path of penicillin by way of lysozyme, and nothing would have diverted him from that course. Even the sulphonamide discoveries, regarded as 'important in the history of mankind' (Prof. R. Hare—*The Birth of Penicillin*, Allen & Unwin 1970) and the flush of hope that suffused the profession in that year of 1936 held shortcomings for Florey, for he saw weaknesses in the new armoury against infectious diseases.

Florey did not falter in his plans. With the prospect of support from several quarters, and with the co-operation of the University in his expansion proposals, he went straight on with building the team necessary for the multi-discipline attack on chemical

* In their post-war monograph, *Antibiotics*, the Oxford group said that Fleming devoted his attention to these agents for three years, 'How completely the possible use of penicillin in the treatment of septic infection was forgotten is shown by the fact that, in his papers on the subject of chemotherapy about this time, penicillin was not once mentioned.'

pathology. He knew what he wanted and he lost no time in showing the ability colleagues referred to as 'his genius for finding the heart of a problem', and what his daughter, Paquita, called 'his uncanny way of making a right decision'.

Florey wrote to Robert Webb, then at the Royal Free Hospital medical school in London, and asked him if he knew of a 'bright young mind' for special work in pathology at his school. Webb found him his 'bright young mind'. This was the Hon. Dr Margaret Jennings, daughter of the Earl of Cottesloe and the wife of a London gastro-enterologist, then in her early thirties and a charming and elegant woman. Webb had known her when she was a student. By chance, she came one day to tell Professor Webb that her husband had taken an appointment at the Radcliffe Infirmary in Oxford and that she would be leaving the Royal Free Hospital to go with him.

Webb enthused to her, 'Then you are just the person we are looking for. What a coincidence!' Professor Webb explained later, 'I told her what Florey wanted and what work she was needed for, and then I wrote Florey at Oxford and told him I was sending him the very person he wanted. I had no idea then what I was doing. She was an extremely loyal and gifted woman and almost from that time on she became his right hand. She was attractive and capable, but I had not the slightest suspicion that one day he would marry her.'

At about the same time Chain suggested an approach to a gifted young biochemist working in Cambridge, Dr Norman Heatley. By the middle of 1936 the team which was to help discover therapeutic penicillin was being drawn together.

With his plans on the brink of being finalized, and satisfied that his position was secure and his future standing safe, Florey yielded to the desire to visit his homeland. His parents were dead, but his sisters were living and Ethel was eager for her relatives to see her two children, Paquita and Charles—who had been born in Sheffield.

So they boarded a ship and made the only journey they were to make together back to Australia. Florey was pleased with his

career in England, but nostalgic for Australia. At thirty-seven he
had won one of the important chairs in Britain in medical science
and he felt he could take a holiday of a few months before he
took his career on to new levels.

As far as was within their character, they made a sentimental
pilgrimage to Adelaide. He went up into the hills at Mitcham to
catch a breath of his old life and walked with his childhood
friend, Mrs Molly Bowen, now married to a St Peter's classmate,
to look at 'Coreega' framed against towering fir trees and eucalypts and flanked by the diminished rose gardens and clumps of
oleander. The fruit trees his father had planted were already
gnarled, some roses were too huge for beauty, and the garden
could not bear comparison with the image he had held of it for
so many years. Reduced in size, intersected by an asphalt road,
and with the old paddocks where they chased the cow and picked
mushrooms built over, he found it sad. As they walked back
down past the church Molly reminded him of the night when he
took her to his first Blue and White Ball at the college and of her
embarrassment that she was eighteen months his senior. It seemed
to Molly that the physical gap of age between them then had
been as unbridgeable as the emotional one she now saw between
Florey and Ethel.

'There was a kind of frozen relationship between them, and it
was a piteous thing to see,' she remembered, adding, 'I could not
reach Floss as I used to.'

Ethel looked much different to her family, changed after ten
years, but they loved the children.

Florey left her in Adelaide and went to Melbourne where he
visited Professor Peter MacCullum and other workers, and talked
about antibacterial concept and the advent of the sulphonamides,
yet to have any impact in Australia.

One of the scientists present at that visit recorded,

He talked about the coming of the sulphonamides, but he
made it very clear he saw drawbacks that did not fit his own
sense of perfection in dealing with infections. He told us, 'What
has happened is wonderful and has shown us that substances
exist which we can use, or adapt, to control bacterial infection

in the blood stream, but they can be very toxic. They are almost useless against staphylococci and pneumococci and we cannot be satisfied.' He explained to us that, since he was not a chemist and could not think of taking on new disciplines, it had become obvious that the whole concept had to be tackled on a multi-discipline basis and that his first assault was to be on a natural substance that dealt with bacteria—and that was lysozyme. For most of us, both lysozyme and sulphonamides were new territory.[8]

When the rounds were finished, Florey became restless and anxious to get back to his new domain at Oxford. He had found little change in the level and scope of the medical research in Australia, only an awareness of its limitations. They took ship and sailed through the Suez Canal and into the Mediterranean where he could wait no longer. He disembarked at Toulon and, leaving Ethel to bring the children home by sea, caught a commercial flight to Paris, stopping to pay a visit to the Pasteur Institute, before continuing on to London.

CHAPTER 5

FLOREY ARRIVED BACK IN OXFORD FULL OF RENEWED
vigour and drive to find his team gathered for the multi-discipline
attack he had planned for so long on the problems of pathology
which interested him—among them the long-standing puzzle of
lysozyme.

Enthusiasm pervaded the Sir William Dunn School of Pathology
and there was—as Dr Heatley noted in after years—a sunny and
bracing atmosphere throughout the laboratories. Soon after his
arrival back in Oxford, Florey received the heartening news that
the Rockefeller Foundation had allocated him $1 280 for equip-
ment to pursue his development of a chemical attack on lysozyme.

But, even with this support from America, the following
months were marked by the continual frustration of important
decisions by the niggardly funding for antibacterial research. In a
country already preparing for war Florey was lashing out again
and again, castigating the blindness of officialdom towards the
needs of research workers and the value of their work. Early in
1937 he was complaining in a letter to the Medical Research
Council, 'I am having the utmost difficulty in finding money for
even relatively small essentials in my research.' The paucity of
funds rubbed his temper raw, with the result that his reputation
as an explosive personality grew. But he did not let the lack of
funds limit his vision or his imagination, and with what money he
had he pursued the elucidation of the ability in the lysozyme
molecule to melt away the bacteria susceptible to its action.

In that year the substance was purified for the first time in
his laboratories and was shown to be a true enzyme capable of
splitting essential components in the walls of bacteria, but these

were bacteria which were harmless to man. In a nearby laboratory, also in 1937, Dr E. P. Abraham obtained lysozyme in a
crystalline form while Chain and his doctoral assistant Leslie
Epstein—a Rhodes scholar from America who was later to change
his name to Falk—worked towards the eventual elucidation of
the substrate, or basis material, in the enzyme.

Florey had pursued these matters since the late 1920s and had
published his first paper on the action of the substance in 1929
but now he could see the trail petering out. It was a long-term
project to which funds had been allocated and it would be taken
on its final logical conclusion, even though—as 1937 came to a
close—it was clear to him that lysozyme would offer nothing that
was of clinical importance. The path which had begun with
Fleming's sneeze in the year Florey had first reached Oxford
began to look a dead end; but it was to be the immediate stepping
stone to penicillin therapy and to the revelation of the astonishing healing power latent in the secretions of the *Penicillium
notatum* mould—the second of Fleming's fortuitous observations.
Florey now had to accept that he had followed the wrong trail
and that with all its mysteries near to complete understanding,
lysozyme would have to be replaced with another line of intellectual inquiry.

At this point Florey and Chain were closer than they had been
since they first began their scientific association, and they were
never again to reach the point of camaraderie. They started the
habit of meeting at the end of each working day to walk home
together across the grassy parklands at the back of the Dunn
building. Chain's home was not far from Florey's house in Parks
Road and they would occasionally invite one another for a drink,
all the while talking of the work that should be done and the
problems to be solved; and the nub of all their discussions was the
antibacterial concept and how they should delve into an almost
virgin field . . . which way would they go . . . what offered them
the richest harvest in knowledge?

But they did not come directly to penicillin. There was no
neon sign pointing down the road they should follow, and no
reason for them to suspect the medical 'Eldorado' waiting in the
humble mould. It was then, as lysozyme tailed off in interest,

that another of the antibacterial substances had to be considered as a replacement in the programme. In general, as they talked, they thought in terms of other enzymes similar to lysozyme but whose action would break down bacteria of more consequence to clinical interest.

These years were the summer of Florey's relationship with Chain and he shared with him his worry and concern at the scarcity of funds for the research they discussed together, and more and more the biochemist began to share his professor's interest in the whole canvas of antibacterial phenomena and its possible use in therapy. The approach was always academic, an exercise aimed at extending pure knowledge.

'We never gave any thought to performing miracles,' said Chain, long afterwards. 'The subject took my interest and I could see at least five years of good solid scientific work on these antibacterial substances.'[1]

There they were, in the summer of 1938, still thrashing about in their exploration for a new path; Florey, a seasoned professor and investigator at the age of forty, unconventional, dedicated to new ideas and the factual proof of them, opposed to speculative theories; and Chain, at thirty-two, gifted with a fast-ranging vision, vitriolic and ambitious, eager to work and an admirer of Florey's positive nature.

Against this background the two scientists blended their minds to attack a problem in the way Florey had envisaged long before in his days in Cambridge—the merging of biology with biochemistry; two minds trained in different disciplines seeking the solution of an intriguing intellectual problem. Florey in his wide-ranging physiology had seen the ability of antibodies and defensive cells to destroy the structure of intruders with chemical keys, as lysozyme could split a key substance in the bacterial walls—and as the mysterious substance from the Penicillium mould could dissolve a thriving culture of bacteria into a transparent liquid. Chain, on the other hand, knew the ways of enzymes and hormones. He had worked on the frontier of biochemistry and shown great flair for striking the heart of a problem. He had the confidence and belief in his skill and knowledge that gave strength to Florey's purpose.

Night after night they would stroll across the grass, kicking
the leaves, and pausing here and there to argue a point of approach.
Then, one evening, they decided to make a full review of all the
older scientific literature for reported examples of bacterial
inhibition, or antagonism among the microbes, to help them
reach a selection of the best prospects. The result of this step was
a rich haul of isolated incidents of discovery that made their final
choice more difficult, and certainly more complex. What it did
reveal was called in an editorial in the *British Medical Journal* 'a
fascinating story of a long series of studies on microbial antagonism going back over sixty years, of which very few users of
penicillin would be aware'.

They uncovered hundreds of examples in a dozen different
countries and the scientific reportage ran a line directly back to
Florey's old boyhood hero—Louis Pasteur. The famous Frenchman, originator of the conception that bacteria caused disease,
had noted with his colleague, Joubert, in 1887, that a culture of a
bacillus causing anthrax was lysed, or dissolved, when contaminated by common airborne bacteria. This was the first reported
incident of what another Frenchman, Vuillemin, was to name
'antibiosis', a word that led, eventually, to the term 'antibiotic',
coined by Waksman of streptomycin fame, in America in 1941,
to denote chemotherapeutic substances basically produced by
natural processes.

Florey found, and reported later when he gave the Lister
memorial lecture in 1945, that in the same year of the Pasteur
observation, a Swiss scientist named Garré, who developed the
culture plate streaking test which Fleming used in 1928, had the
idea that microbial antagonism could be used in therapeutics.
There were many other instances of such work right up to the
end of the century, but of outstanding interest to Florey was that
in 1889 the first attempt was made to develop a practical application when a European scientist named Doehle tried to obtain an
organism that would protect cattle against anthrax infection.
The results, however, were indecisive.

The Oxford research brought to light again the forgotten
work of Emmerich and Löw who showed that an injection of
streptococci into rabbits infected with anthrax saved 60% of

them from death. In what Florey termed 'a remarkable outburst of energy, both in the laboratory and the clinic', Emmerich and Löw introduced the first antibacterial extract, called pyocyanase, which they used in experiments on animals as a bacteria-killing agent effective against a small range of organisms, including some staphylococci. But, while it was afterwards used as an antiseptic, it gained no place in therapy of deep-seated infection because of its highly toxic nature.

About this time a Spanish worker named Gosio went on record with the extraction of the first crystalline antibiotic from a Penicillium mould, the same genus of mould that Fleming found on his culture plate in 1928. Gosio did this work in 1896, 32 years before Fleming's interest was aroused, and produced an antibiotic substance which later was identified as mycophenolic acid. He showed that it was active in inhibiting the growth of the anthrax bacilli, but he did not have enough material to broaden his experiments.

Gosio's mould was a strain known as *Brevi compactum*. That it was not the *Penicillium notatum* strain that landed on Fleming's exposed plate in 1928 may be taken as a tragedy of immense proportion for the human race, especially for the millions who died from common sepsis diseases and for those victims of the First World War who were afflicted by gas gangrene and other infections. The results that would have come from a penicillin-type antibiotic appearing in medicine in the first decade of this century are incalculable. But neither Gosio nor Fleming, and at first neither Florey nor Chain, saw the enormous potency locked behind the chemical barriers they were examining in such detail.

But the two Oxford scientists' search of the world scientific literature revealed that a continuing string of signposts had been erected on a global scale. There were examples reported from Finland, Denmark and Persia, along with others from Switzerland, Spain, Germany, France and Belgium. Even as far away as Australia a bacteriologist named Grieg-Smith, working for the New South Wales Linnaean Society in a room overlooking Sydney harbour at Elizabeth Bay, had noted antibacterial action among a strange class of soil organisms, the actinomycetes. His

6

work was afterwards credited with sparking interest that led to the isolation of actinomycin and then to the eventual discovery of the broad-spectrum antibiotic, streptomycin, by Waksman and others, the first powerful weapon effective against tuberculosis. These were the soil organisms which in the end proved the richest storehouse of antibiotics suitable for use in human beings.

In the mass of data which the Oxford workers compiled, other people were also seen to have come close to earning an imperishable name in medical history: but all missed the accolade eventually to be conferred on Fleming. In the early 1920s, in the annexe of the Pasteur Institute in a suburb of Brussels, Dr André Gratia and his associate woman scientist, Sara Dath, performed a monumental task in collecting and examining many moulds and fungi. Among their cultures of bacteria there came one day the same visitation by *Penicillium notatum* that graced Fleming's plate in the summer of 1928. But the mould that grew on the colony of staphylococci in Brussels was doomed to obscurity and never to be touched by the global publicity eventually given to Fleming's accidental contamination. The conditions for both moulds must have been exquisitely similar, as has been shown by some forensic investigation over the years. But, while the requirements for seeding and culture were all met—to the very point of showing a clear zone of inhibition in the bacteria—the similarity ended there. For while Gratia* and Dath only wrote a short note on their observation, Fleming actually cultured the mould and made observations on its characteristics, which he recorded.

There were hundreds of examples in the literature of observations and investigations as well as many suggestions for their use, not only against bacterial diseases in man but also against certain forms of fungal disease that attack plant life. Along with these was a casebook of accumulated folklore and legend connected with the use of moulds throughout history that made the whole field difficult to ignore as a source of biodynamic phenomena.

*Students of Gratia, when he later became Professor of Bacteriology at Liege University, noted that he often quoted the event as a lesson that every unusual biological phenomenon should be pursued to full understanding by every means possible.[2]

One authority recorded that Chinese people of three thousand years ago applied the crushings of mouldy soya beans to infections and boils, and that primitive peoples around the world had used warm soil as a pack with antiseptic results. One historical source had a Greek king of the sixth century writing of peasant women who treated the infected wounds of his soldiers with mould scraped from cheeses, while in Britain a Suffolk woman was reputed to have magical powers of healing because she grew moulds for treating suppurations and infections.

Many centuries before Europeans reached Australia, some aboriginal tribes had used moulds taken from the sheltered side of eucalypt trees to treat wounds. Sir Charles Kelleway, who directed the Walter and Eliza Hall Institute in Melbourne, related with regret, when Florey's work had made Fleming's observations significant, that a bushman had once brought a smelly bundle of these moulds, wrapped in sacking, to the Institute with the suggestion they should be investigated since they appeared to defeat infection and promote healing. He was thanked politely, regarded as another carrier of folklore tales, and the bundle dropped afterwards into the Institute's ashcan.[3]

The accumulation of data continued week after week at Oxford and, though it was added to by research in later years, Florey and Chain felt in the autumn that they had enough material on which to assess their future research.

The surprising extent of the international reportage of examples of antagonism between microbes displayed a rich field for investigation, but it was one matter to sort out where the brightest prospects lay and another to provide the necessary support for the selected tasks. As they talked on their evening walks Florey made it clear to Chain that he felt hampered and shackled in his planning by lack of financial support.

Recalling these times, Chain commented later, 'It was an absolutely ridiculous situation. On one occasion Florey had to send down a stern message to all heads of sections, warning them not to spend a penny because the research account was overdrawn. It seemed an almost impossible situation in which to start planning a new branch of work.'

In the welter of examples of microbial antagonism which they had found, Florey and Chain, on their evening walks, did not find it an easy task to select their first starters. In the outcome their minds, for various reasons, settled on three chosen substances. Competing with the possibility in the Penicillium mould were certain soil organisms, part of the teeming micro-life in the earth. They chose two organisms of interest. One of these was *Bacillus pyocyaneus* from which Emmerich and Löw had previously extracted the substance they had named pyocyanase. Florey noted, later, that 'Emmerich and Löw applied this substance to lesions of the skin caused by anthrax with, they claimed, some benefit. Although this product was on sale in Germany as recently as 1930, its use in medicine never became widespread.'[4]

At the time—it was 1938—Florey thought that, in co-operation with his gifted biochemist, pyocyanase might produce some new intellectual path into the nature of the chemical warfare between microbes.*

Also holding a place in their interest was a substance called actinomycetin produced by a group of strange organisms of the soil—the actinomycetes, half bacterium and half fungus—from one of which later came a powerful antibiotic against tuberculosis, streptomycin.† Having reached these decisions on areas of interest—the Penicillium mould, pyocyanese and actinomycetin—they agreed that Chain should follow the biochemical path and that Florey would undertake the biological work, provide the systematic backing, and seek funds.

Face to face with the Penicillium report again after nearly ten years and with the memory revived of his exchanges with Murray and Szent-Gyorgyi in Cambridge and the work of Paine in Sheffield another clear indicator, Florey turned his attention to Fleming's original paper with a depth of critical study he had not given when he was immersed in the lysozyme project.

---

* Work on the *Bacillus pyocyaneus* at Oxford was carried out by a Polish-born woman, Miss Schoental, under Chain. In the course of her study she extracted three separate antibacterial substances all of which were toxic to human tissue.
† In the course of events, however, this substance was not immediately pursued at the Sir William Dunn School.

The experience he had gained in antibacterial experiments and the extent of the literature on this subject now gave greater penetration to Florey's approach, and although he then—and afterwards—described his interest as academic and intellectual, those close to him saw a new impatient eagerness as though he glimpsed something more than another intellectual exercise.

Together with Chain, and alone in his office, he spent hours poring over the brief facts Fleming had written, often trying to deduce the meaning of passages or fill in the gaps where Fleming had omitted information. Both he and Chain found the first report incomplete in some details essential to their consideration; the composition of the medium on which the mould had grown, and into which the penicillin had been exuded, was not stated, and the strain of staphylococci was not indicated—it was 'just one of a number of variants'.

Thus the situation which faced Florey and Chain when they commenced their study of penicillin in the latter months of 1938 was something of a laboratory curiosity. It did not differ radically from many of the other paths they could have chosen—with the exception that Fleming's curious mind, his special gift for noting the importance of uncommon phenomena, and his longing to find an antiseptic against the terrible infected wounds he had witnessed in France, had left a trail which, to their minds, held certain attractions.

Substances which were powerful against disease-causing bacteria were common enough, but they had all been found too toxic for systemic use. Fleming's work left enough fact for them to hope for a bland substance from the penicillin mould, and Raistrick's efforts also provided clues.

The final decision to begin work on penicillin rested on two points of appeal in their minds.

To Chain the instability of the active principle in the mould juice which had discouraged Fleming and defeated Raistrick, indicated that it could have extremely interesting biochemical properties, and an unusual molecular structure.

To Florey the allure in the Penicillium mould was that it showed effectiveness against staphylococci which, despite the new sulphonamide drugs, were untouched by any remedy;

and the strange omission of tests against infected animals left a chance that the active substance might strike at bacteria in the living system as effectively as it had done on Fleming's culture plate.

Chain's analytical mind also seized on a further clue from Raistrick's work which raised his confidence that the active principle could be successfully extracted. The London workers had reported that the broth on which mould had grown could be stored for months in sterile conditions at 0°C. At that temperature they found that the penicillin content would remain active.

The biochemist told Florey, 'It seems clear to me that these facts show conditions under which extraction may be made. Cold is the key. If we keep the temperature down and we control the acid levels, then I think we can get, at the very least, a partial purification.'[5]

In the last years of the decade Ethel had become increasingly deaf. Only raised voices, shouting down the curved tortoiseshell hearing trumpet she tried to conceal under little curls of hair, could reach her. Her affliction was a constant source of irritation to Florey. Under the pressures that surrounded him at the time, the effort of communication was a burden that led to irrational reaction; while Ethel, as with so many deaf people, was offended at what she took to be insults to her intelligence. Over the years, since she had joined him in research at Cambridge, she had wanted always to know the path of the development of his work but had been prevented, by the loss of her hearing, from catching every facet and nuance of his explanations, while he had steadily fallen back onto his habitual bluntness. At times, when he was tired and short-tempered and his voice was raised in anger at her, guests at their home would see tears fill her eyes and feel embarrassed at the situation; and some of them, having once experienced the exchanges, vowed never to come to the Florey home again.

But there was always something between them, holding them together, even in bitter argument, and always he wanted to tell Ethel of his advances. The pity of their relationship was that both were such strong-minded people. Ethel's will and resolve, equal to his in the test that was to come with the task of forcing penicillin into medical application, caused them to clash with more fire and hurt than was the case with more compliant wives.

Towards the end of 1938 Florey walked into his Parks Road home one evening to have dinner with Ethel and his daughter, Paquita. He seemed to them more easy in his manner than usual, but restless and eager.

As they ate dinner, with little Charles upstairs asleep, he bent and called down Ethel's trumpet that he had decided to concentrate his research on penicillin. Lysozyme, he said, had to be dropped, and he would turn to the substance that had intrigued him for so long.

As they dined, Florey talked of the long mental path he had followed. Then, Paquita recalls, he said, 'Tonight I came to a final decision, and the moment when I reached that decision I was standing beneath the big old chestnut tree in the park at the back of the building.'[6] Later in the evening he wandered, still restless, back through the night to the laboratories where lights were burning in one of the rooms.

Dr R. Douglas Wright was near the end of his time at Oxford and had taken to the habit of working late at night in order to complete his researches. A massively-built bear of a man, to whom a wry Australian wit had given the nickname of 'Pansy', he was as blunt and as direct in his speech as was Florey. There was an affinity from their first meeting in Australia, in 1936, when Florey had invited the physiologist to study at Oxford, and they collaborated in research on bodily secretions and, together with Dr Margaret Jennings, wrote several papers for publication before Wright left to return to Melbourne University.

'Many nights he would wander back to talk as I worked; he never did seem to have many joyous attractions at home and we would yarn about his work,' said Wright long after. 'On this evening he came in looking tired and very dejected and I spoke to him bluntly, as I always did, and I asked him what he had decided to do. I could talk to him like that. He was the straightest man I ever knew and he would never back off from anyone. If you were straight, he was with you all the way.'

Wright went on to say that, at the time, he knew of the pending decision on the work which would eventually replace lysozyme and he remembered Florey saying, time and again, that he had had penicillin in the back of his mind all during the stages of the lysozyme work.

He said to me that night when I questioned him, 'There is no question, we will now have to go for penicillin. But let's face it; it is obvious that penicillin is a tough project. Some very fine chemists have tried to isolate it and have got nowhere. It could be just another blind alley, and where would I be then?' Then I said that if he had made up his mind about penicillin, what was his worry? And he looked at me for a long moment and said, 'I only hope that I can find some money somewhere. Mellanby might find some, but we've had grants for four years to work on lysozyme and produced nothing—and what he's put up has been a lot of money for this country. My worry is that I've got the bacteriologists and the biologists, and I've got my team together. If the money doesn't come along I might not be able to hold them together, and it would all be finished.[7]

CHAPTER 6

IN HIS LABORATORY ON THE FIRST FLOOR OF THE SIR
William Dunn building Dr Ernst Chain concentrated on the
words he was reading,

... a fluffy white mass which increases rapidly in size and,
after a few days, sporulates, the centre becoming dark green and
later almost black. In four or five days a bright yellow colour
is produced which diffuses into the medium. In certain conditions a reddish-brown colour can be observed in the growth.
In broth the mould grows on the surface as a white fluffy
growth, changing in a few days to a dark felted mass. The broth
becomes bright yellow ... it was shown that in dilutions of
one in up to eight hundred the broth inhibited some species of
bacteria. Staphylococcus, streptococcus, pneumococcus were
the most sensitive. The active broth was ... given intravenously to rabbits and mice and shown to be no more toxic
than ordinary broth and caused no irritation or other unde-
sirable effect when applied to the conjunctiva and to large
ulcerated areas in man.[1]

This was Fleming's paper, published in June 1929, with the
title which showed the bacteriologist's approach, *On the Antibacterial Action of Cultures of a Penicillium With Special Reference
to Their Use in the Isolation of B. influenzae.*
Puzzling over all the promise in these phrases which had not
been fully explored, Dr Chain sat reading in silence, going over
and over the words, a picture forming in his mind of the mould
beginning and growing in the centre of the culture plate, turning

67

from white to blue-green, and then turning darker with age.
Suddenly he was aware of another picture in his mind: a woman
carrying a little glass dish along a corridor, and in the dish was a
culture of blue-green mould. Describing this moment, Dr Chain
said,

> Something seemed to click in my mind, and there was this
> woman—Miss Campbell-Renton who worked for Professor
> Gardner across the corridor. I went at once to find her and ask
> her whether I had seen her carrying a petri dish with a mould
> culture along the corridor that separated our laboratories, and
> she said she had. I asked her if she knew the strain of the mould
> and if, by any chance, it was *Penicillium notatum*. She looked
> surprised and then said 'yes' it was, and that she had been using
> it for some time in the bacteriology lab to separate unwanted
> bacteria from cultures of *B. influenza* which were not sensitive
> to penicillin. I was astounded at my luck in finding the very
> mould about which I had been reading, here, in the same build-
> ing, right under our very noses. I could hardly believe it was
> true. Miss Campbell-Renton agreed to give me a sample and
> told me that it had been obtained from Fleming by Professor
> Dreyer, Florey's predecessor, who had thought for a time that
> it might have some relationship to his interest in bacteriophage
> —but that he had lost interest when it was seen that it had
> nothing to do with that subject.[2]

Chain nurtured his small sample of the mould like a mother a
newborn child. At first he kept its presence in his laboratory a
secret, but later brought Epstein into the task of establishing the
criteria of the growth of the fungus.

In his office across the corridor Florey, still wrestling with the
problems of his internal logistics and finance, was writing a
letter to Sir Edward Mellanby at the Medical Research Council
informing him that he intended to undertake a new line of work
and would need money for its implementation. It was then
exactly two years from the day when the Oxford team would
give their first injection of partially purified penicillin to a human
being.

The date of the letter was 27th January 1939, and he wrote, 'Investigations are planned here on the antibacterial action of certain substances reported in the literature. Our studies will include pyocyanase, actinomycetin and penicillin.' It was brief, but it prepared the ground for the application for a grant that he would make when it became opportune. Unerring scientific instinct, or pure luck, had made Florey indicate his interest in just those three areas of antibacterial action among the teeming microbes from which would come the main flow of antibiotics.

With these events, and with Chain later informing Florey of the existence of the Penicillium mould in his laboratory, just as he was making a formal request for permission to cultivate it, they entered the second month of 1939 with no special portent of the days of medical revolution waiting ahead, and with Florey still engrossed with the problem of money and keeping his team together.

As spring, with all its fateful political events, began to appear, so an atmosphere of presentiment spread both inside and outside the laboratories. The relief and hope that the Munich agreement had brought the previous year were shreds in the chill wind of fact. The intervening months had been no more than a breather. Now all the precursors of war were about the street, with growing piles of sandbags and military convoys, and factory chimneys smoking as they had not done since the 1914–18 conflict. Everywhere were signs of preparation—the handing out of gasmasks to civilians, the exercises in Civil Defence, and the building of air raid shelters. Even at the Dunn School this latter work was put in hand, and the staff excavated and constructed their own shelter at the back of the red-brick building. All the scientists good-humouredly took a hand with pick and shovel and enjoyed the task, with Florey's young son, Charles, being taken on a tour of inspection devised on formal lines. They had fun, and laughed, but, underneath, all felt it was a grim business, which hung a curtain of uncertainty over all there was to do.
For Florey the signs of war added menace to the unity of his team and he feared its stresses would rip them apart before he had

them functioning at peak. He racked his mind for schemes to keep them together as a single grouping, and for new means of obtaining money. In the end the answer to his problem came from an unexpected quarter. It came from Whitehall—from the War Office itself—seeking his services as a consultant on 'poison gas research' to which, if he agreed, he would have to pledge at least a third of his time should the work become necessary. 'I don't quite know what it all means, but I have agreed,' he told his colleagues. It was an approach that brought the idea to his mind of specialized war service for his team.

Informing the War Office and the Medical Research Council, Florey worked out a plan with the Ministry of Health in which his pathologists could become a small war research group, giving special attention to blood transfusions. He proposed that he and Chain should head this group and that Dr Gordon Sanders should be the Transfusions Officer.

The plan was accepted. It ran on a county basis and Florey was allocated transport—a van that would eventually make a crucial journey for his penicillin project—and they all took part in the service from time to time. Ethel, with Sanders and Barnes and the other workers at the school, helped solve some of the problems and lifted the standard of the blood transfusion service in the Oxford area. It gave them contacts at different hospitals that were later to be valuable.

Florey had gone through the first half of the year filling his usual duties on committees and conferences, and tackling the occasional task of being an external examiner at some other university. At one of these, Bristol, he had examined a young graduate with an interest in colour photography, which he had used to illustrate his study of burns. Florey had asked him the usual questions and felt himself liking the young man, passed him, and then forgot him. But he was to see him again during the war when penicillin first came to help pilots and airmen recover from their burns. The young graduate's name was Bodenham.

By the middle of the year Florey's anxieties were at their peak. The team's financial burdens had never been heavier, and what seemed to be the first crack in his team appeared, when the young biochemist who had joined his group from Cambridge, Dr

Norman Heatley, won a grant from the Rockefeller Foundation and planned to use it to study with Lindestrom Lang in Copenhagen.

In the same month, June, Florey became involved in a row with several members of the Nuffield Research Grants Committee. It began over his application for £300 to support the work that Dr Margaret Jennings was doing in collaboration with himself. Florey was told of the rejection of his proposal, and heard that there had been statements and remarks recorded which he considered improper and contemptible. He stormed into the Nuffield offices in a towering rage, demanding that all these remarks be stricken from the record. In the heat of that argument and the tension of the summer, he wrote to Mellanby for help, 'You told me the other day, when you came to the department, that you had to take off your shirt to meet requests—I hope you have another one.' He told Mellanby of the explosion with the Nuffield people and said he had been given an apology—but no money.[3]

'The results that we have obtained from this work with Dr Jennings and Dr R. D. Wright for the past two years have been good. I need her to help me go on with these studies of gut functions and I would hate to close it down.' With his plea for £300 to keep Dr Jennings working with him, he sent details of her qualifications as his collaborator.

Then, like a pot boiling over, he poured out his frustration and revealed how angered he felt and how near the end of his patience he was. He told Mellanby,

> The financial difficulties of trying to keep work going here are more than I am prepared to go on shouldering.
> It seems to me that I have acquired a reputation of being some sort of academic highway robber—I have had to make such frequent approaches for grants. The University has just told me that I must be prepared for further cuts in my funds because they are planning to put some sort of central heating in the building . . . it would seem to me that the University wants to make things as difficult as it can for me to carry on. You will gather that I am fed up.[4]

He pleaded again for the £300 for Dr Margaret Jennings. She
was then thirty-five years old and a valued collaborator in much
of his research work. He wrote Mellanby, 'I hope you can help.
I am not likely to get someone who could help me more effectively.'

Although it seemed that he was ready to throw in his hand,
Mellanby was able to placate him. He talked about that 'barn of
a place in Oxford' and said ... 'you will always have a struggle
of sorts to keep that place running and turning over.' It was one
of Mellanby's prophecies that would be wide of the mark. He
invited Florey to get Dr Jennings to make an application, with
details, and in the end she got £200 for the year. This all happened
in the weeks when the first indications of the sleeping genie of
healing in the penicillin mould were being obtained in Chain's
laboratory.

The height of summer came with the hope of peace at its
lowest point, and in the final days of August the German army
moved into Poland. On that first Sunday of September, in
Southern England, a morning of pale sun and quiet broken by
the first wail of air raid sirens, Neville Chamberlain went to the
microphone and took the nation into war. During those first few
unbelievable days, Florey sat down and composed another letter
to Sir Edward Mellanby to spell out his hopes for a substance that
would defeat an enemy more powerful than Hitler and which, in
the end, would save more lives than were ever taken in all the
wars and all the plagues in human history.

In this letter of 6th September 1939, he told Mellanby of his
proposals and of the possibilities he saw, and he used the revealing
phrase, '... I have long had the feeling that something might be
done along these lines. There exists no really effective substance
against bacteria *in vivo*.'[5]

He wrote,

I enclose certain proposals I think could be carried out by myself and Chain, with his great flair for enzyme work. Work
done over recent years has shown that lysozyme is not suitable
as an antiseptic. There are accounts in the literature of sub-

stances with similar properties and which act on bacteria—
staphylococci, streptococci and pneumococci, and these come
from the Penicillium mould, actinomycetes and certain other
soil bacteria.

I can get the clinical co-operation from Cairns at the
Radcliffe ... and we propose to prepare these substances for
injection and to study their action as antiseptics *in vivo*.

Explaining the viewpoint he held and the prospects he saw,
Florey continued,

There has been some prominence to soil bacteria given in
US medical journals. There is this substance in Penicillium
which was noted by Fleming. Penicillin can easily be prepared
in large amounts and is non-toxic to animals, even in large
doses. Hitherto work done on this substance has been with
crude apparatus and no real attempt has been made to purify it.
In our opinion this can be done rapidly and easily.

Chain's utter confidence manifested itself in this statement.

Florey then came to the nub of his communication. He said
that to make a start on this work he needed £100 to meet the
expenses, and he listed his needs as chemicals for the media on
which the mould would grow, chemicals for extraction work,
glassware and sundries. He then sat back to await the response.

Within a week Mellanby's reply was on his desk with the first
promise of money with which to open the penicillin work.
Mellanby said, 'You can assume that we will give you £25 for
your expenses and will remember your application for £100
when the time comes for a proper decision. It seems to me the
new line of work will be interesting.'

It was hardly better than nothing and it left Florey dejected
and disappointed; but it was not the end of the road.

In those weeks he faced another personal problem presented
to him by Dr Norman Heatley. The young scientist came to him,
uncertain and hesitant, with his Rockefeller travel grant in his
pocket and his plans all set to go to Copenhagen to study with
Lindestrom Lang. The war was dormant in France, and the

Germans and the Allies faced each other across the Maginot Line
with hardly a clash. The optimistic were talking about good sense
prevailing and the war being over by Christmas. Heatley was
unsure of himself and asked what he should do? Should he go to
Copenhagen, as planned, or would it be dangerous? After all
Denmark was not at war.

Florey ran his hand through his hair, and told Heatley it was
hard to advise him but that it was probably best for him not to go
immediately. Meanwhile, if he liked, Heatley could work on the
new penicillin project in Chain's laboratory.

Heatley hesitated. He had worked with Chain since he came
from Cambridge in 1936, and he told Florey he did not want
to continue this arrangement. So Florey made him his personal
assistant.[6]

Heatley went to look at the Penicillium mould growing in
Chain's laboratory. It looked insignificant and small, and without
any hint of the revolution it would cause. The ubiquitous mould
spores had always moved in the atmosphere, settling at random to
perpetuate tiny colonies of fungal life, each to fight its battle for
existence in the microworld. From this little, felted mat of fungal
growth would come a clinical tool of immense value, and never
again would the humble mould be disregarded.

In response to what he learnt from Chain, Heatley realized
there would be need for testing equipment and he spent his first
day on the penicillin project drilling holes into glass dishes as
part of the initial apparatus for measuring antibacterial activity.
It was the 1st October 1939, and he was starting the work that
would take him with Florey across the Atlantic to America, to
help set the wheels turning on a billion-dollar industry, and to put
in motion one of the most intense studies of a single biological
substance in history.

In October, although he did not know it, Florey's troubles of
finding finance for his work had reached their nadir, and soon
there was to be an uptrend from which he would never look
back.

He called Chain to his office one day, and, reviewing the low
level of funds, suggested Chain make a personal application for a
grant and expenses to the Medical Research Council. He also

mentioned to Chain that Dr H. M. Miller of the New York
headquarters of the Rockefeller Foundation was due to visit
Oxford the following month. When Chain raised his head, and
opened his eyes wide and said, 'I suppose you are going to tackle
him for money?' Florey pointed out that Miller represented
not the Foundation's medical science section but the chemical
division. 'Just the same, I'll see that I talk to him,' Florey added.
Chain went away and wrote his first personal application to the
council for funds, and Florey approved it before it went off.
Chain's proposal was based on work 'on the preparation from
certain bacteria and fungi of powerful bactericidal enzymes which
are effective against staphylococci, pneumococci and streptococci,
the work to be done in association with Professor Florey'. They
granted him the £300 personal grant he sought and also gave him
£100 expenses. It was then little more than a month after Florey
had been offered £25.

Early in November Florey found himself at a function in the
university at which Dr H. M. Miller was the guest, and he made it
his business to talk about the difficulty in obtaining equipment,
apparatus and technical staff. Miller was extremely sympathetic.
He said, 'I suppose most people in the States would feel for you
in what you suffer over here. But, honestly, if you ask right now
for money for medical research projects . . . well, the world's
full of them. You'd be right at the end of a very long queue.'
The Rockefeller man raised his eyebrows, and added meaning-
fully, 'But, if anyone was about to put in a plan for an appealing
biochemical project, then I should guess they'd have a much better
chance.'[7]

The 'academic highway robber' of Oxford needed no further
prodding. Within days he had Chain at work framing the proposal which reviewed the biochemical work that had been done
at the School—from the study of metabolic processes in small
tissue fragments, to snake venoms, lysozyme, gland secretion and
other enzymes; and it showed the planned work as a 'chemical
study of the phenomenon of bacterial antagonism with special
consideration to bacteriolytic enzymes'. The review referred to
pyocyanase and to 'The mould Penicillium which produces a
substance strongly bactericidal to staphylococci, streptococci

7

and pneumococci . . . It seems possible, by an appropriate choice
of bacteria, to obtain inhibiting substances against almost any
kind of pathogenic micro-organisms.'

Thus it expressed a guarded hope of a panacea against a broad
range of diseases,

> In view of the possibly great practical significance of antago-
> nistic substances produced by bacteria against bacteria, it is
> proposed to study systematically the chemical fundamentals of
> the phenomenon with the aim of obtaining, in purified state and
> suitable for intravenous injection, bacteriolytic and bactericidal
> substances against pathogenic micro-organisms.
>
> A beginning has already been made here with the purification
> of the bactericidal substances produced by *Penicillium notatum*
> and by *B. pyocyaneus*.[8]

In his covering note Florey said, 'It may also be pointed out
that the work proposed, in addition to its theoretical importance,
may have practical value for therapeutic purposes.'

He said the project naturally followed from lysozyme and that
he wanted money for enlargement and speeding up the study.
He thought it right to say that,

> . . . valuable work already done on biochemical problems has
> been continuously hampered by inadequate research funds and
> assistants, e.g. only one young technician has been available
> for four people. It has often taken months to get special pieces
> of apparatus, owing to the necessity of approaching outside
> bodies—the trustees of which meet at long intervals—for
> relatively small sums of money.
>
> I have been a consistent believer in the growing importance
> of biochemistry to pathology and bacteriology, and for that
> reason have endeavoured to foster it as much as possible.
>
> I have been fortunate in having in the department Dr
> E. Chain who has—I have no hesitation in saying—a very great
> flair for the elucidation of enzymes, as well as other biochemical
> problems. He has been the guiding chemist in all the work so
> far done here, and under the new proposals he would continue

in that capacity. I might also point out that, where necessary, this chemical work is correlated with biological investigations, such as those needing animal experiments.

When he discussed the submission with Chain there was uncertainty on what they should ask for. Eventually Florey rapped the table with his pen, stubbed out a cigarette, and said, 'Well, if we're going to hit the button, we might as well try to ring the bell.'

They asked for wages for three technical workers and £600 for 'one fully qualified biochemist for one year'. They asked for £500 for one year for chemicals and apparatus, and then drew up a long list of equipment they needed, ranging from various centrifuges and electric glassblowers, to a vacuum still and pump, and an ice-crushing machine ... all needed for chilling the mould juice and for extraction of the bactericidal substance—enzyme or some other structure—that attacked bacteria.

The total came to £2 452, made up of £1 670 for wages, and a non-recurring grant for equipment of £782.

At the end of this addendum on costs, Florey wrote, 'I should like to apply for a grant of £1 670 per annum for three years—as a minimum. In the present unsettled state it would no doubt be advantageous to review the position annually, but I should not like the responsibility of organizing the proposed work on less than a presumption of three years duration at least.'9

The document was typed and, with Florey's covering letter to Dr Warren Weaver in New York, it was sent on its way across the Atlantic. Florey had no means of knowing whether or not the report had made the journey safely and he tried to forget the attempt in the busy weeks ahead. It had been his habit for a long time not to give rise to hopes that could easily bring rejection and more despair.

MIRACLE IN A MOULD

DURING THE FIRST WEEKS OF THE WAR THE BLUE-GREEN mould spread itself across the shallow liquid nutrient which Chain had placed into the typical glass petri dishes. He and his doctoral assistant, Leslie Epstein, had nurtured the growth for months, and the sample fungus which Chain had discovered in another part of the building was now spreading from dish to dish.

The dry fronds of the mould—called the mycelium—would appear above the surface, the brush-like tips would drop their seeding spores into the fertile liquid and the growth of the mould would creep outward. Dish after dish was seeded and then incubated into new growth.

When Heatley joined the work at the beginning of October it was already possible to see yellow-gold droplets of a substance rich in penicillin exuding from the dry mycelium. These droplets were their first harvest and they gathered them with pipettes—small glass tubes with the end drawn into a fine nozzle into which the droplets were sucked.

It became essential that there should be some test of precision to determine the amount of penicillin the mould produced in response to their manipulation of its environment and its liquid food—the medium which they called the 'broth'.

Florey had drawn attention to this need on one of his restless promenades through the laboratory, saying that it had to be not only accurate but speedy.

'Unless we get something like this, life will not be long enough for us to find our way,' he commented.

Heatley, with the gift of improvisation which Florey admired, took up the task and produced a device which was an elaboration of a technique which Florey himself had used in his lysozyme work. He cut small hollow cylinders of glass and bored holes in glass plates through which the cylinders could be dropped against cultures of bacteria, and when samples of the mould product were dropped into the cylinders a ring of death was produced among the bacteria circling the bottom of the cylinder. They called this ring the 'zone of inhibition' and its width was a measure of the amount of penicillin in the sample. The technique later became known as the cylinder-plate method and was used for years in the development of antibiotics. It was simple, it was essentially quick and they were able to move on rapidly with the task of nudging the mould into greater efforts.

A study was made of the characteristics of the yellow-gold droplets and it was found they were richer in penicillin than the broth on which the mould fed, but not so much richer that they could ignore the broth altogether. They were able to work out with precision the ideal method of propagating the fungus. They found links between temperature and oxygen requirements, and then studied the relationships between the speed of growth, the thickness of the mould and the level of penicillin yield. Then they searched for correlations between the colour of the mycelium and the underneath or wet part of the mould, and the penicillin level, looking all the time for ways of inducing the mould to put out more penicillin.

At this stage there was none of the urgency, nor the excitement, that was to come. Three scientists were coaxing and coddling a mould growth as part of an academic exercise. It was an intellectual challenge of the kind that science is all about—seeking data from the unknown. The stunning chemotherapeutic power of penicillin had yet to be revealed.

Just the same, Chain, by his very nature, made the work active and brisk. He was brimming with ideas and enthusiasm, and he was constant in his conviction that the mould could be manipulated.

His argument was that the level of the penicillin in the mould broth could be shown to fluctuate and was, therefore, subject to variations by chemical change. It was natural that the base of the change should be chemical since the means by which the fungus fought competing microbes was chemical, and he had only to find by experiment that chemical combination.

Chain's argument was prophetic; its validity would have to wait for proof until two years later when Heatley was working in American laboratories, south of Chicago. But at Oxford nothing the team did improved the yield of penicillin. They changed the conditions of growth, making variation after variation. They innovated with light, temperature, the total environment, but they could produce no increase. They were already growing the Penicillium mould on the type of synthetic broth used by Raistrick's team in 1932—known as the Czapek-Dox medium—which itself was a refinement on the rough digest of bullocks' hearts used by Fleming in 1929, but Chain and Heatley began to seek the ideal nourishment for the spreading mould and started re-arranging its diet.

They changed the base of the synthetic broth by increasing the amounts of glucose, nitrate and other salts, and then they fed the mould *Marmite* and a selection of specially prepared meat extracts. They also tempted it with more sophisticated foods—yeast and malt extract, then peptone, glycerol, and extra glycerol, and more phosphate. Then they went to natural food by adding sucrose and lactate to digest of pure cow and horse muscle, then thioglycollic acid, sodium and ammonium salts, and more oxygen and less oxygen, and a manipulation of carbon dioxide.

Nothing lifted the yield. Nothing broadened the zone of inhibition at the bottom of Heatley's cylinders.

Weeks of patience and detailed work brought them no advance. Then eventually they tried a mixture of extract of boiled brewers' yeast—and got a result. It did not lift the yield of penicillin, but it did speed up the growth of the mould. It was their first result, their first dividend, reducing the time of mould maturity from three weeks to ten days.

Almost at the same time they discovered that they could 'milk' the mould. They could syphon off the broth after ten days and replace it, under sterile conditions, with a fresh broth on which the mould could again feed. The fungus made a surprising response to this tactic. It produced a second crop of penicillin—and this was achieved in two-thirds the time it took to grow its first crop. Still experimenting, Chain and his associates found they could play this trick up to a dozen times.

It seemed a small return against what they had sought, but these discoveries were to prove vital time-savers; they made possible enough material for clinical trials which in turn ensured commercial production in time to meet the massive needs that arose with the invasion of Europe and the peak fighting in the Pacific during the last two years of the war.

They used the broth replacement technique for nearly two years before the contamination of the mould by a stubborn organism made it impracticable. But, by then, the short cut had paid its way.

The first Christmas of the war came and went with the mould still defying their attempts to induce a higher yield of penicillin, and when Dr E. P. Abraham joined the School in January 1940 he was eased, by Florey, into working with Chain on the perplexing problem of extraction and purification. The records of work done by Professor Harold Raistrick and his colleagues at the London School of Hygiene, published in 1932, made the task a daunting one.

Interested in moulds, and their constituents, Raistrick had been a respected authority, with the discovery of no less than sixteen chemical compounds to his credit. He was highly regarded and Florey bluntly expressed his own opinion of him to a colleague, 'He is certainly no slouch.'

On his own testimony it was entirely of his own volition that Raistrick had taken up the task of the chemical isolation of the active substance in the Penicillium mould—a substance that Fleming had apparently failed to identify. With his three co-workers he had succeeded in growing the mould on the synthetic Czapek-Dox broth and went on to find that the active principle they were seeking could be extracted into ether when the watery solution containing the penicillin was slightly acidified.

But when they had reached this stage, and then moved on to bring back the penicillin from the ether for concentration by evaporation, they found penicillin to be an elusive chemical ghost that vanished into thin air. It passed right through the net of infallible chemistry like a wraith and disappeared completely. One of Raistrick's team, the mycologist J. H. V. Charles,* had suspected Fleming's classification of the mould as *Penicillium rubrum* and his suspicions had been confirmed by the world authority, Dr Charles Thom, in America, who had typed Fleming's mould for the first time as *Penicillium notatum*. In recent years, looking back on those days in his London laboratory, Raistrick commented,

We had realized this was a difficult and complex molecule which could be no less destroyed in an acid than in an alkaloid medium. But then this substance which could be so deadly to bacteria just vanished away. So we recorded that it was extremely labile. Of course, we were after the pure acid and not the sodium salts of the thing and it just defied our efforts to crystallize it.

And when in 1939 Ernst Chain—in his search of the literature in the Radcliffe Library at Oxford—had come on Raistrick's paper, he had at first been inclined to view the chance of purifying penicillin as a human drug as very slim indeed.

It had occurred to him then that temperature could be a key factor in Raistrick's failure, and the more he had thought about the process the more he became convinced that, handled carefully, the 'prima donna' molecule could be persuaded to make an appearance in a concentrated extract—always provided the conditions were right. The vital element was that the extraction should be made when the material was cold. Chain had become convinced of this belief and had infected Florey with his unshakeable confidence.

But in the long weeks of winter which came with the New Year they met with disappointment, procedural headaches and failure to isolate the elusive fraction in the mould juice which was active against bacteria. They followed a long and tedious path, and the strong confidence of the previous summer came near to evaporation as the penicillin fraction continued to slip through their fingers.

* The tragic death of Charles—killed in a bus accident—was the first step in halting Raistrick's work which was so close to success.

After weeks of effort, during which he worked like a man possessed, Chain found the pathway that brought them the exciting moment of viewing their first pinch of concentrated activity: a dirty brown powder.

It came from the careful balancing of the level of acidity in the mould juice, from the reduction of temperature in the material with copious use of crushed ice, and from evaporation in the vacuum chamber, concentration and reconcentration of the subsequent powdered material, with Chain watching every step to prevent the active principle from slipping away in the steps of fractionation. In this way came the first tiny mound, the scrap of brown powder, hardly enough to cover a small fingernail.

When they took a fraction of the powder they had teased from the mould's broth and tried it on Heatley's cylinder-plate device, they got their broadest band of death among the bacteria. It was the strongest effect they had yet seen and they began to believe they had come close to a fairly high state of purity.

The exciting moment was memorable, but it did not last long. The success they had won with the first extract through freeze-drying techniques was drawn out and so was limited. Here was an excruciating bottleneck in the production of material for which Florey was waiting impatiently to start his carefully planned programme.

During the weeks of slow toil his mind had gone back again and again to the days at Cambridge when he had worked with Szent-Gyorgyi, the biochemist who had won the Nobel Prize for his work on pure vitamin extraction. Florey remembered him saying, 'Modern biochemistry is now good enough to allow extraction of any naturally occurring substance, provided you have a quick enough test of its character.'

Florey believed that the substance could be won, and when it was available he could begin the extensive bacteriological and pharmacological tests that he considered vital to understanding the nature of the material. But he was faced with the daunting query: could he possibly obtain enough of the drug? There was so little to look at. It was depressing to realize that gallons of mould broth would have to be processed to gain enough concentrate to cover a fingernail.

Although there was an unwritten law that the work was not discussed outside the laboratory, other people had got to hear of their adventure and some scientists were openly scoffing at the viability of the project. So much for so little; so much effort and so much time to grow the mould; so much money down the drain for a scrap of powder; so many months of work which, even if it was successful, might help one patient in ten thousand. They reasoned, as Fleming and Raistrick and the others had reasoned, that it was not worth the trouble.

These arguments could take no account of the tremendous power locked in a trace of penicillin. The project's detractors could not know that, when commercial production eventually commenced in 1943, the drug industry would handle 17 000 gallons of mould broth to win a single pound of penicillin and that this would be capable of a thousand miracles of healing.

They only knew that in the early winter months of 1940 Chain, Abraham and Heatley were reaching into the mould broth by the classical method, which Heatley called the chemical 'front door', and sweeping out their grains of concentrate.

These first miserly, tiny amounts took the team beyond the frontier reached by any previous workers, but the struggle was still only one of high academic and intellectual interest. They could reason that the elucidation of the final substance would lead to a chemical structure which might open up new possibilities of bio-synthesis of unknown consequence, but, even with all that, it was tiring, nagging work that demanded devotion and dedication, which at the time only paid the dividend of a back-ache.

Florey would not let them flag. He constantly upheld them and encouraged them in the struggle, inspiring them by his own faith. He knew the derision that would come with failure, and he engaged in no theatrical fancies. Long years of rigid mental discipline, from the day he began work under Sherrington, allowed him to view experiment only as a means of proving a fact. He had in the back of his mind that, in Sheffield, Paine had used the mould juice to sweep away congenital gonorrhoea from the eyes of newborn children, and that Paine had also saved the sight of a colliery manager afflicted with a staphylococcal

infection. He knew what was happening to bacteria at the end
of Heatley's little cylinders and he was anxious to begin the series
of tests, both bacteriological and pharmacological, which he had
planned so carefully and which he hoped would reveal the true
nature and power of the quarry he had been seeking.

If he had had no faith in what he was doing and had not believed
in himself, Florey needed only to have looked at some of the
facts to have found support for fearing the worst. He could have,
for instance, glanced at the laboratory accounts in his office and
seen them stretched to the limit and, in some cases, running into
the red. Instead, he called in his team, the bacteriologists, chemists,
the pathologists, and told them in detail the paths the study
would follow; Professor A. D. Gardner in bacteriology, Dr
Jean Orr-Ewing, and Dr A. G. Sanders, with Dr Margaret
Jennings as his special assistant; Chain, and Heatley, and Abraham.
They had to confirm and determine that the new extract was
effective against the range of organisms previously reported, and
then they had to go beyond this to a wide range of infective
organisms which might have been overlooked in the incomplete
work Fleming had done.

They were moving, Florey told them, to intimate acquaintance
with the nature and the character of the substance submerged in
the mould juice.

As these first steps got under way fortune suddenly touched
Florey and lifted an enormous load from his mind, casting off the
worry that had been a part of his life for years. It came in a letter
from New York, and he could hardly believe it was true. He could
not help calling Chain immediately and, bubbling with delight,
told him the news.

The Rockefeller Foundation had approved their application
and would meet their request for aid—in full. Money for new
equipment, for the centrifuges, the vacuum pumps, the electric
furnaces and boilers and blowers; wages for two technical
assistants and a mechanic; plus £600 a year 'for one fully qualified
biochemist' and another £500 a year for chemicals and other
apparatus. A magnificent annual grant of £1 670—for the next
five years. And with this, another £1 000 to spend on initial

gearing up for the push into penicillin. It was munificent and, as Chain observed, it was a 'princely sum' for the time.

The assured income of more than £9 000 over the next few years gave them new heart, and added impetus to their work. Two fully-fledged technical workers, G. A. Glister and S. A. Cresswell, were added to the staff and shouldered most of the chores of producing the mould broth.

Florey was elated. Ever since his youth, when the family business had crashed and his father had died, he had not known a time free of the struggle for money.

Now, in one envelope the years of being an academic 'highway robber', a 'bushranger of research', were gone, and there was money to pursue the prize of penicillin or any other naturally occurring substance that showed promise of inhibiting bacteria that were the enemy of man. Florey returned home that evening delighted and exuberant.

Thereafter, the early weeks of 1940 were full of urgent, but still elegant, experiment, and he was repeating his credo—'It is not enough to be good, it has to be superlatively good.'

They put penicillin among human leucocytes—white cells of the blood essential to defence against disease—and studied the reaction to see whether the drug would inhibit their work of clearing away the debris of bacteria dissolved within the system. One by one the team began to answer the key questions: Was penicillin absorbed into the blood from the gut? Would it change its chemical composition when it was in company with the enzymes and hormones of the blood stream and, if it changed, how? What level of dose would be safe, and how could the level in the blood be detected? Could it be maintained or would there have to be continuous doses? Would the body break down the penicillin or would it be excreted in the urine, and would excreted penicillin be metabolized so that it was no longer useful? Could it be taken by mouth or would the stomach acids destroy it completely? How would it behave in the heart? Would the beat slow down or quicken? Could it be injected directly into a loop of the intestine? Would it fail to affect bacteria in the presence of pus in the way sulphonamides had failed? Did it react in any way with sulphonamides?

All the new work was set in motion in an orderly fashion and was planned to create as little disturbance as possible to the research being done in the other laboratories in the school.

As the penicillin studies moved ahead, each with their different demands for active material, so it became more and more apparent that the bottleneck in the production of concentrate of the extracted material was even more serious than Florey had previously supposed. At the end of the second week of March he decided to call Heatley and Chain to a conference to discuss what could be done. This proved to be a momentous occasion, not for the debate it contained, but for the events which it triggered. The talk lasted for most of the day in a free-ranging discussion that was 'at times quite argumentative and marked by brisk exchanges'.[1]

Decades later the scene could be recaptured from the notes: three men, tense and on the trail of a great discovery in medical science, seated in Florey's panelled office while, outside the window, the bare boughs of the trees swung in a cold breeze.

Florey, the leader, was not given to placating people. Always frank and direct, he confronted the fiery biochemist, Chain, who had been aggravated by the torment of the slow process of winning the grains of concentrate on which were pinned their hopes of the grail of chemotherapy. And on the periphery of the continuing argument sat the quiet and unassuming Dr Heatley.

Yet it was Heatley, the notes show, who almost brought the meeting to flashpoint when he interjected that there could be a much improved method of producing the concentrate. In his easy, half-apologetic way he put to the two astonished scientists the results of the intellectual toil in which he had spent the previous days. 'This shy, extraordinarily gifted man', as Chain called him, had mentally followed the molecule through a variety of different chemical pathways and, in the end, had reached a conclusion. It was different from the classical method, a deviation, he told them, that was a kind of chemical backdoor.

Thirty years later, when Florey was dead and Heatley was asked to recall some of the moments of this realization, he said,

'It is curious that what now seems a fairly obvious deduction—that penicillin should be back-extractable from ether into a neutral buffer—had not been reached by Raistrick, his colleague Clutterbuck and the others, and had only been reached with some mental pain and difficulty at Oxford; indeed, when I first proposed it, one member of the group considered the deduction unsound.' That member was Ernst Chain.[2]

In this way the discussion again swirled around and over the quiet head of Heatley, with Florey hammering out reasons why a new method should be tried. In the end Chain capitulated to Heatley, but not entirely. Conceding, with a shrug of the shoulders and a spread of his hands in a gesture of disassociation, the notes record him as stating,

'Then, if you think it will work, why don't you do it yourself? That will surely be the best and quickest way to show that you are wrong.'

Heatley was delighted and waited impatiently for the conference to end so that he could begin the first assembly of his new apparatus.

There was then a lot more talk of the nature of the substance and when they finally dispersed none of them were aware they were on the eve of a day when what they did would touch the lives of millions of people.

On Tuesday, 19th March 1940, Dr Ernst Boris Chain took one of the biggest risks in the whole story of penicillin. This was the day on which his spontaneous action could have masked the bland nature of the drug behind a face of poison and held back the coming of the antibiotic age by an unpredictable period. As it turned out it was the day when fortune touched the gifted scientist so that later he could attest,

'To my mind this was the crucial day in the whole development of penicillin and the day on which everything became possible for us. The barriers were removed to our hopes and our dreams, and the fears that our purified extract would be harmful were all banished.'[3]

Chain's greatest day began with further examination of eighty milligrams of brown powder, a pinch that had come from his painstaking efforts of chemical extraction. A brief test showed him that this material would inhibit a culture of staphylococci even when diluted down to one milligram—one twenty-eight-thousandth of an ounce—in one litre of distilled water. The result showed such high potency that the illusion of near-purity was maintained. Thus, the enormous risk which Chain took could not have dawned on him at that time. Seated at his bench he suddenly made his decision to dissolve the eighty milligrams into two millilitres of water. He carried the solution across the landing, past Florey's door, and down the stairs to where Dr J. M. Barnes worked on studies of cellular pigments. Chain asked Barnes to prepare a hypodermic and inject the material, in equal amounts, into the abdominal linings of two mice.

The sudden request was no surprise to Dr Barnes. He had been working on lethal effects that some staining pigments had been found to have on living cells, and he was the man in the Sir William Dunn School with the most recent experience of injecting mice. It was quite natural that Chain should ask him.

Barnes knew, as did most of the staff at the Sir William Dunn School, that work was progressing on the Penicillium mould, but he knew little of the details. He felt no great interest, nor excitement, and took it as a natural thing that Chain should ask for a test of the toxicity of a substance. In the free and easy relationships that existed in the School, it did not occur to him to question whether or not Florey had been consulted. He just took two mice, blew away the fur from their stomachs and slid the needle home. Long afterwards he said, 'We stood together and watched them for a while, but when they showed no sign of deterioration, I lost interest. I had been interested in substances that killed and this result meant nothing to me. The incident was forgotten until I met Chain in 1952 and he reminded me. When I looked up my notes there was a very brief reference, but nothing more.'

Chain, however, did not lose interest. He sat fascinated by the actions of the two mice in the cage, watching and waiting for some faltering motion, some tiny gesture in their behaviour to suggest that the concentrated material coursing through their systems was destroying vital cells or blocking nerve paths.

Fleming's claim that the crude mould broth filtrate was non-toxic had been stated more than a decade before, but this had referred to a mixture that was weak compared with the potent chemicals now running through the veins of these two mice. Chain feared that, in high concentration, this substance might be deadly to man. He knew that in his own laboratory, Miss Schoental had obtained an antibacterial substance from *Pyocyaneus bacilli* which had proved toxic; and the literature they had combed for weeks had been studded with gems of antibacterial promise that had proved to be paste when taken into life forms.

Chain could not take his eyes from the animals for fear he would miss some slight stagger, some movement of sudden distress. Even if the substance were slow to strike down the mice it would be bound to be classified, with all the past experiences of cellular products, as harmful to man. The promise left in Fleming's uncompleted work and neglected discovery would be illusory, and biochemistry would be marked by one more fallen castle.

He sat on, watching the two small animals in their actions, and his hopes rose higher as the minutes passed by. For two hours he sat. Then, seeing no change he rose, smiled his thanks at Barnes, and walked out. Seven years to the month after he had left Berlin to avoid the terror and the intimidation which Hitler's 'Brownshirts' had been heaping on his race Chain felt he stood on the brink of a great new contribution to medical knowledge. Unable to keep the news to himself for even a moment, he made directly for Florey's office.

He did not know for some time how big the risk had been; not until the staggering truth was revealed that his high purity concentrate was, in fact, a solution that held 99% rubbish.

The injection had not been intended as a test of penicillin's healing power but as a toxicity test. Any one of the hundreds of compounds and elements in that 99% of unwanted matter could have been toxic to the animals, and the 1% of penicillin would have been thought to have been the cause. But nothing among the proteins, the fats, sugars, carbohydrates—or the 1% of penicillin —was toxic, and the result raised the team's sights towards the protection tests which Florey was then planning.

On that same day as Chain watched the mice and then had taken his tale to Florey, Heatley spent the hours bent over his new task of developing the solvent transfer process which would not only speed the production of penicillin, but would also enable the team to reach a higher concentration and eliminate many of the difficult and unwanted fractions. It was the process which would be subsequently adopted as the main extraction technique by the great American drug houses.

Heatley's method of reversing the chemical path which Chain had followed and of extracting the penicillin from the mould juice into ether and then passing it back through a chemically neutral buffer material produced a superior extract and it was with this improved material that Florey began his own toxic reaction tests on mice, rats, cats and rabbits.

Week after week in the early months of 1940 he carefully built his acquaintance with the substance into deeper understanding of its potential; and then, as the laboratory workers won an increasing supply of the drug, he moved towards the testing of its power to defeat infectious bacteria in the living system. By mid-May he was ready to begin his mice protection tests.

Just before ten, on the morning of Saturday, 25th May 1940, Florey left his home to walk across the grass in University Parks, Oxford, to where the red brick of the Sir William Dunn School building was warming up in the sun.

It was the start of a lovely summer, but the political atmosphere was charged with the gloom and danger of the coming defeat across the Channel. Two weeks before, the Nazi blitz had opened on Holland and Belgium. Defenceless Rotterdam had been mercilessly bombed, Stukas had machine-gunned helpless refugees, creating panic and terror, and with the British and French forces committed to Belgium, Guderian's wedge of armour had closed a steel ring behind their backs.

On this day of tests on mice, the morning news had told of the German armoured columns at Calais, that Boulogne had gone and Dunkirk was encircled. Churchill, who had taken over from Chamberlain on 10th May, had offered nothing but blood, toil, tears and sweat, and the first small boats were already carrying the evacuated troops back across the Channel to England.

The tide of events had had its effect on the work at Florey's laboratories and, in the emergency, he made every day a working day. Weekends were gone—a thing of the past. They would begin a crucial experiment on that day—a Saturday—a thing that would have been unthinkable in peace time.

A sunny Saturday morning in Oxford—and waiting for Florey in room 46 of the cool building was James Kent with eight white Swiss albino mice in glass-topped cages, together with culture preparation of nearly 1 000 million swarming bacteria made highly virulent by consecutive passaging through other animals. These were the type of haemolytic streptococci which had caused death by puerperal fever to more than two mothers in every thousand childbirths.

The experimental procedure had been carefully planned and, as always, Kent knew every piece of equipment, every service expected of him. They kept precisely to their time schedule. As Kent held the first mouse for its peritoneal injection and Florey slipped home the needle with its lethal cargo, the hands on the clock stood at eleven. Into each animal went a volume of infective material calculated to contain upwards of 110 million bacteria, and these were deposited inside the abdominal lining to make the task of the drug more exacting.

Four of the mice were set aside as controls, and so were doomed to die without the protection of penicillin. The other four mice Florey separated into two compartments. One pair labelled Group B were given a single dose of penicillin, a tiny scrap in a drop of distilled water. Their protection against 110 million streptococci was one-fifth of one milligram of powder.

Group A received half of this amount initially, but at periods of about two hours during the day this dose was repeated, the last being due at ten in the evening. Florey planned to give this final dose three and a half hours after the previous injection.

When the first injections were completed and what remained of the infective material had been cleared away and destroyed, Kent made the tea as he had done so many times during the previous thirteen years, using the Bunsen burner to boil the water. Then they sat together in silence munching sandwiches and steadily watching the mice in their cages.

In all they had used a tiny 50 milligrams of extract, an amount about equal to a week's production by the laboratory staff, and

though the Oxford unit of measurement of penicillin activity
had yet to be devised, it was afterwards calculated that this entire
test consumed little more than 200 units.

Throughout the long, quiet afternoon Florey sat and watched
the mice continuously, his keen and experienced eye searching for
clues in the scamper and scurry among the litter at the bottom of
the cages. Then, at six-thirty he turned and, in a rare gesture, put
his hand on Kent's shoulder and told him to go home.

Kent left the building feeling no surge of excitement. To him it
had been one of many experiments with the professor over the
years, and realization of the importance of that Saturday's work
would not come until much later.

Soon after Kent had gone Florey was joined by Heatley.
Together the two men carefully studied the condition of the mice.
Heatley noted that he could already detect signs of distress in the
four untreated controls. Their fur was bedraggled and their
movements were slower than those of the other mice. Nearly
eight hours after being infected with the virulent bacteria, which
would have increased by many millions, this was only to be
expected; but, as yet, there were no signs of distress in the treated
mice. Florey suggested they should have an evening meal and said
he would go home to eat. Heatley made a few notes and then went
out to a small, local restaurant.

When Florey returned to the laboratory for the final penicillin
injection in the Group A pair, Heatley was not there. It was ten
o'clock and he picked out the two mice and injected the final
wisp of drug into muscle tissue and then returned them to the
cage. Standing back, he could see the evidence taking shape. The
four control mice were obviously ill, the other four were all well
and lively. Only one of the two which had received a single
injection was a little listless. He stopped to write the note on the
observation,

'Both mice in Group A are very well. Of the Group B pair,
one is in good condition, cleaning itself and eating biscuit. The
other is not quite as lively. The four controls are the worse for
wear and their breathing is laboured and they look very sick.'[4]
Then he went home to bed.

Heatley came back for his night's stint at the laboratory some time after eleven, feeling unwell for having eaten not one, but two, dinners. For as he had left the dining-room, he had bumped into a cousin whom he had not met for some years and had allowed himself to be dragged off for drinks and then, protesting, had eaten a second meal accompanied by a liberal supply of fine wine which had been pressed on him. Back at the laboratory he refreshed himself by splashing water on his face and then sat down to study the mice. His heavy evening did not affect his accuracy nor his ability to record what he saw, and the notes are graphic in the tale they tell,

'At three minutes to midnight the first of the four controls died. The creature staggered to its feet, lurched about for a second or two and then fell down. It twitched once or twice and then died.'

Within ninety minutes he was recording the deaths of two more of the untreated mice. This was just before half past one in the morning. The last mouse held out for almost two more hours. Then, 'At precisely 3.28 a.m. it began to move about drunkenly and with each inspiration, lifted its head and opened its mouth widely. The breathing was erratic, and then the animal fell, twitched several times and was dead.'⁵

The four mice protected with penicillin were still alive and well: only one from Group B did not look completely well.

Heatley completed his record and prepared to go home. He made no attempt to remove the dead mice. They were contagious with a bacteria even more virulent than when they had been injected, and he was too tired for the precautions which were necessary. Florey had called a conference with Chain in the morning, at eleven, and he felt badly in need of sleep.

As he began cycling home through the blacked-out streets it was nearly four and, elated at the success, his head brimming with excited thoughts of the possibilities of what he had just seen, he ran into an elderly air-raid warden. The man was angry and wanted an explanation from Heatley of 'what he was up to'.

The tired scientist smiled and apologized, and rode off home thinking of the four white mice. He could not have explained to the warden how millions of bacteria had been quelled with a scrap of brown powder. It would have sounded too much like a miracle.

On the Sunday morning Florey stood in the laboratory with the evidence of success before him. Four white mice lay still and dead in the bottom of the cage. The other four were still living, and only the one, which had had a single, minute injection, looked unwell. This was the mouse that would live for two more days; the other three were to be counted survivors.

Florey was joined by his two colleagues. Chain was thrilled and almost dancing with excitement; Heatley was brooding and moody from lack of sleep and too much food.

Florey said, 'I suppose that we could say that it seems like a miracle.'

Chain enthused, 'Of course it does. It *is* a miracle.'

Florey then told them that he had planned mass tests using batches of up to fifty mice in a series of experiments, some of which would last for two days or more, and that he would want very much more material.

Chain asked Heatley, 'Could you start by lifting production of mould broth up to 200 litres a week?'

In his depressed state Heatley was taken aback, but he said he would try. He caught his first vision of the mad days that were coming, with the wild scramble to grow more and more mould. Florey then fixed his eye and said,

'This is the point, Heatley. We want a lot of the stuff for these mice, I know. But we are going to have to move on to man. Until we get to that stage this is all just as much a laboratory curio as was Fleming's mould. Remember, a man is three thousand times as big as a mouse.'[6]

Heatley afterwards said of this moment, 'It was typical of Florey's drive that a mere twenty-six hours after beginning the experiment, and before its completion, he had his plans ready to increase production of penicillin by all means possible.'[7]

'It is clear cut,' Florey said using his favourite phrase when deciding to go all out to increase production of the penicillin mould. 'This experiment has been striking, even dramatic, but it was imperfect. We shall do it twice more to eliminate chance of a freak result and then go on to mass trials with different organisms. We shall need a clear picture of the size of dose, its duration and the optimal effect.'

It was also clear-cut that there would be no waste of time. With the exciting possibilities of the new drug displayed by the four mice still scampering through the chaff in the glass cage, his immediate demand was for a fresh supply of purified extract within twenty hours—enough to undertake a slightly expanded trial, and then a similar supply within the next twenty-four hours for a further trial. From eight mice Florey planned to increase to ten and then to sixteen and then on to hundreds, using different strains of disease-causing bacteria.

Florey was already deeply involved in research with other workers; research from which he would produce that year a run of articles for learned journals that ranged from observations on the action of lymphocytes in a rabbit's ears, the influence of drugs on nerves and enzymes in the intestines, contraction of blood vessels, secretions in the thoracic duct, to the influence of the vagus nerve on the secretion of mucus in the stomach—this last in collaboration with Dr Margaret Jennings. Amid all this he made a detached assessment of the value of the new extract, but could not say what unseen power was at work in the fragments of chemistry scratched out from a mould growth that had the ability to touch against the cell walls of bacteria. But the mice tests had established the presence of an agent that would move through a living system and maintain its power to dissolve agents of infectious disease.

CHAPTER 8

BEFORE MID-DAY ON 27TH MAY, KENT HAD TEN WHITE albino mice ready, and Dr Jennings joined Florey in the task of infecting all ten with a similar strain of streptococcus to that he had used in the first trial. Six of these ten mice were given tiny injections of penicillin and they all lived. Three of the four untreated mice died within the first three days.

The next day, before this experiment was completed, Florey started the third test, with sixteen mice each receiving large doses of streptococci. Six of the mice were set aside for the bacteria to overwhelm their capacity to produce antibody. Within twenty-two hours they were all dead from virulent infection. All the treated mice survived the first days, but by the third day five of them were dead and the rest collapsed at different times until the last one died nineteen days later.

Now Florey was left with a neat sum. A certain activity of penicillin seemed to equal a given amount of bacteria and he could see the shape and form of the treatment technique that would prove the most effective method. When he assessed the quantity that he would need for the series of mass tests that would lead on to the use of penicillin by man, the total seemed almost frightening.

'We seemed to be faced with an almost impossible task,' he said later.

He called into consultation everyone he thought might help and he told them, bluntly, 'Talk penicillin.' How could the wastage of space and time in culture, growth and extraction be circumvented?

They discussed the unwieldy shape of fashioned glassware,

and though this material was ideal it was expensive, and so they argued that the answer was to find some firm which not only could, but would, in war-time, make the ceramic containers they needed. But—where was the firm and where was the time?

Up against this nagging problem that barred his path, Florey threw up his hands in perplexed anger and snapped,

'Use any damn thing, anything that will fit and in which the stuff will grow. Try anything, but get it done as quickly as possible.'

The result of this remark was an incredible collection of paraphernalia for the attack on the problems of growth and penicillin yield. From the time of the first mice protection tests during the last week-end in May, the team extended their equipment in the penicillin work to an assortment of astonishing variety and originality. Receptacles were spread about the laboratories like used articles in a jumble sale, each filled with its shallow draught of nutrient liquid on which the blue-green mould was growing.

There were tin trays, quart-size milk bottles and biscuit tins—lacquered and varnished against the destructive contact of penicillin on metal—and some tins with pipes soldered to them; there were china meat-dishes and sedate Erlenmeyer cone-shaped flasks, which were so wasteful of space in the incubators where the cultures were grown and in the autoclaves where sterilizing took place; there were china plates, a dog bath, pie dishes and a variety of urinary vessels from the hospitals—including bed bottles and the old-fashioned bedpans with the side spout and the removable lid. These last were so successful that the team based their eventual mould vessels on their design.

Amid this scene of confusion there were rows of gallon-size lemonade flagons with screw tops, a bronze letter-box, a lavatory cistern, a hand-made disc-paddle wheel and a milk cooler and separator; there were milk churns, a domestic bath, and stirrup pumps borrowed from the fire watchers, and Heath Robinson contraptions of tubes and glass fitted into battered bookcases long ago discarded from the Bodleian Library up the road. With it all was a maze of tubes, pipes, filtration columns, taps, flow valves and aquarium pumps of the type that blow bubbles through water.

Then, just while the team were frantically trying to produce more penicillin from this makeshift factory, the head of the Medical Research Council, Sir Edward Mellanby, arrived unexpectedly at the Sir William Dunn building. He came with the air of an emperor inspecting part of his realm and announced in his overbearing way that he had 'dropped in while in Oxford'. It was the 5th of June.

From the old days in Sheffield Florey knew this man who had come to influence the allocation of British funds for medical science—that he was brilliant, but intolerant, inclined to be suspicious, and often huffy and dogmatic, but rarely, if ever, impromptu or haphazard. It was plain to Florey that Mellanby, intrigued by lack of specific information and probably hearing some muttered reference to the strange happenings at the School, had come to 'sniff out' the facts.

Mellanby could dominate many people, and some feared him for the power he had over allocation of research funds. He could explode as he had done on a previous visit when, leaning over the shoulder of Dr Brian Maegraith—later Professor of Tropical Medicine at Liverpool—he had shouted in that man's face, 'Good God! Do you call *that* research?' And Maegraith had earned Florey's respect with a very blunt Australian reply.

Florey, too, was well able to stand up to Mellanby who was to be kept completely in the dark on penicillin until Florey was satisfied they could go into print. Mellanby knew the three subjects Florey had listed in the application for money made the previous year, but he was left to make his own guess as to which of these Florey's team was pursuing. All he was told was that promising progress had been made. Mellanby could see all their research, except penicillin. Florey's intransigence was well-based. He could not break his edict on secrecy at the top and still expect it to apply down his whole staff structure. Besides, Mellanby had not had much time—or money—for naturally-occurring bacterial inhibitors after the advent of the sulphonamides.

But of far more importance than these reasons was that to allow Mellanby to view the penicillin area at the School would be to invite an angry outburst. No one could predict the effect it would have on this stern and passionate man of classical science. The very sight of the place might have sent him into a towering rage, and so he was given a vague verbal indication of how the research was going, taken to lunch, and then escorted back to the London train.

Florey was determined Mellanby should not be allowed to know what was developing before he had reached some plateau of attainment, but he desperately needed more hands at the work, and on 11th June, he wrote to Mellanby, 'As I told you recently we have been working with a substance that gives the greatest promise of being an important chemotherapeutic agent. We don't want anything said about it at this time, but I need further help from you . . .'[1]

He sought—and later obtained—permission to transfer people, working on grants, from other research over to the penicillin project. But he still did not tell Mellanby that they were working on penicillin.

The time in which they were living was itself a trial; the country standing alone against Nazi Germany, the food rationing, queues for simple necessities, nights on air-raid duties, or fire watching, with tin helmets and gas masks in cardboard boxes and no street lights—all these adding to the anxiety that came out of the danger each day brought nearer. With the time-consuming chores of nursing the mould and extracting the concentrate, the days passed quickly, and it was the end of June before Heatley could inform Florey that enough of the material was on hand for the big mice trials.

Nearly three hundred Swiss albino mice had been bred for the work, and over the next weeks Kent produced these in batches of between fifty and seventy-five—which was the largest number used in a single experiment. Florey arranged for his bacteriologists to produce a fearsome array of test organisms, and he, Dr Margaret Jennings and Kent, had to use the utmost precaution to avoid infection themselves.

For one experiment Florey chose a strain of the gas gangrene organism—*Clostridium septique*—that had ravaged and killed millions of wounded in the battles of history; in another he used the staphylococcal agent commonly feared as 'golden Staph'; and in a third, a streptococcus that produced a fierce infection which caused a type of pneumonia. They spent hours infecting the mice, not with the mere 110 million bacteria of the first experiment, but with doses calculated to contain up to 750 million.

In some of these experiments the treatment of the protected mice was continuous for five to ten days, and Kent was Florey's constant companion, assisting, holding mice for injection—and recording details. Florey found him an old stretcher-bed in the roof and, wrapped in a blanket, Kent would snatch brief catnaps during the night.

In Florey's office across the hall, built into a huge wall cupboard, was the pull-out bed which his predecessor had had constructed. As each injection period ended Florey would lie down there under a cover and rest. In less than three hours his copperfaced pocket watch would sound the alarm and he would walk into the laboratory to shake Kent by the shoulder.

Day after day, night after night, batches of mice running and dying among the litter in the cages were piecing together for him a life-and-death pattern from which he could see emerging the unbelievable power of a revolutionary new drug. He was meticulous to show that this substance was not merely the antiseptic of which Fleming had dreamed ten years before, but a wonderful systemic agent that would seek out infection in any part of the body and destroy the damaging organism but remain harmless to the living cells.

He explained later, 'A really true chemotherapeutic effect can only be shown if the curative doses are given at some distance from the infective site and given some time after the infection.[2] He used the gas gangrene organisms for muscle and intravenous injections and applied the penicillin at a distant site. In these particular tests the untreated mice were all dead within seventeen hours. Of the twenty-five mice treated with tiny sequential doses, twenty-four were still alive ten days later and were counted as survivors.

The exhausting weeks left Florey haggard from lack of sleep; notwithstanding, he was thrilled and delighted. He told his staff

he was grateful for their efforts and said openly for the first time
that they could now claim to have discovered penicillin as a true
chemotherapeutic agent of considerable power.

'I must confess these mice tests have given me my most exciting
moments,' he said.

The full power of the drug had not yet been revealed. The team
only knew that in their hands was a remarkable substance which
would have to be used on a human patient before it had value.
This meant many more months of toil—not only in production,
but in refinement of its chemical and therapeutic nature. Among
the many problems to be solved was the one of measurement.
They decided that their standard measure should be denoted by
the activity of penicillin in a cubic centimetre of water needed
to stop the growth of bacteria in a circle 2·5 centimetres across
when the cylinder-plate method was used against cultures of
Staphylococcus aureus. This was the 'Oxford unit', later adopted
as the international standard.

With this work under way the members of the team would meet
for morning tea. Florey would join them and the talk would run
over the work and the war news. Concern was mounting in the
country at the threat of invasion, with the entry of Italy into the
conflict, and the broken spirit of the French leaders, and thoughts
were entertained by some of the team on how their secret was to be
kept—and how it would be preserved—if the Germans crossed
the Channel and occupied Britain.

The only hope seemed to lie across the sea, possibly in America
where, at that time—although the President was sympathetic—
many Americans were closing their eyes—and some their hearts,
as Heatley was to find—to the embattled British people. If the
worst happened, the group of scientists agreed, and only one
man got away across the Atlantic, then he would take the secret
with him in his head, and the vital mould spores *in his clothes*.

There was no general direction from Florey, only individual
action, and Florey himself rubbed a handful of mould into the
lining of his raincoat while Heatley daubed it across the pockets of
his suit. As long as these clothes were not sent to be dry-cleaned,
access to the mould was assured. Spores shaken from the material
over a dish of nutrient could awaken the mould to life again and

it would begin producing penicillin in a new culture. Satisfied they had done what they could to perpetuate their work, they then commenced the task of reporting the details of their experiments. They wrote their paper, couching their remarks in tight but explicit phrases, and sent it off to the *Lancet* with the names of the authors in alphabetical order. Florey was meticulous in giving his team credit, as he was for the rest of his life. The alphabetical arrangement put him second to Chain, and then came Gardner, Heatley, Jennings, Orr-Ewing and Sanders.[3]

The title of the paper was *Penicillin as a Chemotherapeutic Agent* and the editor of *Lancet* buried it inside the edition of 24th August 1940 on page 226. Sandwiched between a review of chest injuries and a report on a case of meningitis, it ran to about two full pages, including a graph on the large-scale mice trials.

The paper opened with these words,

In recent years interest in chemotherapeutic effects has been almost exclusively focused on the sulphonamides and their derivatives. There are, however, other possibilities, notably those connected with naturally occurring substances.

It has been known for a long time that a number of bacteria and moulds inhibit the growth of pathogenic micro-organisms. Little, however, has been done to purify or to determine the properties of any of these substances . . .

The article referred to work by Dubos* in America and the authors stated that following their own study on lysozyme it had occurred 'to two of us' that it would be profitable to conduct a

* Dr René Dubos was working on bacterial antagonism at the Rockefeller Medical Institute. He had devised a brilliant approach, and had managed to isolate a substance that was antibacterial from a spore-forming soil bacterium called *Bacillus brevis*. He had obtained a compound which was active against staphylococci, called tyrothricin, but which was shown to contain two substances—gramacidin and tyrocidine, both of which were obtained in crystalline form. It was gramacidin that was the germ-killer and although it proved, as did so many, to be too toxic for injection into man it was used successfully for the task which Fleming had thought penicillin might be used—for topical application as an antiseptic. Dubos was responsible for a first-class piece of scientific work, but it was not crowned with the same fortune that fell on the penicillin workers and so was destined to fill a minor place in the antibiotic story.

systematic investigation. This had included, they said, 'a promising mould' on which Fleming had reported in 1929. Fleming had shown that the mould broth—which he had called penicillin—was useful in the isolation of certain types of bacteria. Fleming's report had indicated that agents causing diseases—such as gonorrhoea, pneumonia, diphtheria, meningitis and others—had been inhibited in test tubes and that an injection of a filtrate of this crude broth into a healthy animal had produced no sign of toxicity.*

In this classic paper the Oxford team noted the brief efforts that had been made, and then announced,

'During the last year, methods have been devised here (Sir William Dunn School) for obtaining a considerable yield of penicillin and for rapid assay of its antibacterial power. From the culture medium a brown powder has been obtained which is freely soluble in water. It and its solution are stable for a considerable time, and though it is not a pure substance, its antibacterial activity is very great . . .'

The authors called it 'our preparation', but still gave it the name of penicillin and described its action in the living systems of mice as a truly systemic drug.

'From all the above tests it was clear that this substance possessed qualities which made it suitable for trial as a therapeutic agent . . .', and then using Florey's favourite phrase, the paper stated, 'the results are clear cut . . . it would seem a reasonable hope that all organisms inhibited in high dilution in vitro will be found to be dealt with *in vivo*'.†

* The authors did not here question why Fleming had not taken the logical scientific step of injecting the substance into diseased animals, but their puzzlement at this omission was voiced many times in the years that followed. Exactly thirty years later—almost to the very day—Dr Norman Heatley wrote in *Nature*, 'Perhaps one's astonishment that Fleming abandoned penicillin is partly founded on a fallacy, namely the oft-repeated legend—which Fleming himself did not correct—that he knew all the time that penicillin would turn out to have remarkable curative properties.' And Professor Chain, knighted by this time, when lecturing in Australia, said, 'The evidence exposes the popular figure of Fleming as a myth.'

† It was a hope that came true in unexpected measure, for one organism causing a world-wide scourge, that was not dealt with *in vitro*—in the test tube—turned out to be highly sensitive to penicillin in living systems: syphilis.

9

The team ended their paper with a quiet acknowledgement of aid and gave their thanks in this way, 'In addition to the facilities provided by the University, we have had financial assistance from the Rockefeller Foundation, the Medical Research Council and the Nuffield Trust.'

The preference given to the Rockefeller Foundation acted like a detonator in Mellanby's London office, and he was soon writing furiously, and rebuking Florey in high dudgeon.[4]

There is great interest here in your report and it seems you are on to a very good subject. But you gave a great boost to the Rockefeller people and it seemed that the MRC had played a minor role.

I doubt whether this accords with the facts and, since you mention the Rockefeller money, you should mention the grants given to other members of your team by the MRC. You have received:

Yourself—£50 expenses; Chain—£300 and £100 expenses; Jennings—£200, and Orr-Ewing—£200 and £350.

I doubt whether the Rockefeller is supporting you to that extent. It seems to me that your method of dealing with this is wrong tactics, partly because these Rockefeller grants in this country follow discussions between O'Brien (Rockefeller) and myself, and partly because if you have a good thing in your own country you might as well give it the proper credit and not follow those people who, in cases of research, find it more convenient to give foreigners boosts than their own colleagues.

And having said that I salute you:—Mellanby.

Florey accepted the rebuke and explained that the editor of the *Lancet* had cut down his acknowledgments to people and bodies. Having said that, his reply showed he was annoyed,

The negotiations with the Rockefeller people were started not through O'Brien at all but with their chemical people and, in the end, they gave us $5 000 for the year (£1 200) and, in addition, had given Heatley £300. And, by the way, the £50 you credit to me was for the tail-end work on lysozyme.

By my reckoning the MRC help for penicillin for the year was £300 for Chain, £200 for Jennings, and with other small matters would not go above a maximum of £800. We got £1 200 from the Rockefeller so there was very good reason to thank them. I have always expressed my gratitude for help which the Medical Research Council has given me but, on the other hand, I am not aware of having asked you to finance anything which did not produce the results anticipated.

Mellanby, being the man he was, still had to take issue, but he ended his next letter with the words, 'If you can get penicillin to cure cases of human bacterial infection I will forgive you a good deal more than your misdeeds in the present instance.'

The publication of the Oxford report in the *Lancet* coincided with the appearance of waves of German bombers over Southern England that marked the opening of the Battle of Britain and it is impossible to know now which made the greater impact on Alexander Fleming at the time. Casually turning the pages of his copy of *Lancet*, he saw the heading that must have awakened many memories, *Penicillin as a chemotherapeutic agent*.

The thoughts and feelings that must have flooded through him as he read the preliminary review, with the tremendous possibility for the reduction of human suffering it foreshadowed, must surely have been an experience given to few.

In the extraordinary public relations phenomenon, which has gone as far as naming a crater on the moon after him, the picture of Fleming bending over his contaminated culture plate has become as immortal as that of Newton beneath the apple tree. No one has been able to re-create the real moment of truth, however, not even Fleming himself. The emotions, the flood of thought that surely came to him at that moment—long after he had given up his interest in penicillin as a healer of man, and after years during which he had not mentioned the name of penicillin in lectures or written papers—have gone to the grave with him. According to members of the Oxford team, Fleming telephoned Florey on the following Sunday and said he wanted to visit the

Dunn laboratories on the Monday morning. Florey grinned widely when he told Chain that Fleming was coming. Chain was astonished.

'Fleming?' he said, puzzled. Then, as realization struck him, 'Good God; I thought he was dead.'

Fleming stood on Florey's doorstep the following morning, a short, white-haired man with a gay little bow tie, and immediately staked his personal claim to penicillin.

'Hullo,' he said, holding out his hand, 'I hear you've been doing things with my old penicillin. I'd be interested to look around.' It was the longest sentence he was to say to them that day.

Florey and Chain took him through the laboratories and explained the step-by-step procedures of the extraction techniques and gave him a tiny sample of their purified concentrate. They found him quiet and non-committal, and Chain suspected that he did not understand his explanations of the concentration methods. Chain said afterwards to Florey, 'He looked a lot, but he said very little.'[5]

Fleming went back to London leaving no comment or word of praise that remained in the minds of the Oxford team for the work that was to lift him to world fame. He never returned. Whether he saw the picture dimly, or not at all, is not known, for other than in a letter with samples of his own preserved Penicillium mould, sent later in 1940, he failed to leave any record of his visit to the place where the chemotherapeutic power of penicillin was discovered. The great new era of public medicine, the blessing that the molecules in his old neglected mould would bring to tens of thousands of wounded men, the Nobel Prize for medicine, and emotional people kissing his hand and the hem of his clothing—all these things were in front of him, but he could not then have glimpsed them.

This is apparent from the statement Fleming made, and which tended to confirm Chain's suspicion of his lack of grasp of the subject—when he told a gathering of medical men in that same year of 1940,

'Penicillin has not yet been tried in war surgery and it will not be tried until some chemist comes along and finds out what it is and, if possible, manufactures it.'[6]

When they noted this statement in the monograph which they began writing in 1945 on the history of penicillin, the Oxford team limited their comment to the following,

'Fortunately this view, in the event, was not justified.'[7]

THE HUNDRED-MILE STRETCH OF TWISTING ROAD BETWEEN Stoke-on-Trent and Oxford was perilous with sheets of black ice.

It was two days before Christmas 1940, and Dr Norman Heatley, tense and numb with cold, sat over the steering wheel of the van listening to the chink of one hundred and seventy ceramic culture pots as the vehicle hit each bump in the road.

Twenty yards ahead the roadway vanished in a white haze through which the headlights of the approaching vehicles burst with a distracting glare. There were piles of snow and slush lining the route, and no traffic signs or names of towns to guide him as these had all been removed in anticipation of the invasion.

He had to feel his way along the road, travelling not much more than twenty miles an hour—for fear a sudden jolt might crack one of the precious pots for which Florey was waiting in Oxford. Hour after hour he eased his way along, determined that the cargo would reach the laboratories undamaged.

Heatley had carefully packed the culture vessels flat, with their short, angled spouts criss-crossed as they would be when they held their charges of nutrient broth and matted mould. The loading had been slow and was achieved with frozen fingers after a laborious drive from Oxford to the factory, and when he reached Oxford on the return journey he had driven two hundred miles and had spent nearly eleven hours on the road.

Florey was acutely conscious of time slipping away and so the journey had been made in a van borrowed from their emergency health service. It was a trip Heatley was to make twice more, once in a blinding snow storm, to make sure their six hundred culture vessels arrived safely and as quickly as possible.

The rectangular pots were the outcome of many months of frustration and effort, and each one was carried into the laboratory with care and reverence; for on these and the several hundred that were to follow Florey was dependent for enough penicillin extract to begin his first trials on human beings.

Through the summer months after Dunkirk and in the long autumn which brought the German bomber onslaught on England—first by day and then by night—the team's lives had been dominated by the struggle to obtain a few hundred milligrams of powder for their experiments—chemical, biological and pharmacological. Florey found progress agonizingly slow, and firm after firm was approached in vain for the help that he sought. He asked for glass vessels at first but learned rapidly that, while this was ideal material, they were out of the question. The best he was offered was a few hundred vessels for £500 and delivery in six months—perhaps!

These costs, conditions and delays Florey could not accept. Together with Heatley he worked out the style and line of vessel they thought could be made of a material known in the trade as slipware—clay vessels which were kiln-baked after shaping. But finding a factory that could produce them in the middle of the devastation of the blitz was not easy.

Florey found a way out when he remembered a friend he had in Stoke—Dr J. P. Stock, a consulting physician who, he felt, would know the local scene in his part of the Potteries. He sent Stock a letter of explanation and sketches of their requirements and Stock reacted immediately and effectively. Within two days he replied to Florey by telegram saying that the Burslem firm of James MacIntyre and Co. Ltd were ready to help. At Florey's request Heatley caught a train north the next day—30th October —and spent hours of aggravation in the carriage because of bomb damage to the railway line, not reaching his destination until late at night. On the following morning he was heartened to find that craftsmen had already fashioned three pots which they were ready to fire—only minor adjustments by knife were needed and the project was under way.

These first three vessels reached Oxford in November and
Florey approved them and then placed his order for a total of
six hundred at a cost of £300.

When MacIntyre and Co. had the first batch ready, transport
difficulties threatened to hold up delivery until the New Year, so
Florey asked Heatley to take the van and collect them. He could
not waste the days because, he told his team, it had been made
clear to him in his discussions with industry that, without proof of
a startling kind coming from tests on human beings, there was no
hope at all of drug companies beginning commercial production.

The arrival of Heatley with the one hundred and seventy
culture vessels was Florey's first step in turning his laboratories—
with all their prized reputation as a world-class research centre—
into a makeshift penicillin-producing factory. He would not be
defeated. On Christmas Eve the team started the task of large-
scale production.

The culture vessels were all washed and then charged, each
with its litre of nutrient broth, and stacked in serried racks, up-
right, for their sterilization in the heat of the autoclave. They
finished this work in the evening and their only festivity was a
quick drink and a 'Happy Christmas' all round. Next morning
Florey was back in the building with Heatley and the work of
seeding the vessels with spores ejected from syringes began, and
then all the vessels were stacked again into incubators for
culturing.

Ethel spent a lonely Christmas in the three-storied house across
the park. Her home was a vault of silence. The children had gone
and Florey was spending all his time in the laboratory. The war
had created this void in Ethel's life. The bombing, and Florey's
engrossment with penicillin, had led her to agree that the children
should be evacuated to America where they would live for the
rest of the war. Florey had written to his friend John Fulton, in
New Haven, Connecticut, and he and his wife had thrown open
their childless house to the Florey children. Ethel had planned to
go with them but had been prevented from doing so because she
was a trained doctor and would be needed in Britain. Long
afterwards Paquita recalled the scene of their parting,

Joseph Florey's shoe factory in Adelaide, early 1900's (*South Australian Archives*)

The house in Adelaide where Howard Florey was born on 24th September 1898 (*South Australian Archives*)

Howard Florey as a young man (*Mrs Brebner*)

Ethel Florey as a young woman (*Mrs Brebner*)

Penicillium notatum mould growing in a petri dish at Florey's laboratories at Oxford (*Sir William Dunn School, Oxford*)

Florey injecting penicillin into a mouse (*Reportagebild, Sweden*)

The second penicillin extraction plant at the Sir William Dunn School of Pathology, Oxford (*Dr A. G. Sanders*)

a) Extraction of penicillin into amyl acetate

b) Separating the penicillin-rich amyl acetate from culture fluid

c) Re-extraction of
penicillin into water

d) Second cycle of
concentration, using
chloroform instead of
amyl acetate

Dr Ernst Chain at work in his laboratory at Oxford (*Keystone, London*)

'We went by ship from Liverpool and crossed the Atlantic in convoy. But Dad didn't like fuss or emotional bother so he and mother just came to the station when we caught the train in London and saw us off from there. He just kissed us goodbye and told us to be good, but mother was terribly cut up and cried because she felt it was a dreadful thing for us to go alone.'[1]

But they went: talkative and companionable Paquita, aged ten, chaperoning her quiet five-year-old brother Charles.

So Ethel lost four precious years of her children's lives and this was a gap that nothing could adequately fill. Her reward was penicillin, and a period of slogging and, at times, heartbreaking effort which in the end rightfully earned her an imperishable place in medical history.

In the months that followed the departure of Paquita and Charles the last traces of the laughing girl with the long swinging walk dissolved into a woman scientist with a resolve and a will as formidable as that of her husband; and what Ethel did and the way she worked left its mark in dozens of British hospitals and war casualty wards, and on medical practice.

Her husband said of her, despite the worsening of their relationship in later years, 'It must never be forgotten that if it wasn't for Ethel penicillin would not have been introduced into medical practice when it was.'[2]

Heatley's delivery of the last of the slipware pots, known thereafter by Florey as the 'jerries', brought Florey's large-scale production capacity to a planned 500 litres of mould broth a week, from which he hoped to extract between one hundred thousand and two hundred thousand units of penicillin. By modern measurement of antibiotic dosage this would be, at the most, a tenth of what would be used to clear up an infection of gonorrhoea. But even this modest target was to prove elusive and Florey's plans were undermined again and again by unexpected snags and developments. At times the delays and frustrations broke his rigid control and he lapsed into angry impatience.

The problems came not only in handling the amount of material on a large scale, but from the chemical behaviour of the Penicillium mould. In the first place, Florey and his team had to face the fact that they could not possibly work up to 500 litres a week by hand on their existing flow process unless they wanted a continuance of the excruciating problem of extraction. The existing system of tubes and coils running through sheathings of crushed ice was therefore abandoned. Instead of the cold being brought to the material, the material was taken to the cold, by creating a cold room in which the penicillin could be worked. The team wore thick clothing and fur-lined boots, and carried out the extraction process in sub-zero temperatures. They had problems, too, of emulsion forming in the flowing material, and in controlling the acid and the temperature levels. Then Heatley, aided by Glister and James Kent, erected a battery of six contraptions that was a supreme test of ingenuity and improvisation.

These six assemblies of tubes and bottles, set in wooden frames, were basic units working in parallel in which showers of cooled broth from jets were passed down a glass tube containing amyl acetate. These droplets yielded their penicillin to the acetate and fell to the bottom where they were discarded into the drains. Fresh solvent was passed continuously into the tubes at the bottom, slowly forcing the penicillin-rich solvent to the top where it was collected into gallon jars, after which it was dealt with by hand. They called it a counter-flow operation and Heatley rigged the six contraptions with an automatic system that turned on coloured lights and rang a bell when the jars were full. Not only did this speed up the process of making the precious substance but it turned out penicillin ten times more powerful than any previous extraction.

The apparatus had a capacity of handling twelve litres an hour, but each of the six frames quickly earned pet names for their temperamental behaviour. Just the same, they were a long step towards large-scale production for human trials, and they gave wonderful service for the year in which they were in use.

The work was not easy. It made inroads on the team's reserves, and shortened tempers, and the material was coming out in such meagre amounts that each wisp or particle was washed from the containers or rinsed from the syringes. The merest trace of penicillin was chemical gold to them. Florey saw the struggle was a trial to his colleagues and, after discussing it with Chain, made his first move towards recruiting more staff for his 'factory'. On 7th December he again wrote to Mellanby with another urgent appeal for money. This time he wanted £5 a week to meet the wages for two young women who would take over some of the chores in the cold room extraction plant and the handling of the culture pots.

The application was put before a formal meeting of the Medical Research Council along with Florey's request for approval of the expenditure for the 600 culture pots, and Mellanby's account of this meeting provided Florey with one of the merriest moments he had enjoyed in years.

Mellanby told him that, when he raised the subject of money for 'mould pots' so that more penicillin could be produced, one elderly member, who was not a scientist, but was there to see that public money was not wasted, misheard the word *moulds* for *moles*. He must have had a mental picture of public money being used to finance little moles sitting on pots making penicillin, and when he protested against the feasibility of such a project the usually staid gathering dissolved into an uproar.

Florey got the money for his pots and they awarded him £5 a week for two women assistants. Two girls with nursing experience, Ruth Callow—a sister of Chain's assistant—and Claire Khan, took on a tough and demanding job with such success that Florey decided to seek more women workers, and another letter went off to Mellanby outlining the requirement for girls with nursing or technical experience, 'Bright, but not graduate standard for we don't want them so clever that they think they can improve on our methods.' He suggested that there should be an approach to the Royal Air Force to ask whether they could spare three girls for this work.

Mellanby wrote to the Air Ministry and, from there, Air Marshal Sir Harold Whittingham dealt succinctly with the request. The RAF was under great pressure and not even three girls could be spared. 'We are absorbing every girl we can find for training as nursing aides and therefore we are unable to meet your request.'[3]

Florey said they should try the Army and Mellanby pulled a string with a highly-placed friend at the War Office—but with no result. The Army, too, could not spare a single girl from its resources, but did hint that half a dozen soldiers might be made available.

In the end Florey, when he was ready to settle for three men, found himself in trouble with the University over the question of employer-employee liabilities.

Eventually the difficulties were overcome when the two young women were joined by four others to form the group which became known as the 'Oxford Penicillin Girls'. The new names were: Betty Cooke, Peggy Gardner, Megan Lankester and Patricia McKegney. Their devotion helped to lift the output of therapeutic penicillin by a thousand-fold and to make it available in quantities sufficient to save the first human lives.

But the increase in production did not mean the end of all their difficulties and soon afterwards biological snags began to appear. The first was a hammer blow. The mould stopped producing penicillin.

After a period of investigation that pinned down the trouble to the sudden chemical change in the mould, the team had to revise their methods of culture. Future delays in production by this cause were overcome by sub-culturing spores that showed a higher yield and storing them in the refrigerator against further mutational changes.

They had no sooner surmounted this problem when trouble began over the technique of syphoning off the broth medium beneath the fungal mat. This was being done as much as a dozen times and each syphoning exposed the fungus to the millions of bacteria in the air; some were capable of producing the penicillinase enzyme which could eradicate a crop of penicillin as quickly as penicillin itself could deal with bacteria. The microworld from which they were garnering the precious substance was working against them. This problem posed Florey and his team with a recurring challenge that added tremendously to their burdens.

Florey wrote later, 'The months spent in increasing output and in accumulating stocks, with all their disappointments and their trials, are not likely to be forgotten by those involved. The possibility that the drug might be of value in treating war injuries had by this time provided us with a powerful stimulus to persevere.'

The continuing difficulties created a foreboding that, for all their labours and inventiveness, they might one day find themselves against an insurmountable barrier. Then they would have to turn, as Fleming had already done, to the hope that it would prove possible to elucidate the structure of the active molecule and then make it by synthesis. Florey set aside amounts of his precious stockpile for analytical studies and the Oxford scientists began a long and fascinating investigation that in the end revealed the structure of the penicillin molecule.

Towards the end of January Florey assessed the stockpile he had collected for human experiments and felt he was close to the stage when he could make his first move. Then, on the edge of decision, he paused.

The hesitation came out of his dislike of being an arbiter of life, and not out of doubt of his science. Throughout his career he had shrunk from involvement with patients—even when Ethel needed treatment—because he felt himself incapable of being detached from their suffering.

Now he faced the moment when penicillin, injected into a human vein for the first time, would mingle in a living system. The penicillin would mix with lymphocytes, leucocytes, antibodies and hormones. What would happen?

The hesitation could only be momentary. His patient work had built up a casebook of data on how the drug could be expected to act in the environment of the human body. He was among the world's best judges of physiological probability and he thought his experiments had given extensive insight into dose levels, frequency and method.

At this stage he consulted his friend, Professor Hugh Cairns, now a brilliant neuro-surgeon and a power in the organization of the Radcliffe Infirmary.

He immediately gave Florey's project his support and swung his influence behind it. As a result Florey immediately went to see the Professor of Medicine, L. J. Witt, and was explaining his requirements when there was a knock on the door and a young man put his head inside to ask Witt a question.

Witt seized on the interruption with delight and said to Florey, his face alight with inspiration, 'Why, Florey, here is the very man you need.'

In this way Dr C. M. Fletcher, Nuffield Research Fellow, working at the Radcliffe with the status of Registrar, was carried into medical history and had his name carved into a commemorative stone in a rose garden at Magdalen College.

Fletcher had heard of Florey but had never met him. He had read the paper on the animal experiments in the *Lancet* the previous August, but had not thought it much to enthuse about. He was, however, impressed with Florey's quiet power. He said, in recollecting the meeting,

'It didn't thrill me at all to be drawn into this. I thought it was another chore but I was happy enough to do the work. I was glad to meet Florey and he struck me as a man of quality—a Rolls-Royce of a man.'[4]

Florey's instructions to Fletcher were terse and to the point. He would look through the hospital for some patient on whom penicillin could be tested for toxicity—ethically. When he had someone, he would be given 100 milligrams of the new drug and he would inject it as soon as possible.

She was a woman in her forties and she was beyond human help. The carcinoma that had been in her amputated breast had sown colonies of cancer cells about her body, and she had only a month or two to live.

Fletcher was direct in his approach and told her that it would not be of help to her, but she agreed and he injected 100 milligrams of the substance intravenously.

'Had she declined I should have just kept walking round the hospital until I found someone else. There was never any question of making her a guinea pig nor did we put a notice on the board calling for volunteers,' Dr Fletcher said. For some unknown reason the injection was not recorded in the woman's case notes and this left a trace of uncertainty about the identity of the first person in Britain to be injected with penicillin.

Only the sudden fever—the trembling and the steeply rising temperature—she showed two hours later left a clue to her name.

The resultant 'spike' in her temperature chart, plus the cause of death two months later, made it highly probable that this was Mrs Elva Akers, of Oxford. Her name rang a bell years later in Fletcher's mind when an attempt was made to name this person in the story of penicillin. But no definite record of the event was kept.

When Fletcher carried his report of the toxic reaction to the Sir William Dunn building, it caused consternation and some dismay. Several of Florey's team confessed themselves stunned at the result. Florey found it incredible and thought at first that the fever was peculiar to this particular patient. He asked Fletcher to go through the process again with a different patient but, when this second volunteer was found and the toxic effect of the drug recurred, he tackled the problem in his own laboratory.

The detective work commenced immediately and Florey's first results, using rabbits, pointed to a toxic fraction—a pyrogen —which Dr Abraham was able to eliminate by passing the material several times through the purifying process. Once the toxic fraction had been detected, and removed, then events moved fast.

Fletcher carried out a series of tests with the drug, using various methods of application, on a number of patients, proving that the intravenous drip system was the most effective way of treating deep-seated infection. Florey himself, hearing of a case at another Oxford hospital—then known as the Wingfield-Morris Hospital—experimented with internal application.

The patient, a man named Edward Reynolds, suffered from osteomyelitis caused by bacteria attacking the bones of his right leg. Florey put a tube down the man's throat in an attempt to carry the penicillin into the duodenum, avoiding the destructive acids in the stomach. No penicillin activity was detected in the man's blood, or his urine, and Florey discounted the case as a record of treatment.

By this time Ethel was working at the Radcliffe Infirmary and, through her, the plight of Constable Albert Alexander came to Florey's attention.

Albert Alexander had been a burly forty-three-year-old officer in the County Constabulary before bacteria entered his system through a scratch at the side of his mouth, caused by a rose thorn.

When Heatley was driving back to Oxford with the first culture pots on 23rd December Alexander was already fighting for his life. He was host to a primary infection by the murderous *Staphylococcus aureus*, and to a secondary infection by *Streptococcus pyogenes*—both of which were strains Florey had used in his successful mice tests.

With a misplaced faith physicians at the Infirmary had pumped nineteen grams of sulphapyridine into him over a period of a week. This achieved nothing more than a drug rash. During Christmas and into the New Year the bacteria ran riot, and by mid-January Alexander's doctors were incising multiple abscesses on his scalp. The sockets of his eyes became pools of virulence and the attack was so bad that surgeons took away his right eye and then lanced the swollen mess of his left eye to relieve the pain caused by pressure. The infection was attacking his bones and fresh abscesses broke out. He was emaciated and near to death when they took penicillin to him. This was on 12th February 1941, four months after his admission to hospital.[5]

The first injections of penicillin were intravenous and were repeated every few hours. Florey stood with Ethel for a while at the bedside and Florey's manner indicated he already had doubts. He afterwards described the case as 'forlorn', but he organized his team into a relay service so that every scrap of penicillin could be brought to the man's aid.

Each time Alexander passed urine into an attached bottle it was unclipped and the member of the team in attendance at the bedside would cycle through the streets of Oxford, with the bottle of urine, back to the laboratory where Chain, Abraham or Heatley would re-extract the penicillin for re-injection into the constable's veins. Ethel, Sanders, Fletcher and others, were all couriers in what some people grimly called the 'P-patrol'.

But with each journey, with each injection, they lost a part of their precious stock. Sometimes the penicillin in Alexander's urine would be little more than half the amount injected. Sometimes it was less than half. More was lost in the re-extraction process, and both the patient and the team were fighting a battle of diminishing returns. At the end of the third day they became entirely dependent on the penicillin they could extract from his urine.

Already by the fourth day the change in Alexander was remarkable. He was making a striking recovery. The suppurations from his head wounds and from his eyes were drying up, and his fever was gone. With his temperature normal he had a return of appetite, and these improvements continued into the fifth day. Then his case notes show a grim entry,

'Penicillin supply exhausted. Total administered: 4·4 grammes in five days.'

These words were the patient's death warrant. Though he fought to hold his ground for ten more days, he then deteriorated in condition. His lungs became suffused with fresh infection and he died on 15th March, one calendar month from the start of penicillin treatment.

Alexander was their first case of recognized specific treatment against severe sepsis and he died not because penicillin had failed but because Florey and his Oxford team could not supply enough of the drug. The dose was too small, treatment came too late, and then had to cease before all infection had been quelled. But, even though he died, Constable Albert Alexander did make a contribution to medical advance, and Florey made a point of this in his notes, 'If this forlorn case had value it was that it showed that penicillin could be given over five days without toxic effect in man.'[6]

It was little consolation to Florey and his team, but if he felt defeated and downcast at the outcome he still drew a logical conclusion from the case, and told his colleagues, 'This will not happen again. We shall not go into any other case unless we are sure that we have enough penicillin. Until we are sure, we shall treat only children.'

The case of Albert Alexander gained an historic place in medicine, despite the defeat, since it showed the latent power of penicillin. As such it became recognized as the opening of the age of antibiotics, and more than a quarter of a century later Florey gave his approval—unwillingly because he found no place for such things in medical science—to the wording of a plaque which was erected in the foyer of the Radcliffe Infirmary. Florey did not live to see it erected. But the text has since informed many thousands of waiting patients that the first systemic treatment of a human being with penicillin occurred within those walls. It contains two errors.

In the text on the plaque the word 'systematically' was used wrongly for the word 'systemically'; and the Radcliffe Infirmary was not the first place where penicillin had been injected into a human being.

The first injection actually took place at the Presbyterian Hospital in New York, four months prior to the start of treatment on the Oxford policeman and more than three months before Dr Fletcher's injection of the woman dying of cancer.

For more than thirty years the evidence of this medically historic event rested unnoticed among the clinical and laboratory notes of a small group of researchers from Columbia University led by a dynamic and persevering physician who was America's pioneer of penicillin therapy.

Unknown to his countrymen and recognized by very few of his scientific colleagues he, nevertheless, was the first physician to inject a penicillin preparation into a human being.

Dr Martin Henry Dawson had conducted a personal crusade against rheumatic disease and the fatal heart condition of bacterial endocarditis, and was fired by Florey's paper on penicillin in the *Lancet*. For years he had faced the disease of bacterial endocarditis as an implacable foe and whenever one of his cases was diagnosed as having this affliction which attacked cardiac tissues and pitted and ate away the delicate valves of the heart, Dawson had come to regard it as a death sentence. When the power of penicillin was described in the Oxford report, Dawson caught the first gleam of hope and in a burst of energy and initiative, motivated the steps which led to the first production of penicillin extract in America. Dawson became co-ordinator and clinician for the project, Gladys Hobby handled the microbiology and Karl Meyer did the chemical extraction work. They suffered all the setbacks which Florey and his team had gone through. But they knew a substance could be won that was active against bacteria causing the piteously hopeless cases which Dawson was constantly facing—and within a week of reading the *Lancet* report Dawson had obtained his first Penicillium culture.

A search of the literature revealed that an American worker had tried his hand with Fleming's mould in 1935. Dr Roger Reid, then a graduate at Pennsylvania State College and writing his doctoral thesis, had confirmed Fleming's findings and also Raistrick's conclusion that the active substance was highly unstable. Reid had obtained his samples from Fleming and although he was unable to extract an active preparation, he had to his credit, maintained them without mutation. He received several other requests for transfers when the Oxford report reached America, one of these was from Dr J. M. McGuire, of Eli Lilly Company, in Indiana. But neither McGuire, nor any other worker, moved with the rapidity of Martin Dawson.

Dr Gladys Hobby was on vacation when the August 1940 issue of the *Lancet* had reached Dawson in New York, and she returned to find that an air of excitement had filled the laboratory where she worked with Dawson and Dr Meyer.

'Henry Dawson had immediately begun work on this new prospect and I was at once caught up in his eager search . . .' she said later.[7]

Brief notes the small team compiled at that time display the speed and urgency with which they tackled their new project,

Early work of Dawson, Hobby, Meyer: first studies on fermentation of penicillin started 23rd September 1940. The culture used on this day was from Roger Reid, of the Johns Hopkins Hospital. Culture had been received from Fleming in 1935. First series of flasks showed activity after 4 days and first sensitivity tests, using green streptococci from cases of subacute bacterial endocarditis, were run on 30th September.

Within a week of putting Reid's culture to growth Dawson had confirmed that the substance in the mould broth was lethal to the organisms killing his heart patients. Within three more days

he had a filtrate of the penicillin broth in the veins of experimentally diseased mice and was embarked on a series of toxicity
tests.

Dr Karl Meyer, following the path Ernst Chain, Norman
Heatley, and others, had beaten in Oxford, won his first concentrated extract on 7th October 1940, less than five weeks after the
Lancet report reached America and within two weeks of the start
of the first fermentation studies in New York.

Dawson waited only eight days for Meyer to increase his tiny
amount of penicillin extract; then, as Dr Hobby recorded, 'Henry
Dawson was full of excitement . . . his interest in rheumatic
disease and in subacute bacterial endocarditis provided the stimulus. Early in that fall, on 15th October 1940, the first doses of
penicillin were administered intracutaneously to Mr Aaron
Alston at the Presbyterian Hospital in New York City.'[8]

Nothing was recorded to reveal anything of Mr Alston's
history, the first man to be injected with penicillin, but it is
known that he died and lack of success in the first attempts to
influence the course of subacute endocarditis is told in the following words,

'Obviously, the drug preparations were extremely crude and,
moreover, extremely low in potency.'

There was no success in that first attempt, but Dawson was
heartened that there was no sign of toxic reaction—and he knew
that the mould extract, given in sufficient amount, would conquer the bacterial infections in which he was specializing.

In his eagerness to amass every scrap of penicillin he wrote to
Ernst Chain at Oxford, seeking a higher-yielding mould. Chain
acted immediately and Dawson was writing back to him on
28th October saying,

Thank you for the prompt reply . . . it must be extremely
difficult for you to carry on scientific work in England under
present conditions and I feel it more than trite on my part to
express the unbounded admiration which all Americans feel
for the stand Britain is making. Your report has occasioned
the very greatest interest here, and, with the assistance of Dr
Karl Meyer, we have been able to get started on this problem. I

hesitate asking for information before your work is published, but if you are prepared to release any data on the preparation of your extract we are naturally anxious to know about it . . . My inquiry is prompted by my desire to treat, if possible, a patient with subacute bacterial endocarditis in whom I am more than ordinarily interested . . .[9]

To meet the cost of despatch Dawson sent Chain an international money order for five dollars. The mould from Chain arrived safely, but the five dollars spent on sending it were as the resultant note shows wasted, 'Culture received direct from Dr Chain and acknowledged on 28th October, . . . it showed purplish-red sporulation on arrival; one subculture grew with greyish-green sporulation; it never produced any penicillin in our hands.'

Dawson's team had to rely entirely on Roger Reid's sample and they grew the mould in hundreds of bottles which, because of the limited space in their own laboratory, they stacked in rows in different classrooms in the Columbia University College. Gladys Hobby described the scene.

As the students took occupation so we moved the bottles and apparatus from classroom to classroom. The excitement even spread to some of the patients in the hospital wards. Frequently, we carried culture flasks and the assay plates to the bedsides of some of the people we were treating and they took a share in some of the experiments. Many of them were as interested in the work as we were. They were well aware that the drug might never help them, but they also knew that it might help others. Most of our emphasis was on subacute bacterial endocarditis, but some attempts were made to study the effects of penicillin on other infections.

Karl Meyer's early chemical studies deserved far more credit than they have ever been given. Working with fantastically small amounts of active penicillin and with quite inadequate facilities, he isolated all the material with which we worked during those early significant months. Without his considerable talents we could have accomplished essentially nothing.[10]

The entire period was an exciting one and, as the winter passed into the spring of 1941, Dawson began to compose the first professional report on the use of clinical penicillin in America. Above his own name, and those of Dr Hobby and Dr Meyer, he presented the paper to a meeting of the Society for Clinical Investigation on 5th May 1941, and in this document he announced,

'Penicillin has been administered to four patients with subacute bacterial endocarditis and to eight patients with chronic staphylococcal blepharitis. Sufficient material was not available for adequate therapy in the cases of subacute endocarditis. However, no serious toxic effects were observed. The results in the local eye infections were most satisfactory. One patient who proved resistant to sulfathiazol showed a prompt response. Further clinical trials are under way . . .'*

In a hand-written summary to this paper Dawson added, '. . . it would appear that penicillin is a chemotherapeutic agent of great potential significance.'

As Dawson delivered that first American paper on penicillin therapy, tragedy loomed over him, for he knew then that he suffered from incurable myasthenia gravis, the disease which would gradually strip him of muscular power. It lent greater urgency to his mind and he fought against the condition as the months went by. His co-worker, Gladys Hobby, wrote, 'he died early in 1945. In the years in between he worked quite regularly, but obviously he was not as productive as he would have been. He was a brilliant man, and, I believe, the first to realize the true clinical importance of penicillin, at least in the United States.'[11]

Later, she recalled,

I believe Henry Dawson unquestionably treated the first patients with penicillin in the USA. The paper was presented in collaboration with Karl Meyer, and myself, in May 1941, and the last paragraph read, 'Clinical use of penicillin has been hampered by two facts. (1) The small yield. (2) The desire to provide as much material as possible to the chemist for analysis.

* Earlier in the year Dawson had recorded, '11th January 1941: penicillin administered to patients', but on that occasion he had probably been too eager to reach a conclusion to record the results.

However, a number of cases have been treated with satisfactory results. Penicillin has been proven to be effective in
man when given by the intravenous or intramuscular route,
or when applied locally ... the number of cases so far treated
is small, but the results are highly encouraging.

CHAPTER 10

ALEXANDER'S DEATH IN OXFORD UNDERSCORED THE
paradox that Florey faced in the spring of 1941. He needed a
triumph in penicillin treatment to encourage a start to commercial
production so that there could be sufficient penicillin for more
compelling clinical trials. He had failed to win his triumph
because there had not been enough penicillin.

He drew his consolation from the proof of non-toxicity of the
drug, but this was no conquest of disease that would sway
opinion where it mattered. He wrote his view on this situation as,
'. . . something of a vicious circle, for without more extensive
clinical demonstration . . . it seemed unlikely that any firm would
undertake large-scale preparation of the drug, while without a
larger scale of working it was an almost superhuman effort to
prepare enough of the drug for the requisite clinical trials.'

There had not been enough penicillin to save Alexander, so
Florey came to depend heavily on the cases that followed in the
next two months. These other early cases were all disappointing
and the case of Johnny Cox was, especially, an entirely unexpected
blow.

Previous to Cox's case there had been two others, but Florey
considered neither of them to be really satisfactory proof of the
pure systemic power of penicillin. The first was a fourteen-year-
old lad whose leg became infected when a steel pin had been
inserted into a broken bone. Florey cleared up the infection well
enough but when surgeons removed the pin two weeks later
infection broke out, and he discounted the case as satisfactory.

After this case Florey treated, purely by chance, the husband
of a cleaner at his laboratories. John Hawkins, aged forty-three,

suffered from a large carbuncle on his shoulder and chronic nasal
and bronchial catarrh. He, too, recorded a reversal of condition,
but the result could not be called dramatic in an age when the sulphonamides were doing similar things.

Thus, when the team came to Johnny Cox and registered a
complete defeat of the staphylococci that had entered his body
through measle spots, they felt they had their first real triumph
in this four-and-a-half-year-old boy.

Johnny Cox was admitted to the Radcliffe Infirmary on 13th
May and was at that time moribund and comatose from bacterial
attack on his lungs, liver, eyes and spinal fluid. He was treated
from the day he entered hospital with an intravenous drip of
penicillin and in nine days was back to life, talking and smiling
in his hospital cot, obviously convalescent.

Then, in the early hours of 27th May, the night sister at the
Radcliffe was aghast to see Johnny suddenly vomit and go into
convulsions. Thinking they were facing a resurgence of infection,
he was given a total of two grams of penicillin, but it was without effect. His temperature soared to 106 degrees, and by the end
of May he was dead.

The autopsy completely exonerated penicillin. The drug had
cleared the abscesses in his lungs and had conquered the bacteria
in every corner of his body, but it could not repair the damage
done to the walls of a vital artery running beside his spine.
Weakened by the intensity of the *Staphylococcus aureus,* the
artery had swollen under the pressure of the child's new surge of
life and had burst. He had been killed not by infection but by the
aneurism caused by the infection before penicillin treatment.

The case notes said, 'Before this vascular accident, the patient
had been restored from a moribund condition to apparent convalescence. No toxic effects from penicillin were noted.'[1]

Two successful cases followed this disappointment. A fourteen-
year-old boy who had injured his leg and suffered from staphylococcal infection, and so was extremely ill, made a good recovery
after ten days of penicillin treatment, and a six-month-old baby
boy, with an infection of the urinary tract, was cured by the first
oral use of minute doses of the drug.

After this came several cases of topical, or surface, applications, and all of these were successful—including a treatment of Florey himself. Fletcher had devised a technique where a small plastic bag could be placed over an eye so that it could be flushed with a wash of penicillin—to treat ulcers and similar infections. When Florey awoke one morning with one eye swollen with con-junctivitis, he became a patient of Fletcher and gained 'much relief and a rapid clearing of the infection'. On another occasion he also took penicillin when with an infection of his throat identi-fied as streptococcal, he gargled with the crude mould juice.

'It tasted foul,' he told his colleagues. 'But it did the trick.'

During the harrowing weeks of these clinical trials Florey faced new problems and found himself under steadily growing pressures. The lack of firm and convincing evidence of the power of penicillin added weight to arguments that they should not waste their meagre stocks of the drug on inconclusive clinical tests that would influence nobody outside their own circle, but should use their supply to make an all-out attack on the chemical nature of the penicillin molecule in the hope that it would lend itself to synthesis.

Florey, however, regarded synthesis as only a hope; on the other hand he knew for certain that the mould produced penicillin, and that penicillin could cure people of a whole variety of infectious diseases—if it was given in sufficient quantity. So he allocated the major part of the available drug to the human trials and set aside a small part for the analytical and chemical probing which Chain and Abraham had started soon after the end of the mice tests. Here again the work was severely limited by the amount of drug available. For weeks Florey haunted public officials and industrial executives, but had won little more than polite interest. The battering industry was suffering from the German air onslaught; the almost total diversion of the chemical industry to war production; the engrossment of government officials with survival; these were all against any chance of success in inducing a start to commercial production of a new and half-proved drug.

The possibility of penicillin's value for treating battle casualties had always been behind the solid perseverance in Florey and his team and this was increased when, in the middle of his first human trials, Florey received information in a private letter that alerted him to enemy interest in the drug and helped to sharpen his awareness of the need for full-scale production.

He sent the letter off to Sir Edward Mellanby, as head of the Government's Medical Research Council, with these words,

> I enclose this letter for you to see and it seems very undesirable to me that the Swiss should be allowed access to penicillin and that, through them, it should go to the Germans.* I think it would be well worth while to issue instructions to the National Type Collection Laboratories telling them not to issue sample cultures of *Penicillium notatum* to anyone with possible enemy connections.
>
> You might also think it worth while sending a note to Fleming and anyone else who might have the mould, although I do not know anyone else myself.[2]

Mellanby was quite unperturbed at the disclosure of an interest in the mould emanating from neutral Switzerland, or at the prospect that it might travel to Germany from there.

He wrote back to Florey, 'This does not seem to be a really serious matter to me and is nothing for you to worry about. After all, you are so far ahead it seems that no one else can compete with you.'

Mellanby's lack of appreciation of the military potential of the drug served to firm Florey's resolve on the plan that had been taking shape in his mind as he met the continual rebuffs of industry and authority. But there was one question which plagued him in those days of 1941 that had to be settled before he could instigate this plan—which was to take the discovery across the Atlantic to America and seek help there for its mass production. He had to settle the question of rights and patents.

Chain had been vehemently advocating protection of their work and his pressure on Florey had been incessant until the very word 'patent' touched a raw nerve at the Sir William Dunn School. Among Florey's staff there was a division of opinion,

---

* Penicillin development in Germany and Japan during the Second World War is described in an appendix at the end of this book.

but the German-born biochemist had a wide-ranging vision that
saw—against a background of the years when their work had
been based on penny-pinching budgets—a prospective income that
could be used to finance a broad and especially skilful exploration
of the biodynamic substances which were already known to exist
in the chemical conflicts in the microworld. Commenting on his
view of this Chain said later,

> I could not believe that we would not find other substances
> of equal, perhaps even greater, versatility than penicillin. It was
> just too much to accept that Fleming had stumbled on the only
> antibiotic of use to man—the odds of this happening were
> astronomical. I saw a whole tremendous virgin field and we
> were the leaders and would remain so if we got enough money.
> I argued our position again and again with Florey and we had
> bitter fights.

There were other opinions in his group on the ethics involved,
and so Florey took the question to the authorities. He caught a
train to London and sought a ruling from the President of the
Royal Society, Sir Henry Dale, the man who had been chairman
of a meeting in London thirteen years before at which Alexander
Fleming had read a paper on an interesting contamination of a
culture plate. As head of the Medical Research Council, Mellanby
was also consulted.

It was never divulged how these two eminent men reached
their finding. Whether they themselves made the decision after
conferring, or whether they consulted higher authority, did not
emerge, but they were firm in the ruling that it would be entirely
unethical for a medical scientist to seek monetary benefit from his
work by covering it with patent rights, especially in the case of
the development of a naturally-occurring phenomenon. One of
the phrases that remained in Florey's memory from their ruling
was, 'the people have paid for this work and they should have the
benefits made freely available to them'.

Chain exploded with anger at the decision and ranted against a
ruling which he considered to be idiotic and out of touch with
reality. Florey was unmoved by the outburst. His way ahead had

been cleared and he wasted no time on useless argument. His approach at that time was later explained by a life-long friend in whom he confided.

His objective was to get penicillin made in bulk in time to help the war wounded, and he followed that path. Having got his decision from the two top-shots in the scientific world he knew he could not be justly accused of quixotic neglect, even though there were malicious statements that he handed penicillin to the Americans on a platter. After he got his ruling he never felt badly about the patents question, although he said, many times, when he felt the need to give help to people and organizations he considered worthy, that if he had had his just dues for penicillin he could have made good use of the money.[3]

When the first days of summer came in 1941, Florey went once more to London to gain further assurance that his proposal to seek mass production in America was both understood and authorized. He got the green light in writing a week later from Mellanby,

Dear Florey: After discussing this with you, I have come to the conclusion that the only way that this most important matter (of penicillin production) may be pursued is for you and Heatley to go to the United States of America for three months.
This is a subject of the highest medical importance and it is quite clear that you cannot get this substance made by firms in this country. I regard it as most important that you go to America and get the facilities there under way.[4]

The letter from Mellanby cleared the way for Florey's proposal to enlist the vast resources in the United States, and he determined to make use of every possible contact—academic, industrial and governmental. But though he felt it wise to obtain the green light from Mellanby he did not ask him for the air tickets. Weeks before, so certain was he that his human casebook would show penicillin a success, he had written to Dr Warren Weaver at the

Rockefeller Foundation Headquarters on 49th Street, New York. This same man who had received his application eighteen months before for the money to back his work on the penicillin problem had no hesitation in again throwing Rockefeller resources behind the scientist.

The journey had been planned in the greatest secrecy and had been given a cloak-and-dagger atmosphere before it even started. Florey caught Heatley by the sleeve one day and, cautioning him to secrecy, asked him whether he would like to travel with him to America. 'I'm not telling you to go, I'm asking. Would you like to come and help me ginger up penicillin production over there?'

The two scientists worked up to the day of their departure and, just before he and Heatley quietly left, Florey completed the second article on penicillin to go to *Lancet*. In the alphabetical order, which he insisted should apply, first place was given to Abraham, and Fletcher's name came in ahead of Florey.

The review was eventually published in August 1941 when Florey was still in America—a year after the first revelation of their work—and this time gave great detail of the technique they had developed for growing the mould, and their method of assay, before passing on to large-scale production in the laboratories, extraction processes, and the biological tests, including the first six human patients. It was an impressive ten-page document dealing with original scientific work of the highest order. Florey and Heatley carried copies of the typescript with them when they left for the United States.

The critical eyes that looked at the bare details in America thought the human results were a slim foundation for massive industrial action, but the two scientists had both seen wonderful transformations, even though the patients in two of the six cases had died. Heatley recorded, '. . . the response to penicillin was considered almost miraculous. It seemed that penicillin had vast clinical potentialities, especially in time of war.'

Florey's objective assessment was written later,

From these cases it was clear that substantial doses of penicillin were not toxic to man—in fact, one of the most striking features was the improved appetite and feeling of well-being in these gravely ill patients within two or three days of the beginning of treatment—and there were very good indications that the drug could control the most severe infections. The effect on staphylococcal infection was especially important as the sulphonamides were of limited use against the staphylococcus.

The results of these trials were so favourable that further expansion of the work—whatever the difficulties—was imperative.[5]

The first leg of an air journey to America in 1941 was usually made down the dangerous corridor to Lisbon. It was perilous because German fighters ranged westward from air bases in north-west France and paid scant respect to neutral boundaries. In Britain the strictest precautions were applied to maintain the secrecy of departing aircraft.

Cautioned against loose talk of their journey, Florey and Heatley made an unobtrusive exit from Oxford on 26th June and caught a train to Bristol, where they spent a night made restless by the activity of bombers and the wail of air-raid sirens. They were up at first light and were driven to the airstrip at Whitchurch where they took off at sunrise for an undisclosed destination. All the aircraft's windows were blacked out. They flew for about a half-hour and then landed at an airfield, the location of which they never discovered. The only information Florey could gather that morning was that the name of the pilot was Captain Parmentier and he remembered that because it was the name of a horse which had raced in Australia.

At the unknown airfield, as they transferred to a larger plane, they looked around and could see the early sun gleaming on sand dunes piled high beyond the field. But there was no sign of sea, or of river flat, and nothing to indicate where they were.

Again the aircraft was blacked out and they took off in an unknown direction for an encapsulated flight to Lisbon. It was cool and dark in the cabin. Florey sat with his briefcase carefully balanced on his knees. Inside it were the vital mould samples and some penicillin extract, in vials wrapped in cotton wool, and with them were the notebooks and the typescripts of the *Lancet* report on the first human trials.

They arrived in Lisbon several hours later with a change of engine noise and a brief scream of heated rubber as the tyres met the runway. Then the door opened to blinding sun. A brief walk across a super-heated tarmac to where two smiling faces waited to greet them and the tension of the first stage of the voyage was gone. The two representatives of the Rockefeller Foundation were Dr Hunter, who took charge of their formalities, and a Mr Makinski, who thrust a small wad of Portuguese paper money into their hands and then sent off telegrams to their families announcing their safe arrival.

They were taken by car through the broad and busy streets of a city untouched by war and were installed in the comfort of the Hotel Tivoli on the *Avenida da Liberdade*. With the recent indication of enemy interest in the penicillin mould, and the warnings of authority still in his ears on the dangers of espionage in this neutral city, Florey was cautious from the moment of arrival. The idle and solitary men he had been cautioned against were not in evidence in the small foyer of the Tivoli, but Florey took no chances.

He went straight to the proprietor-manager, Dr Joaquim Gonzales Machaz, and, handing him the briefcase, stood by until the safe was securely locked again.

'It must not be handed out to anyone but me,' he told the mystified hotelier.

Each morning the hotel manager had to assure Florey of the safety of the case before the two British scientists would leave the hotel to stroll to the American airline office to check whether their names were on the list for the evening flight. Afterwards, they would wander back along the broad avenue of one of the finest promenades in Europe, sitting sometimes in the shade of the trees lining the route, enjoying the white blaze of the sculptures and statues against the cool green of the parks and gardens.

They enjoyed the Lisbon shops, the food and the colour of the fruit—the bananas, grapes and oranges in the windows—and they ate all the things that had disappeared from their wartime lives. Florey loved to walk in the sun and to take off his hat and

feel it beat on his scalp. He revelled in the light and the clear air
that reminded him of his homeland.

On the fourth morning in Lisbon they learned that the interlude
was over, and in the evening they stepped aboard a Clipper
aircraft, with KLM markings, to begin the exhausting flight, via
the Azores and Bermuda, to America. There, Rockefeller agents
waited to greet them and escort them to the New Weston Hotel
on 49th Street, not far from the Rockefeller Centre.

NEW YORK WAS ON THE EVE OF CELEBRATING ITS LAST peaceful Fourth of July for five years when Florey and Heatley arrived. The city was like a concrete oven, the temperature climbing through the nineties; but, though the heat was tiring after the long journey from Lisbon in the bumping aircraft, Florey wasted no time in rest. Soon after they had booked into their hotel, the two scientists were walking through the baking city to the huge Rockefeller pile on 49th Street—the first chore was to inform Dr Alan Gregg, head of the Foundation's natural sciences division, of the latest stage in the work Rockefeller was supporting.

At first, Heatley regarded this duty as routine, but he was soon to change his mind. Once shown into Gregg's spacious office Florey set about his task of accounting how the Rockefeller money had been spent. For almost an hour Dr Gregg and Heatley sat enthralled with Florey's narration of the discovery of the enormous healing power in the penicillin mould. Florey sat and talked, without notes and without hesitation, despite his tiredness, and he traced the concept through, step by step, from the early investigations to the saving of the first lives a few weeks before, touching on the heartbreak of Albert Alexander, the tragedy of Johnny Cox, and reviewing the material which would appear in the following month's issue of the *Lancet*. When he had finished, he thanked Dr Gregg for his support and his faith and laid a copy of the coming *Lancet* report on his desk.

Like Gregg, Heatley had sat silent through the whole impressive parade of fact, the event burning into his mind so that it was always sharp and clear in recall.

I remember him best of all for that performance—and he was so tired after that long journey. He was very lucid in the presentation of his facts, and fully explanatory. It was un-emotional, but still very telling, and in a startling sort of way it revealed the wide grasp of his scientific mind.

Even though I knew the subject well, he showed me new facets, and I realized suddenly how great a man he was. None of us in the penicillin team could have matched him, and he was so clearly the leader. I count that hour in Gregg's office as one of the great experiences of my life.[1]

Florey had to repeat his narrative many times across America expounding the facts, and the possibilities, to leaders of the drug industry, to scientists and executives, to public servants and friends, in a long propaganda tour for penicillin. His mission to America was to obtain the penicillin extract from ten thousand litres of mould juice—an undertaking on an industrial scale which afterwards became known to leading workers as 'Florey's kilo'. He sought this amount with the intention of conducting extensive clinical trials in Oxford with his wife, Ethel. These would be designed to convince industry, the government and the doubting medical profession, that massive support should be given to the large-scale production of penicillin. With only the thin casebook of the first clinical results, Florey knew many people looked askance at the product. The ratios of two thousand litres of mould juice for one single treatment, plus many man-hours and the risk that airborne organisms could destroy weeks of work in seconds, were frightening facts for the economic minds of pharmaceutical executives.

But, first of all, after fulfilling his duty to Rockefeller, he left New York and went north to New Haven, in Connecticut, where the Fultons were harbouring his children, taking Heatley with him despite Heatley's protest that he would be intruding. There he spent Independence Day 1941, with his children and friends; eleven-year-old Paquita, still trying to settle into the American way of life, and five-year-old Charles, completely at home with his second mother. Fulton's love of people, and his joviality, made them welcome, and, when he heard the story of penicillin, his ebullience was unrestrained. His enthusiasm contrasted with Florey's calm and cool manner in recounting the details.

John Fulton, enthused into action, began telephoning and discussing and arranging the first steps by which Florey was to gain the aid of American resources. Florey sat back and rested for the first time in more than five years and slept a lot.

The Fulton home, a stone and wood mansion overlooking the water, had the same look and feeling that he had known in 'Coreega' when the old home had been full of family and voices. He found restfulness listening to the children playing, left Fulton to make arrangements for the gruelling schedule ahead.

The idyll lasted four days and then Fulton took him south, with Heatley, to a hurried meeting with the President of the National Academy, Professor Ross Harrison.

With sublime simplicity Harrison linked the question of an anti-bacterial substance produced from moulds not with any branch of medical science but with the man whose name was synonymous with moulds and fungi, Dr Charles Thom, a scientist in the Department of Agriculture's bureau of plant industry. It could only have been inspiration that sent the questing pathologist to a man working in agricultural science, but it was a first step that led to many thrilling developments.

Dr Thom worked in Beltsville, Maryland, and when Florey walked into his office with his briefcase it was the second time the Fleming strain of *Penicillium notatum* had been carried across Thom's threshold. In the corner of his room there stood a cabinet holding a file with the note:

5112—H. Raistrick.
Received 14 May 1930
5112.1—*P. rubrum* isolated by Fleming.
British collection No. 3127. Cultured Dox-glucose
   agar, April 25th 1930=*P. notatum*.

This had been the finding sought by Raistrick in 1930 which had corrected Fleming's mistaken information that his penicillin strain was red.

Thom's reaction to the story of the potential for human

healing that lurked in the mould, and to Florey's outline of his
reason for being in America, was to call in Dr Percy Wells, then
acting head of the department's Bureau of Agricultural Chemistry
and Engineering. Facing the two hard-headed American government scientists, Florey pulled no punches. He had no compunc-
tion in saying that America was bound for war and that the lives
of thousands of men could be saved by the action of penicillin
against gas gangrene alone—taking no account of the various
other types of war wounds subject to infection. He also faced
them with the grim fact of the limit to penicillin production from
the best known Penicillium strain.

He told them that he could only get two units per millilitre,
at the most, and he could lose 60% of that in the extraction
process. It meant, he said, that two thousand litres of mould broth
was needed to treat one single case of sepsis.[2]

He admitted that, as things stood, the cost of such penicillin
would be high and the number of people that could be treated
would be low. It was clear to each of them in Thom's office that
day that without new development and advance in research, the
prospects were not bright.

Wells thought for a moment and then suggested that Florey
should go out west to see the new Northern Regional Research
Laboratories at Peoria. There was a strong team out there, he told
Florey, with wide experience in fermentation and the creation of
chemicals from organisms in ferment. It was the only step he
knew that could be of any help to the British scientists, and
Florey at once agreed to go.

Wells thus made the proposal which was to assure the future
of penicillin production and set a group of little-known agricultural scientists on a hectic trail that would last out the war and
put their names into the history of American medicine.

The day of Florey's decision to visit the Regional Research
Laboratories was 9th July 1941. The same day Dr Wells sent the
first of many cables that would flow in the coming years on the
subject of penicillin. He sent it to Dr Orville May, Director of
the Northern Regional Research Laboratory, at the mid-West
town of Peoria, on the banks of the Illinois River,

'Thom has introduced Heatley and Florey of Oxford. Here to

investigate pilot scale production of bacteriostatic material from
Fleming Penicillium in connection with medical defence plans.
Can you arrange for shallow pan set-up to establish laboratory
results?'[3]

When he received this message, Dr May consulted the director
of the laboratories dealing with fermentation, Dr Robert D.
Coghill, the leader of a group of about twenty people.

Three years after this event, the name of Robert D. Coghill
became nationally synonymous with the story of penicillin,
when the extraordinary wave of public fervour swept the mass
media and the drug itself was associated with the word 'magic'.
But on this day of Wells' cable, few people outside his own
university and professional circle had heard of Dr Coghill. Heading a strong group of research workers with extensive experience
in persuading moulds, yeasts and even bacteria, to produce
chemicals in fermentation, he was the chief of a team that Florey,
with his love of banter, afterwards referred to as the 'magic
mould merchants'. In that month of July 1941, they were mainly
involved with fermentation to produce suitable acids attached to
which there was a strong interest, because of the international
situation, in the possibility of converting glycol into butadeine
and synthetic rubber. They also had inherited from Dr Charles
Thom a superb collection of moulds, *Aspergilli* and *Pencillia*.

'But we none of us knew a thing about penicillin and until that
day the cable arrived we have never heard the name of Florey.
It was all very new to us,' Dr Coghill recorded.[4]

They sent their reply to Wells, 'Pan-set and organisms available
Heatley and Florey experimentation. Details of work, of course,
unknown. Suggest they visit Peoria for discussions. Laboratory
in position to co-operate immediately.'

Three years later Coghill described penicillin as a Cinderella
who came to Peoria to steal the limelight from the two elder
sisters, the sulpha girls, 'When, in time, penicillin became
adorned in raiments of thirty million dollar production plants, and
attended by thousands of scientific and technological footmen,
and fanfares galore, we would sometimes wake in fear that midnight would strike, and the unbelievable would be gone, leaving
us holding an empty, useless glass vessel.'

Florey and Heatley reached Chicago on 13th July and the following morning boarded the 'Peoria Rocket' and rattled their way across 180 miles of track to the blazing heat of the mid-West town. Coghill met them and escorted them to the local hotel, the two scientists looking out of place wearing their English clothes in the dusty, wheat town setting.

There was no welcoming lunch. There was no government money for such frippery: and they did not come as important people. No one had heard of them before. They lunched alone and afterwards walked over to the laboratory to talk to the waiting Americans on their problems and ideas.

In an air-conditioned office they found Dr Orville May, the director, and Dr Coghill and his deputy, Dr G. E. Ward. For the rest of that afternoon Florey again related the development and the clinical applications of the Oxford penicillin, its potential and its present limitations. The problem was discussed among the five men, ending with Coghill's undertaking to set 'one of his best men to work on the problem, provided Dr Heatley would stay in Peoria to teach them the ways of the Penicillium mould and the techniques and methods of his assay process'. At this, Florey opened his briefcase and laid on the table a culture of Fleming's original *Penicillium notatum* and a sample of the Oxford extract, and British and American co-operation in the production of penicillin moved to first base.

During the discussion that afternoon on the path the work should take, Robert Coghill suggested, for the first time, that production by deep submerged culture might be an answer to the low yields achieved by surface growth of the mould. They also agreed that there should be no personal rewards for any individual taking part in the work at Peoria, and that any benefits should be shared equally by the Northern Regional Research Laboratories and the Rockefeller Foundation: both sides later signed this agreement.[5]

In the morning, Florey climbed aboard the train to Chicago, on his way to try and interest the drug companies. In his usual blunt manner, and without formal farewell, he nodded and said, 'You'll be all right, Heatley. I'll be back in a week or two to see how you are getting along.'

Dr Andrew J. Moyer was chosen to partner Heatley in the penicillin task. It was an unfortunate choice for the quiet, gifted Englishman. Moyer was a tough man, with strong forearms, a long nose, a tight mouth, and a grim visage; and he was fervidly anti-British. He had no hesitation in telling Heatley that Britain was dragging America into an unwanted war and that, if the Germans shed British blood until the gutters ran red, it was all that Britain deserved.

Moyer was a dedicated scientist, with intense determination and a sense of history. He was also very secretive and was always covering his written notes even when his chief, Dr Coghill, came into the room. Heatley's self-effacing and gentle manner made him liked by the Peoria people and, in the end, Moyer forgave him for being British and they had a working relationship in which Heatley was tolerated with a smile.

Their work began in difficulty, not only from the personal and awkward situation caused by Moyer's bitter isolationism, but because of the mould spores themselves.

The Penicillium mould spores which they had brought from England proved recalcitrant, unwilling to grow as they had done in Oxford, and Heatley blamed this behaviour on damage done to the samples in the weeks of heat and travel. It made the start of the work slow but, eventually, overcoming unsuitable climatic conditions in the mid-West summer, the scraps of white fluff gradually took hold, then the blue-green appeared and the first gold droplets of penicillin oozed from the spreading mycelium. Working together during those few months of the summer and autumn, Heatley and Moyer retraced the steps first followed by Chain two years before, attempting to prove that diet and environmental manipulation could induce the organism to increase its manufacture of penicillin. In Peoria, however, the factors which had been lacking in Oxford were on hand, and fortune was once again about to touch penicillin.

Among the variety of tasks assigned to the mid-West scientists was the seeking of industrial uses for surplus cereal crops, chiefly wheat and corn-maize, and one special headache was a difficult, gluey mess left over from the process of extracting starch from corn. Many hours had been spent on this viscous substance, and even its disposal presented them with problems. It was called 'corn steep liquor'.

When it was mixed with a little lactose and used as a nutrient bed on which to grow the Penicillium mould it had what Coghill called, 'a magical effect'. It immediately caused a ten-fold jump in the penicillin yield.

This single advance at once reduced Florey's requirement of two thousand litres of mould juice for the treatment of one case of sepsis to a mere two hundred litres; furthermore, it opened a new potential for commercial production. It was only the beginning of the role which the mid-Western laboratory was to play in the antibiotic age, and it gave new heart to the research. Coghill wrote of the discovery,

> Penicillin has often been referred to as a miracle drug but one of the least understood miracles connected with it is that Florey and Heatley were directed to our laboratory in Peoria. I do not say this because I feel we were smarter or knew more than other fermentation people, but because it was—I am certain—the *only* laboratory where the corn steep liquor magic would have been discovered.
>
> Moreover, it was no flash of genius with us, as has sometimes been alleged, but a simple routine procedure. We had tried corn steep liquor in every fermentation study we ever started.
>
> The discovery of its key place as a Penicillium medium was fore-ordained and inevitable, once the problem has been assigned to the Peoria Fermentation Division.[6]

The road to the corn steep liquor transformation had been a straight one: from Fulton, to Harrison, through him to Thom and then Wells and finally to Peoria—the 'only place' in America where it was certain to be revealed. From there the drive of science could not be stopped, and Peoria became the nerve centre for the American work. And as Heatley and Moyer worked, it became gradually apparent that they could not accept the astronomical chance that the earth's highest yielding strain of mould organism had fallen on Fleming's culture plate; and though they found nothing immediately that would replace the

Fleming *notatum* in Peoria's collection they remained convinced of the possibility of finding such a mould. At the same time there came a fresh and crucial approach to Coghill's prophetic observation—which Florey had noted at their first meeting—that penicillin might be grown, not by the cumbersome and restrictive surface bottle culture, but deep inside thousands of gallons of liquid nutrient, in big tanks stirred to oxygenate the mixture.

At Heatley's request, Moyer had shown him how to operate two rotating drums which had been used for other fermentation experiments. These were filled with the nutrient medium and each drum was seeded by Heatley with spores from the *notatum* mould and set to revolving and turning for about a week.

Heatley found the mould produced penicillin under these conditions; but it gave only half the yield achieved in surface culture. He discussed this finding with Moyer and from then on it became clear that Fleming's mould strain would soon fall by the wayside, and would, having performed its role of leading medical science into rich yields of knowledge, revert to its former role of a laboratory curiosity.

Coghill's drive soon had the penicillin team at Peoria expanding beyond the preliminary inquiry which Moyer and Heatley had conducted; but the research and interest in the whole project also began to extend beyond Illinois and America, to take on a global aspect in a search for the elusive organism that could outpace the *Penicillium notatum*. Heading this world search was Dr Kenneth Raper, the curator of collections at Peoria.

Raper soon caught the ear, and the co-operation, of someone in the Pentagon and orders went out to crews of the Army Transport Command in many parts of the world. Puzzled pilots were told to snatch small samples of soil from wherever they were based—and exotic samples came from far away lands, from Venezuela and Zanzibar, from Australia and the East, from Europe and China. Organisms were cultured from these soils and the long process of antibacterial tests was started.[7] The search was on for the fungus that would not only grow the drug in thousands of glass bottles, but also for an organism that would do its best work and give higher yields of penicillin when submerged in deep tanks. The work was demanding, but the American drive for an answer was unrelenting. It was inevitable that the growing impetus would, in the end, advance penicillin to another milestone.

Florey returned briefly to Peoria in August, attended a party in Robert Coghill's home, and then took Heatley off to Canada to support him in an attempt to win further co-operation. For weeks he had fought his way into executive offices of the drug houses, meeting indifference, disbelief, incredulity, and, in a few cases, a ready and sympathetic ear. The experience had left him disgruntled and angry. He told Heatley, and, later, other colleagues, that he had often been treated as a sort of 'carpetbag salesman' trying to promote a crazy idea for some ulterior motive. He had sown a few seeds, however, and he later paid a tribute to those firms where they had borne some fruit, listing them as Merck's, Pfizer's and Squibb's. By mischance, he did not learn that at Upjohn's Kalamazoo, a young scientist, named Evans, intrigued by his 1940 paper in *Lancet*, was already growing the Penicillium mould, a sample of which he had obtained from Thom.

Florey carried Heatley off to Toronto to the respected and wealthy Connaught Laboratories where, he hoped, some of the several hundred workers could be turned to penicillin production to support enlarged and more convincing clinical trials. Unlike America, Canada was then at war, and it was his hope that some effort could be made there to push along a protective drug that would deal with situations and organisms which the sulphas left untouched.

At the Connaught building he and Heatley conferred with the new Director, Dr R. D. Defries, who called in Dr Ronald Hare, a former colleague of Fleming at St Mary's, London.* In later years, Hare recorded that he had then already come across the Oxford article in the August 1940 *Lancet* and 'found it one of the most astonishing papers he had ever read and that, exactly a year later, Florey handed him a typed copy of the second and fully explanatory article then appearing in print in London. Florey also

* Professor Hare's book *The Birth of Penicillin* refers to this incident in some detail.

told them, he recalled, the incredible story of the Oxford Penicillin epic: how the mould had been grown, and how the penicillin had been extracted at the Sir William Dunn School and experimentally tested in human patients.[8]

The Connaught workers rejected the proposal that they should join the penicillin work. Their reasons were several and, according to Hare, they found the prospect of growing the mould and extracting the active substance 'formidable'—that other people were then investigating penicillin and that their chemists advised that synthesis of the drug was likely. Hare also wrote that there was a further requirement in the ' "proof" of penicillin'; that, at that time, it had only been tried against staphylococcal infection—although the *Lancet* article he had read in August 1940 had shown its powerful effect against the gangrene organisms, and others, and the typed copy of the 1941 *Lancet* paper which he was given showed a use of penicillin in the human trials against haemolytic streptococcus.

Florey could accept that the Connaught people found the task faced by his own smaller group at Oxford to be, despite their greater resources, a formidable one, but he held the other reasons for rejection to be fallacious. He never forgave them—and maintained a dislike of Dr Defries.

Bitterly disappointed at the outcome of his visit to Toronto, Florey turned back to the drug industry in the eastern United States while Heatley went back to Peoria.

The disappointment Florey felt about his visit was partly allayed by the welcome, and the work, of a handful of American scientists who had followed his reports and believed with him in the potential of chemotherapy. In New York he met and talked with Dr René Dubos, the man whose brilliant work on gramacidin had interested some American investigators in the subject of chemotherapy.

Dubos introduced Florey to the American followers of his penicillin therapy. At the College of Physicians and Surgeons at Columbia University, and at the Presbyterian Hospital in New York, he met Dr Martin Henry Dawson and his chief colleagues— Dr Gladys Hobby and Dr Karl Meyer. For the previous eight months they had suffered the tedium of penicillin production on a laboratory scale, and when Florey looked at their array of equipment and the hundreds of bottles he knew so well what it had cost Dawson and his colleagues to struggle from the first mould sample to extraction of active substances.

In Rochester, at the famous Mayo Clinic, Florey also met a brilliant young worker, Dr Wallace E. Herrell. Herrell had been stimulated into following the same path the Oxford team had trod the previous year after hearing Dawson's paper on his experiments with injecting penicillin into his patients at the Presbyterian Hospital in New York, which had been read only a month before Florey's arrival in America, but the importance of which was to be hidden for thirty years.

Florey was also told that Dr A. Newton Richards, the man Florey had chosen to work with fifteen years before when he had been given a Rockefeller Foundation Travel Grant, had been appointed chairman of the Medical Research Committee in the Office of Scientific Research and Development operating under the command of Dr Vannevar Bush. From this information Florey was able to seek out Richards in the city of Philadelphia, where he was vice-president for medical affairs at the University and, on 7th August 1941, over dinner at a quaint old club over-looking Rittenhouse Square, he achieved the master-stroke from which flowed all the fame and success that came to penicillin by the end of the Second World War.

Florey's casebook was as slim for Richards as it was for many others to whom it had been presented in America and in Canada. But Richards knew his man from the months they had spent together in 1926, and he saw a value of judgment behind the calm voice and the cool eyes that others had not seen. Twenty years after this meeting and his decision to produce penicillin in commercial quantities, Richards sat at lunch in the same Ritten-house club with a senior executive from Merck's, Mr Osgood Nichols who later revealed their conversation.

'I asked Richards how it happened that, despite all the scepticism about penicillin at that time, he had decided to take a chance on Florey,' Nichols said. 'The 1941 *Lancet* article on the first human trials had then not yet been published, and I had seen some memoranda at Merck's from so-called experts urging Merck's not to waste time on it. Richards' eyes, normally a soft, but startlingly bright blue, turned disdainful, "Florey is a scientist, and a scientist like that doesn't tell a lie", he answered me curtly.'[9]

In New York and elsewhere decisions and events were shaping a future in which the drug would eventually rise to hold a high priority as a strategic material. The shock of Pearl Harbour was still months away, but the feeling of war filled the air in America as many people came to realize the world threat behind Hitler's massive onslaught on Russia. Before Florey and Heatley had crossed the Atlantic, President Roosevelt had announced that America would take over the occupation of Iceland and, during the weeks following the two men's return from Toronto, there were U-boat attacks on shipping in American waters. Roosevelt warned the Axis to keep their ships clear of US defence zones, and soon after this came the sinking of an American destroyer, the USS *Kearns*, with the loss of American lives, for which a German U-boat claimed the 'victory'. Even in the mid-West, at Peoria, it was accepted that the entry of the United States into the war was only a matter of time.

It was against this background that Dr Richards met Florey and heard his story of the Penicillium mould and the need to brew thousands of litres of medium for a single dose of the new drug. Florey would not gloss over the difficulties of the small yield and high cost: a situation which meant that few patients would benefit from work that would consume much money and effort. Despite its existing production drawbacks, the picture he painted for Richards of penicillin, was of the only known drug that could wipe away diseases which no sulphonamide would reach.

With his broad knowledge of pharmacology, Richards knew the hope of relief from suffering his visitor was holding out—this man he would recognize publicly as a 'rough colonial genius' in one of the most prized of all the tributes Florey received. The tempo of the war was bound to mount, and penicillin would be needed by thousands of wounded men. These were strong arguments that Florey had to advance but it was enough for Richards that Florey was convinced the task should be pursued, and he accepted that there was little time to lose.

Florey presented his case just two years after he had written to Mellanby asking for £100 for the chemicals on which to grow his first crop of penicillin producing mould. So now he pressed Richards for action: and he sought assurances and asked Richards to give the backing of his new office to the venture.

Dr Norman Heatley later commented on Richards' response with these words, 'One wonders whether this fateful assurance would have been given so freely had the chairman, Dr A. N. Richards, not known of Florey's calibre from the time, some fifteen years before, when the two had collaborated in Richards' laboratory.'

Richards' decision to expedite unified action on penicillin placed his name among the people whose imagination made possible the plan to put penicillin ashore with the Allied troops on D-Day, 1944.

Florey paid his own tribute to the qualities Richards showed in facing the penicillin decision, 'Dr Richards deserves great credit for his courage in deciding to recommend the expenditure of large sums of government money on the project of producing penicillin, for his decision rested in the first instance on the experimental results and the few clinical trials from Oxford, and on the opinion of the Oxford workers that synthesis of penicillin, in the near future, did not appear likely.'

Once he'd made his decision, Dr Richards acted with alacrity. He called in drug industry leaders reported to him by Florey as having shown interest and told them the government was interested too. He said they would be performing a national service in sponsoring research on the penicillin production problem inside their own organizations, and he spoke of the possibility of official support for production of a drug that had little to do with the matter of profit. The men he called in were from Merck's, Pfizer's, Squibb's and Lederle, and he placed the matter squarely before them so effectively that they all arranged to meet again in December, two months ahead.

When this day arrived, America was at war and the project took on a new urgency in the eyes of the chairman of the government's Medical Research Committee. They met in the quiet setting of the University Club in New York and Dr Vannevar

Bush, head of the OSRD and already with the atomic bomb in his
care, took special note of the meeting. From his office Dr Baird
Hastings and Dr Mansfield Clark attended, while nine representatives were there from the drug companies, along with the solid
figure of Dr Robert Coghill from Peoria.

It was December 17th, ten days after Pearl Harbour, and it was
a gathering credited with the decision to produce penicillin in
large volume. But the meeting began in a dismal and doubtful
way. Dr Coghill wrote from his notes,

> The drug houses were obviously afraid to pool their informa-
> tion for fear of prosecution under the Sherman anti-trust
> laws. George Merck also said that while the co-operation of
> the drug industry was forthcoming, with the best fermentation
> and recovery yields they had been able to obtain it was not
> humanly possible to produce the 'kilo' of penicillin requested
> by Florey. The other people there did not dispute this point of
> view.

The question of anti-trust offences was not resolved for more
than two years, though they were never applied to the project;
but the answer to Merck's assessment of yield waited in Coghill's
pocket and was produced when Richards called for his comments.
He told them about corn steep liquor.

> If there was any one time that we could claim the antibiotic
> industry was born, then we could say it was on this day. This
> was the real turning point. I told them what Heatley and
> Moyer had done at Peoria, of the corn steep liquor transforma-
> tion and of the adjustments in trace metals and lactose, and
> George Merck said that if these facts were substantiated then
> it would revolutionize the situation and industry could meet
> its objectives and turn out Florey's 'kilo' of extract for him.

Reflecting on this meeting, Dr Coghill said later,

> It was still a tremendous gamble for both industrialists and
> government representatives, and I am convinced that it was

one which would never have been taken in peace-time. One can only speculate, of course, but I have the conviction that, but for the war, we might not have had penicillin available as a widely used drug today, and, without the lead and the knowledge and know-how we all got from penicillin, it is very questionable whether the other important antibiotics would have followed. The gamble did not just rest on industrial interests, but also on government, both in America and England, when co-operative programmes were put in hand. In some cases, factories were built by governments and run by private enterprises, and, in America, the decision led to enabling industry to make a gamble with a fifteen-cent dollar by the imposition of approximately eighty-five per cent excess profit taxes. It was a gamble involving millions and the dice was thrown that afternoon of the December meeting. That is why I believe that the antibiotic industry was born that day—and that the corn steep liquor prevented it from being a stillbirth. A child was born in England and was raised to adulthood in the United States—a not uncommon result of wars.

The results given to the New York December meeting by Coghill were the outcome of four months of intensive application by both Heatley and Moyer in the late summer and autumn at the mid-West laboratories at Peoria. These efforts, however, were only a start to the giant strides that were to follow. The revelation of the corn steep liquor transformation was given at the New York meeting, but well before then it had started the scientists at Peoria searching for means and methods that would give even higher yields—a search that would isolate mould organisms and grow them in a medium far more effective and sophisticated than the broth which had been used at Oxford.

CHAPTER 12

WHEN FLOREY RETURNED TO OXFORD AT THE END OF
September 1941, the seeds of the coming age of antibiotic
therapy had been already sown across America.

Spores of the Penicillium mould which he had taken with
him and had been hibernating in various American culture
stores had been awakened in research laboratories and were
already producing the first trickle of the drug that was to become
a river under the demands of the impending war. Most of this
activity was known to Florey, but he still felt disappointment
with the immediate outcome of his visit.

Dr Robert Coghill estimated that, at the existing levels of
purity, Florey had been asking for a 'kilo that would contain
activity of about forty million Oxford units'. This amount would
have allowed Florey to put in hand a clinical trial on more than
eighty patients with treatment of infections ranging from the
superficial to the utmost severity and was many times in excess of
the amount which had been won in the toil at the Oxford
laboratories. It was a hope that was never realized. Florey's 'kilo'
was demolished with the bombs that blasted Pearl Harbour just
over two months after his return to Oxford. It never came to
light again in the swift appreciation by American minds of
strategic value of penicillin in war, and of all the drug houses
Florey had tried to persuade to his cause in the dying days of
American peace—many of whom were soon clamouring for a
place in the government-sponsored penicillin programme—
only Merck's of Rahway, New Jersey, kept faith with him,
though on a much smaller scale than they had hoped. Merck's
was the one corporation which had sought Florey's advice and

made arrangements for him to visit their plant but they, with the rush of events which war brought, could send him only half a million units—one-eightieth of what he had hoped for, and only a third of the amount necessary to treat a case of streptococcal meningitis.

The arrival of the package from Merck's raised hopes at the Oxford laboratories. It was so large Florey thought at first that it must contain the 'kilo' of penicillin extract for which he had campaigned. He wrote to Heatley soon afterwards, 'As soon as I picked up the damn packet I knew I was wrong—it was so light. Inside the box was a smaller box and within that, in large amounts of packing, was the precious material.' He recognized that the trials he had planned to conduct with Ethel would be limited to British resources, and that the mass tests would have to be conducted by American physicians; his consolation was that the results would be the same.[1]

The American mission had not produced the immediate answer he sought for his 'imperative expansion' and he confessed to friends at Oxford, 'We are caught in that same circle of circumstances—we do not have enough of the drug for convincing proof that more should be produced. We can only use the poverty of our resources to spur us on to greater efforts.'[2]

The greater efforts he called for from his struggling group in South Parks Road, Oxford were answered with a determination and dedication that made the year 1942 a time of crucial development in the introduction of the drug, both to the battlefield and in civilian hospitals, as well as for the treatment of infected burns of the airmen defending Britain against the German *Luftwaffe*. The former Animal Building at the Sir William Dunn School was converted into a penicillin production centre, and the ingenuity of Dr Gordon Sanders was turned to the designing and building of the second generation extraction plant, apparatus which he scaled to handle increased brewing of the mould juice. When the news of Pearl Harbour came, they decided not to wait for 'Florey's kilo' from America and the wisdom of the decision came home to Florey when they learned later that, by the following June, the American pilot plants had produced enough of the drug for only ten cases of systemic sepsis.

Sanders built his new apparatus with the toiling James Kent. Their contraption was a masterpiece of improvisation, which mixed acidified mould juice with amyl acetate and then broke the resulting emulsion with a centrifuge action. To do this they lifted the cooled brew by pump, through a filter, and into a bank of four milk churns. This was, then, the world's largest penicillin plant.

Along with the increased output of material they had recorded a dramatic jump in the level of activity, following Heatley's news from Peoria of the marvellous effect of growing the Penicillium mould on corn steep liquor.

To enable the Oxford workers to check results from the corn steep liquor produced in the American mid-West against similar medium produced from their own resources, Heatley went to great trouble in surmounting the war-time difficulties of shipping goods across the perilous Atlantic. Eventually he was able to place a 62 lb. drum of the corn steep liquor from Peoria on the SS *Arabian Prince* which sailed in convoy and landed the drum safely in Liverpool early in 1942. Florey wrote to Heatley that the results had aroused great excitement among his staff. Later the firm of Watherspoon & Co. Ltd of Paisley Scotland, began shipping corn steep liquor supplies to the Sir William Dunn School of Pathology in Oxford—to Florey's makeshift penicillin factory. As a medium for growing penicillin, corn steep liquor was never surpassed—even in the massive deep submerged growth tanks which were built at the end of the War.

The immediate result in Oxford was remarkable compared with the yields they had experienced in the struggling days of 1940 when activity was as low as two units per milligram of extract. Soon they were achieving a retrieval of up to 60% of the original penicillin placed by the mould into the corn steep liquor which reached as high as 400 units a milligram of prepared material. With Sanders' bank of ten-gallon milk churns and further improvements in the conversion steps they eventually recorded as much as 1 300 units per milligram.

As these developments were under way in his own establishment in the first months of 1942 Florey's hopes for a speedy introduction into civil and military medical practice were dim, and interest in the new drug was confined to a very limited circle. The period following his return from America did hold its reward and encouragements, however. At the November meeting of the Royal Society he was rewarded for his long service to science with election to fellowship. This highly prized honour lifted both his standing and his spirits and helped him to forget for a while the restrictions on work which he was now convinced was vital.

He was personally delighted to be able at the age of forty-three to write the letters *F.R.S.* after his name, because, as penicillin was still then, to the main body of science, an unproven curiosity, the honour, it was recognized, came from the regard of his scientific peers and his standing before the work on penicillin commenced, and from the long haul of first-class, original contributions he had made since he emerged from Sherrington's guidance in 1924. For these reasons it was a special pride to him to be admitted to the premier scientific body in the British world; but it did not alter the pursuit in which he was engaged. The slog to produce penicillin at Oxford did not falter and, with Ethel at his side, he set about the daunting task of locating the special cases needed for their programme.

The initial difficulties came from the need to convince medical authorities, physicians and surgeons that they should co-operate in the proving trials, and from finding all too often the truth of Fleming's observation that the medical profession had become tired of hearing 'too many alarms'. Florey felt keenly the lack of appreciation among medical practitioners. At times, their attitude and disregard annoyed him into caustic comment, and, soon after he left America he was penning his aggravation on this matter to a director of Merck's, Dr Randolph T. Major,

... with a new compound like this it is very difficult to induce surgeons to give one the cases for treatment at the earliest possible moment. They will treat the patients surgically according to their accepted procedure; they will give them all the sulphonamide drugs they have ever heard of in succession, and, then, when all these have failed, they will suggest that, perhaps, penicillin might be tried. This, in effect, is asking one to resuscitate a corpse.[3]

Then encouragement came his way when Imperial Chemical Industries opened a pilot-scale production unit and were able to start sending small amounts of penicillin to Florey for Ethel to use in the expanding clinical trials. Florey also made use of this event to stir American firms into greater activity and through Heatley he had notes on increased British action on penicillin circulated to interested firms in the United States, calling into effect the spirit of industrial competition.

Florey and Ethel started their labours by sacrificing what remained of their home life. Ethel lived for nothing else but the hunt for proof of penicillin and devoted herself to the task with a steely application that astonished many of the professionals with whom she came into contact. Her home became a casual dormitory where she and her husband sometimes saw each other when they were in Oxford together.

Kent, married to the Florey's house-maid, Doris, was looking for a home at a time when houses were being bombed by the thousands. Ethel, viewing her childless home and its continual emptiness, invited them to take over the top floor of the house in Parks Road and convert it to an apartment. Kent accepted the offer—and he and Doris lived there for the following fifteen years.

They moved in as the clinical tasks expanded to include, eventually, fifteen cases of severe systemic infections, which were treated to determine the most effective method of administration of penicillin, and more than one hundred and seventy topical applications which covered a carefully selected broad spectrum of infectious illnesses and injuries. They started with two cases, in Oxford's Radcliffe Infirmary, in which they sought to find a method for successful administration of the drug by mouth.

'For a course of treatment likely to extend over many days in a patient seriously ill, administration by mouth would be the most convenient,' they wrote into their case notes. 'Penicillin is absorbed from the intestinal canal, but the acid gastric juice will destroy at least part during its passage through the stomach. This might be avoided by enclosing the drug in a suitable capsule or by using a duodenal tube.'[4]

In those first two cases the team had no success and, deterred by the loss of nearly one million units of penicillin without definite results, Florey and Ethel decided to return to muscular and intravenous injections and the successful drip method. Their attack on deep-seated infections took them beyond the hospitals in Oxford into other centres and they treated some cases in military establishments, one of them in association with Florey's old friend and fellow Rhodes scholar from South Australia, Hugh Cairns, by then a high-ranking consultant surgeon with the army.

The cases often ran over weeks. On one occasion Florey and Ethel worked to save a thirty-four-year-old airman who was close to death with multiple outbreaks of exuding staphylococcal infections, lung abcesses, signs of osteomyelitis and bronchopneumonia—by giving him continuous penicillin injections ranging from one every two hours to one every four hours, for sixteen days. They commented in the case notes they later published under their joint names, 'As he had no other treatment till well on the way to convalescence, his recovery from the very severe infection . . . may reasonably be attributed to penicillin.'5

They later reported on a single attempt to defeat the resistant bacteria in a case of subacute bacterial endocarditis in a young man of twenty-four they found dying in the Radcliffe Infirmary. In dealing with this disease they used more of the drug than had ever before been given to a human being—a total of more than four and a half million units, administered over a whole month. They found the agent attacking the heart tissues to be *Streptococcus viridans,* the same organism Florey had used in his mice tests two years before. The man was soon eating again and putting on weight and 'became bright and anxious to get up'.

By then they had exhausted their stock but he seemed so much better and looked so well they probably would have stopped the penicillin anyway. Yet three weeks later his heart began to swell, his blood cultures were again positive from the isolated bacteria that had hidden in the heart tissue away from the penicillin, and he died.

Florey and Ethel wrote, 'It would probably have been better to give very large doses initially, but it must be admitted that this case does not give grounds for the belief that penicillin will cure subacute bacterial endocarditis ... the patient had, by present standards, a very large dose of penicillin continued for a month. Even these doses produced only temporary effect.'

It was a defeat, but there was the hope, realized that same year, that since an overdose of penicillin produced little or no toxic effect, the heart infection could be swamped with the drug and the hidden bacteria destroyed. Their joint paper made the point, 'As penicillin is at present so difficult to make in quantity, we have been tempted to find the minimum effective instead of the optimal dose ... it is quite possible that some good results will be obtained with less dosage than recommended ... but if penicillin ever becomes available in quantity, the above dosages will probably be considered small.'

Heatley returned to Oxford in the middle of 1942 at the end of a complete year spent, first at Peoria, and then at Merck's in New Jersey. He had new ideas to help increase production of concentrate, but, at best, the scant supplies being won from the Oxford laboratories for the clinical trials were no more than 10% pure penicillin. It was the greatest good fortune that none of the impurities injected into the patients was of a toxic nature.

Florey and Ethel also noted that, with the exception of two of the staphylococcal infections referred to them, all their cases were considered hopeless after other treatments, including the use of sulphonamides, yet 'without surgical interference ... the evidence is that with adequate dosage it is possible to eliminate all infection. One may look forward to the time when osteomyelitis treated early will no longer be a surgical condition.'

They agreed that they had come to the point where some attempt should be made to send penicillin to war. Only a small amount for military topical use was available at first, and they sealed this into glass vials and took it to London to Major-General L. T. Poole, the Director of Pathology at the War Office, and it was flown with accompanying data and dosage instructions to the Central Pathological Laboratory of the Middle East Forces near Cairo. They also took their penicillin powder to one or two cases of topical infection at the Princess Mary's Royal

Air Force Hospital at Halton, in Buckinghamshire, and to the
101st General Military Hospital near Oxford.

At Halton Florey visited the burns unit in which the noted
plastic surgeon, Sir Archibald McIndoe, took a direct interest, and
there he met again Flight Lieutenant Dennis Bodenham who
reminded Florey that he had been one of his examiners at Bristol
University in April 1939.

Later, when he was an internationally-known plastic surgeon,
Dennis Bodenham recalled the meeting,

I knew him at once, but though he said he remembered me
I don't really know that he did. I reminded him that he had
asked me a very awkward question about the island associated
with the name of Hippocrates, and I drew his attention to my
interest in burns and photography. Because of this interest he
gave me some penicillin which I had read about in the *Lancet*.
It was quite infinitesimal—not enough to fill a small salt spoon,
a sort of muddy brown powder. I chose four cases of airmen
with burns—more than half the burns we got had nothing to
do with combat—and tried the powder on these men with
startling and quite dramatic results.

For the first time in our experience we were able to attain a
completely sterile burn wound—something we had considered
impossible. It was exciting, enormously dramatic. But I knew
how precious this stuff was, more precious than gold dust, and
how difficult it was to obtain. The idea that we might ever get
enough to use in full-scale treatment never entered my head.

Soon afterwards Bodenham was appointed the RAF's Penicillin
Officer and so had frequent contact with Florey, often driving
across to Oxford to report results and collect further miniscule
supplies.

I got samples from him of different potency and he was
always kind and helpful considering I was a very junior officer
and he was a great man. As time went on I got more and more
penicillin, and once got a miracle cure of gonorrhoea with a
mere sixty thousand units. I flew all over the country with

penicillin for systemic use—the lives of pilots and flying crew
were very, very precious to us in those days, and we did everything we could to save them. But those first four small burns
were always the most significant results for me.[6]

Bodenham made a personal issue of relieving wounded air crew
of the pain of constant injections. As he began treating more
extensive burns and more critical cases he came to realize the
dread with which an injured man faced the prospect of repeated
injections.

He used himself as a guinea pig, injecting himself dozens of
times to find the 'kindest way to give penicillin to a man in pain'.
He thought of the impurities in the substance and how they
might be reduced, and of the frequent doses needed to maintain
a constant level of penicillin in the blood—Florey had said that
trying to keep this level was as constant a struggle as 'trying to
keep a bath full with the plug out'.

'Through thinking about these things,' Bodenham said later,
'I came upon the idea to use procaine. First, I used it before the
penicillin injection and then I decided to try it at the same time
with the penicillin—and what happened was another one of
those accidental discoveries. In some unexplained way the procaine slowed down the absorption of penicillin into the blood.
We found we could get away with a single injection a day instead
of one every two hours. The result, of course, was highly interesting. One American interest tried to cover it with a patent until
we were able to prove that we discovered it at Halton before
anyone else.'

Bodenham went further; he also mixed penicillin with sulphonamide powders and produced a cream for use on burns. This
proved highly effective in the days when penicillin was extremely
scarce and before it was able to make significant contributions
to techniques of plastic surgery and skin grafting. He saw a man
who had clung to life for six months with infected leg burns
walk after only days. He saw, too, infective meningitis in the
brains of injured pilots swept away with a power he could not
believe, and he saw new horizons open for plastic surgery on men
who had suffered horrible disfigurement.

Bodenham was not a fighter pilot, nor the leader of a bomber crew, but the RAF's Penicillin Officer who represented the service in the eventful Therapeutic Trials programme. They gave him no decoration and little advance in rank; but he did not mind. He saw the muddy brown powder go yellow with higher purity, and then reach full crystalline white; and he saw the death warrants of generalized septicaemia and meningitis abolished and the fear of gangrene removed, and he worked with the man and woman who forced acceptance of this wonder substance on a sceptical profession. That was enough reward for him.

Dr Ethel Florey went many times to the Halton Hospital, and to a lot of other hospitals. She took a tremendous load from her husband's shoulders in the second series of clinical trials and this set her on a career of pioneering antibiotic treatment, eventually composing a massive work—under her name alone—from thousands of cases and results, many of which were undertaken when all other treatments had failed.

She spent many weeks in the Birmingham Accident Hospital, asking for infectious cases which had defeated the efforts of doctors and surgeons. One surgeon who worked with her in those days left a memory of this forty-one-year-old Australian woman doctor, handicapped by deafness, carefully supervising her charges, smiling at the disbelief of sisters and doctors who had never seen the wonder of the drug at work—working to the small hours of the morning with complete control of the case. The surgeon wrote,

Mrs Florey knew she had to prove that this new drug was good. Not everyone was ready to accept that as a fact. Her devotion was tremendous and she concerned herself with not only the selection, but also the close supervision of her cases. She also assumed the demanding task of dispensing the precious penicillin and she was meticulous that not a grain was wasted, working late into the night to prepare her doses and going to great lengths to prevent contamination by those bacteria in the air which could produce the enzymes destructive to the potency of the drug. It was heartening to see her and to hear her quiet assurances to the patients, although always it was difficult to communicate with her. More than anyone else, she proved that penicillin worked in civilian medicine.[7]

Eventually, after months of work, Florey and Ethel compiled their massive—and convincing—case list. Yet ironically the one single case included in that list with which Ethel had no connection, and Florey only marginally, was a dramatic story of recovery from death that sent the name of penicillin ringing around the world.

This historic case took place in the wards in that same hospital at Paddington, London, where the antibacterial action of the mould, *Penicillium notatum,* had been noticed and recorded, but unexploited, some fourteen years earlier.

The patient was a fifty-two-year-old man, a close friend of the family of Professor Alexander Fleming, and he had been taken ill with fever some seven weeks before. During the first three weeks of the illness the clinical signs of meningitis began to appear with frontal headache, drowsiness and vomiting. Fleming tapped the spinal fluid but did not succeed in isolating a causative organism, and while this searching went on the man began to sink rapidly. Fleming treated him with solid doses of sulphapyridine and then, some ten days before the final crisis, the frail body of the patient became racked with constant hiccoughs. After these had lasted for four days the patient dropped into coma broken by fits of restlessness. Fleming took another spinal fluid sample and, taking it up to the same small laboratory where he had seen the action of the mould in 1928, he tried again to detect the infective organism that was destroying the brain tissue of his family friend. He grew a culture of non-haemolytic streptococci. It was a bacteria that was resistant to sulphathiazole but which, tested against his Penicillium mould in a glass dish, showed that it was sensitive to penicillin. The work revealed clearly that there was only one answer. There was little time left. His friend was then moribund and was being given oxygen to keep him alive. But Fleming had no penicillin.

For the first time in his career Fleming faced a case which he knew could be saved only by the extract of the mould on which he had reported so long ago. Yet the demands of this treatment were completely beyond his resources, and he knew of only one source where he might obtain the drug needed to save the life of his dying friend.

Early in the morning of 5th August, Fleming took up the telephone and called Florey in Oxford to ask for a supply of penicillin. He then had no knowledge of how much of the drug would be needed; he had never been faced with the prospect of using concentrated penicillin in the treatment of systemic infection. He sought Florey's full help, and he got it. Florey knew the drug intimately. He knew that intensity of dose was the key to treating deep-seated bacterial infection. His entire penicillin stock, at that time, was in the refrigerator at the Dunn School—a total of one million three hundred thousand units. It was all he had, and it had been earmarked for a systemic treatment of one of his clinical cases. But he offered it to Fleming on the condition that he could include the case notes within the list he and Ethel were compiling—Fleming was only too ready to agree.

Florey caught the early train to London and walked into St Mary's with the penicillin powder inside the glass vials in his briefcase. He instructed Fleming on preparation, on methods of dosing and on the drug's effectiveness against streptococci in general systemic use, and said that it had not yet been used intra-thecally—by direct injection into the spinal cavity. He then left the case in Fleming's hands.

For the first six days of the penicillin treatment Fleming gave injections of the drug into muscle tissue every two or three hours. But it was clear from the results and from cavity fluid tests, that the penicillin was not passing readily from the blood flow into the cerebral spinal fluids which harboured the streptococci.

On 11th August, seven days after the start of the treatment, Fleming injected the first penicillin ever to be placed direct into the spinal cavity of a human being. It was taking a risk, but the outcome almost immediately justified the gamble. He used five thousand units on the first injection and then repeated it a number of times until one hundred and twenty-five thousand of Florey's Oxford units had erased the last of the bacteria from the fluid. A few days later when recovery was certain Fleming ceased administering penicillin and his friend was discharged from the hospital, according to Fleming's notes '... with no abnormal signs or symptoms'.*8

Three days before the telephone call from Fleming asking for a supply of penicillin, Florey had received a letter from his old professor-teacher, Sir Charles Sherrington, and with it the copy of a lecture Sherrington had given in Oxford in which he had mentioned Florey's work. It was 2nd August 1942. The publicity bubble had yet to burst, and penicillin was still only an interesting curiosity among medical scientists. Florey wrote to thank Sherrington for his kindness, to say how sorry he was not to have seen him, and how glad he was to know that the great man was still in high spirits. He continued his letter,

We are all pretty busy here—we've had forty-eight weeks of teaching this year, guiding through the medical students. A certain amount of research is going on, but it is a matter of filling in large numbers of forms these days to keep anyone on the job.

The penicillin work is moving along and we have a fairly substantial plant for making it here. It is most tantalizing, really, as there is for me no doubt that we really have a most potent weapon against all common sepsis. My wife is doing the clinical work and is getting astonishing results—almost miraculous, some of them. Our last case was a cavernous sinus thrombosis caused by staphylococcus. From the moment we gave the drug he started to improve—he was comatose at one

* Fleming made a brief public reference to this case when he attended a meeting of the Royal Society of Arts in November 1944, at which Florey was invited to lecture on penicillin, its initial discovery, development and clinical application, and the prospects which the work held out for medicine. It was in a comment after this lecture that Fleming said, 'You have heard today some of the triumphs of penicillin in war wounds and in the diseases of ordinary life. I also have had some experience of the merits of penicillin, but none more impressive than the first dangerously ill patient I treated. He was a friend of mine who had meningitis. None of the ordinary drugs had any effect and he appeared to be on the point of death. Through the kindness of Professor Florey I obtained some of the concentrated penicillin and injected it into the muscle and the spine. In a week the man was practically well. This is not exceptional—but the first time one sees that sort of thing it makes a great impression.'

stage. In a week he was peevish because he was not allowed a
newspaper.

I am afraid the synthesis of the substance is rather distant,
but if, say, the price of two bombers and the same energy was
sunk into the project, we could really get enough to do a
considerable amount.

We also have another lot of antibacterial substances from
plants and moulds under investigation and, apart from the
prospect of some immediate use in the war, these substances
are full of interest and open up quite a vista . . .[9]

Money equal to the cost of two bombers . . . other substances
with antibacterial promise foreshadowing the coming of the
antibiotic epoch . . . increased effort . . . all these became reality,
but not from the months of slaving in hospital wards and in the
laboratories in South Parks Road, Oxford, but from the impact on
Alexander Fleming of his first real experience of penicillin at work.
For the remarkable recovery of his friend had as equally a dramatic effect on Fleming himself and he was soon causing strong
interest not only in government circles but in Fleet Street; and
the flurry of publicity and newspaper enthusiasm that ensued
was to catch Florey off balance and initially frighten him into
retreat.

Fleming's first move was to discuss his renewed interest with
Raistrick and to ask his advice on how he could best obtain
government action to sponsor penicillin production. Solid
Raistrick, in his dour Yorkshire manner, said he had no special
contacts with the Government and then, in a brave gesture, said,
'Why not go to the very top? With all this publicity Churchill
is bound to be interested. You don't happen to know *him*, do
you?' Fleming said he did not know Churchill, but he did know
one of his ministers. When he told this story Raistrick added,
'He told me that Sir Andrew Duncan was a fellow member of a
club—a sort of Scottish club in London—so I suggested he should
buttonhole him. He did—and Duncan threw his top civil servant
into the deep end, straight away.' The Scottish club to which
Fleming had alluded was the Ayrshire Society.[10]

Three years and three weeks from the time he received Sir Edward Mellanby's letter saying he could assume he would get £25 towards his new work on penicillin, Florey sat at a table in the Ministry of Supply and heard a British Government spokesman say,

'Gentlemen, the Government will provide whatever financial means are required. All available knowledge and expertise will be pooled so that this drug can be produced without delay on a factory scale. Nothing will be allowed to stand in the way.'[11]

Sir Cecil Weir, permanent head of the Department of Supply, spoke these words in his office in Portland House, a brief walk from where Edward Mellanby had received that classic letter from Florey in the first week of the war. 'I have long had the feeling that something might be done along these lines . . .'[12]

The statement came too late to save Florey from later criticism that he had 'taken it on a platter and handed it to the Americans, free'. But, no need now to scratch for money. The long months of exertion and late nights for his penicillin team could be relaxed, and he and Ethel need not go on burning out their health with monumental and lonely battles with an unbelieving medical profession. In a single statement the team had the enormous power and backing of authority—the Government, the armed services, industry.

They were all there at the meeting in Weir's office on 25th September 1942. Fleming and Raistrick and Florey (Weir recorded their presence as 'the greatest authorities on penicillin'); Major-General L. T. Poole, the army's senior pathologist; Quigg, Cronshaw and Scott of ICI; a consortium of brains from the Therapeutic Research Corporation, formed by industry as a war group, Drs Maxwell, Carr, Pyman and Trevan; the influential civil servant, Sir Russell Wilkinson; and Arthur Mortimer who became the first chairman of the General Penicillin Committee, formed that day, until the chair was taken over by the President of the Royal Society, Sir Henry Dale, who occupied the position until the end of the war.

Sir Cecil Weir wrote a postscript to the meeting in his diary, 'We can find it fortunate to do these things in war. But why must it only be in war-time? There is a lesson in this case which I believe will not be without its effect.'

What Florey had been seeking so long came about with the penicillin rescue of a dying man in St Mary's Hospital and Fleming's proclivity for public relations—a tendency he showed he possessed in strength as time went on. His friend had barely left the hospital before the story of the 'miracle recovery' was in the newspapers, and Fleming was being photographed at his microscope in his white coat. That the news had been leaked to the press appalled Florey, but Chain was amused and chortled later, 'The British hospitals were struggling for their pennies, remember. Then, here suddenly, was a pot of gold for St Mary's. It was an opportunity to be grasped—and, if I had been the manager of the hospital, I might have done the same.'

The first news treatment was restrained, but exciting, and *The Times*, in sober vein, drew attention to the 'allure of the new drug' in an editorial which revealed the painful gap of thirteen years from the finding of the mould and 'the discovery in Oxford that purified preparations are much more richly endowed with bactericidal properties than is the crude substance'. It remarked that the drug could be diluted millions of times and still remain effective and that, because of its potentiality, 'methods for producing penicillin on a large scale should be developed as quickly as possible'. It also said that the mice trials carried out at Oxford had shown the drug to be 'innocuous to man'.

The Times editorial observed carefully the military slogan 'no names, no pack drill,' but it reckoned without a voice that could thunder as effectively as its own. In his office in the Inoculation Department of St Mary's Hospital, Paddington, Sir Almroth Wright, then in his eighties and engrossed in his studies of immunity *in vitro*, took up a partisan pen to claim the prize of penicillin for the establishment which he had ruled as an unquestioned disciplinarian for thirty years. The heavy-browed old man—variously described as 'a dictator', one 'whose doctrines could not safely be doubted by his staff', one who liked to 'dominate his team'—was also a cantankerous and difficult octogenarian with a strong sense of territorial possession. He believed *The Times* had slighted his establishment and denuded it of a right to fame. So he took up his pen and told the editor in one paragraph where the true honour should be directed for the life-saving qualities that the Oxford workers had discovered in the drug. He wrote on 30th August,

> Sir: In the leading article on penicillin in your issue yesterday you refrained from putting the laurel wreath for this discovery round anybody's brow. I would, with your permission, supplement your article by pointing out that, on the principle *palman qui meruit ferat,* it should be decreed to Professor Alexander Fleming of this laboratory. For he is the discoverer of penicillin and was the author also of the original suggestion that this substance might prove to have important applications in medicine.[13]

Credit where credit is due, his Latin tag demanded.

The publication of this letter was a declaration of open season for the news media and Fleming was besieged in his laboratory in the brick tower above Praed Street. There and then began the legend of the visitation of the wonderful mould and the long years that Fleming had spent crying as a lone voice, his words falling on the deaf ears of the unyielding medical profession; and that he had known from the beginning that in the mould lay the greatest medical discovery in history and that, in time, 'some chemist would come along' and release it like a genie from a bottle. It was a story so easy to tell, with a hero at odds with a villainous profession, that even Fleming's official biographer drew old Sir Almroth Wright into this picture as an opponent of Fleming's belief.

This claim was strongly discounted by Professor Ronald Hare in his book *The Birth of Penicillin.* Hare, a long-term colleague of Fleming's and a life friend, rejected the suggestion that Sir Almroth Wright stood in Fleming's way and described the idea as the creation of a novelist seeking a villain to oppose his hero. Hare went even further and challenging many of Fleming's subsequent statements as 'unfortunate' broke down much of the legend surrounding Fleming and the discovery of the penicillin mould. He also drew attention to the absence of Fleming from the crucial undertakings which led to the introduction of clinical penicillin and industrial production.

The legend still persisted, however, and in the year following Hare's book the BBC televised a film about Fleming which included many of the old fallacies. He was, for instance, shown arguing the case for antibiotics in 1928 when the word was not coined until 1941 by Waksman in America; he was seen in the film speaking excitedly of the Oxford achievement in 1940 as being due to the freeze-drying method when this was not mentioned in the original *Lancet* article; and among other things he was pictured preparing a penicillin injection for the Oxford policeman, Albert Alexander, who was the patient of the Oxford team in the Radcliffe Infirmary. Once set in train in the vigorous manner of the media the legend was built up so rapidly in those early years that Fleming was unable to resist the flow of events although at times he did protest that he did not 'invent penicillin—Nature did it and all I did was draw attention to it'.

However, the professional ranks of scientific medicine, noted increasingly, as the legend grew coincidentally with the power of penicillin to treat a wider range of disease, that Fleming did nothing really to reconcile his belief of its efficacy with the long gap of neglect.

It was a shock to Florey when the news corps arrived at the front door of the Sir William Dunn School. He immediately escaped through the back with instructions to his secretary, Mrs Turner, to 'send them packing. I won't talk to them now. Tell them to come back next Thursday and I may give them ten minutes.'

A deep abhorrence of the media stayed with Florey for the rest of his life. It always pleased him to sit quietly reading a newspaper at airports, unrecognized by newsmen hunting film stars or political arrivals. It was an unworldly attitude, and it was this naïvety that cost him and his team true public recognition of their gift to human life. Dr E. P. Abraham made this point in tribute to his chief when Florey died, saying that while Florey's down-to-earth personality made penicillin available in war-time to save many lives he, nevertheless 'showed an instinctive aversion to publicity and it was never appreciated by the general public that the experimental work in his department, which owed so much to his initiative and drive, had produced the crucial results responsible for the introduction of penicillin into medicine'.[14]

There was another aspect to Florey's horror of the publicity given to penicillin in the later summer of 1942. He told a colleague at the Dunn School, 'I fear disruptions to our work and to my schedule and I hate getting involved in committees. But, more than all this, it is utterly wrong to write about this drug as "magic". It is not a cure-all and it is cruel to raise hope among the dying and their relatives that such a substance exists and then to tell them that they cannot have it supplied.'[15]

Among all this upheaval, with its effect on his work, Florey received the first report from the commander of the Middle East Pathological laboratory, Major R. J. V. Pulvertaft: a secretly circulated paper reporting on how penicillin had been used on battle casualties.

CHAPTER 13

MEANWHILE, THE AMERICAN EPOCH OF ANTIBIOTIC medicine which had been opened by Dawson was continued at the bedside of a dying woman in the Yale-New Haven Medical Center on a cold afternoon in March 1942. As the strong Atlantic winds swept through the Connecticut town on Saturday 14th, a needle carrying the first successful systemic use of penicillin slipped home into the weakened veins of Mrs Ogden Miller, the thirty-three-year-old wife of Yale's director of athletics, and editor of the Yale *Alumni Bulletin*.

Mrs Ogden Miller was close to death after an exhausting month-long battle against infection which was destroying her life processes—despite heavy doses of sulphonamide drugs. She was additionally weakened by the shock of operations aimed at limiting the spread of the streptococcal septicaemia—the age-old enemy of childbirth which had killed millions of women. Mrs Ogden Miller had also suffered the trauma of a miscarriage, and for those climactic four weeks in her existence, the fever of the battle had sent her temperature close to 106 degrees. Surgeons had tied off some of her main veins, and then, in a bid to shut off a suspected main source of primary infection, they cut away the tissue in which they thought the bacteria were breeding; but, in vain. In each cubic centimetre of this poor woman's blood there were as many as 100 of these destroying agents and her whole being was burnt out with the fever of the battle.

The supply of penicillin which saved the life of Mrs Ogden Miller was reckoned to be at least a half of the total supply in the United States at that time. It had been produced by Heatley and Dr Max Tishler at Merck's, and what took it into the hands of her doctor, John Bumstead, was Fulton's association with Florey. For John Bumstead was John Fulton's physician and, watching his patient slipping away, went in desperation to see Fulton who recorded the events in his diary,

> Knowing that I knew Florey and that we had his children with us, Bumstead asked on Thursday whether it might be possible to get some penicillin and try it as a last resort. I wired Dr Heatley (Dr Florey's assistant who is still in this country helping to get the production of penicillin organized). The Medical Director of Merck's replied that it had not yet been given as a clinical trial and implied that their limited supply was in the hands of Professor A. N. Richards, chairman of the Committee on Medical Research. I ran Richards to earth on the telephone on Thursday evening in Washington and he said he had turned the penicillin over to Dr Perrin Long, chairman of the NRC committee on chemotherapy. Long got in touch with Bumstead with the fortunate result that he released 5·5 grams, the first, I believe, to be made available for clinical trial.[1]

The package from Rahway arrived with no instructions on dosage or preparation, and with no experience of penicillin extract Dr Bumstead was at loss how to begin. He spent much time on that crucial Saturday morning telephoning medical men with Merck's to enlist their aid but found only one man at his bench, Dr Norman Heatley, the biochemist from Oxford. Heatley tried to avoid donning the mantle of medical adviser and toured the empty laboratories to find someone else, but without success. In the end he telephoned back to New Haven to the anxiously waiting Dr Bumstead to advise on preparation, and dosage based on the Oxford experience and the activity of the preparation which he had himself extracted.[2] They gave the patient a small dose at first to test for any toxic reaction. Her temperature was over 105 degrees. The opening dose was tolerated well and they gave her injections of a larger amount each four hours. Dr Fulton recorded the spectacular outcome, 'By 9 a.m. Sunday, less than 24 hours later, her temperature was normal for the first time in four weeks. She has eaten several enormous meals, also for the first time in four weeks.

'It really looks as though Florey has made a ten-strike of the first water; and I am glad that we have had the opportunity to make the first clinical trial of the American extract here.'[3]

It was a first step—a giant step towards recovery.

On the Monday—less than 48 hours later—Dr Bumstead was so elated he came close to falling into error which might have led to a resurgence of the infection and to tragedy for the patient. He wanted to reduce the dose. At his rooms at Rahway that evening, Dr Heatley wrote into his diary for the day,

> A phone call from Dr Bumstead, New Haven, saying that his patient's temperature had been down to normal since yesterday morning, that the penicillin was completely free from any harmful effect (200 mg dose) and that blood culture count was reduced from 100–150 colonies per cc to 1 colony per cc. He wanted to reduce the dose—but I urged him not to.[4]

Bumstead heeded the warning and maintained the dosage: but, a week later, Fulton, conscious of the limited supply of the drug, wrote in his diary,

> It is still too soon to say she is cured, but the response has been most dramatic. The 5 grams of penicillin which were used have cost many thousands of dollars to produce, since they are still in the experimental stage . . . on Sunday, Dr Norman Heatley, who came over with Florey from England, came up to New Haven to carry back to Merck's the week's urine, as nearly 70% of the penicillin is completely unchanged and can be recovered. He expects to get about 3 grams back which will be an enormous saving. If other cases respond this way, millions of dollars will be invested in the production of the new drug.[5]

At the Merck plant in New Jersey, Dr Norman Heatley ran the same gauntlet with the extraction of penicillin from Mrs Ogden Miller's urine as he had done exactly one year before, in

Oxford. Albert Alexander had died on 15th March 1941, but, on that day, the following year, there was enough to record America's first penicillin victory.

Three years later, when Alexander Fleming was conducted on his triumphal tour of America, under the auspices of the British Council and during which he collected a cheque for $100 000, he was taken to meet Mrs Ogden Miller and to receive her thanks. Posing for his picture with her, Fleming proudly told reporters, 'She is my most important patient.'[6]

The struggle in America to produce satisfactory amounts of penicillin by growing the mould in bottles was pursued in several industrial and government research laboratories in the early months of 1942, and out of this slow beginning came a rising tide of clinical and experimental observations. A document produced by the OSRD's Committee for Medical Research was able to say of this period, 'This study was co-ordinated by a committee consisting of Chester S. Keefer, Francis G. Blake, E. K. Marshall, Jnr, John S. Lockwood and W. Barry Wood, Jnr, and was carried out with extraordinary competence in selected clinics; by March 1943, the results of treatment of 200 cases with penicillin were available.'

Among these first two hundred cases were the triumphs at the Mayo Clinic, won by Dr Herrell and his associates with the first scraps of crude penicillin extract produced at the huge Abbott complex at North Chicago. Herrell's cases were the first to be published in American scientific literature and he spoke freely of them as dramatic results that 'looked like miracles'.[7]

His first two patients also had the right to believe that their lives were due to miracles; but all of them owed the success of their penicillin treatment to a quiet, sandy-haired scientist named McCorquodale who had worked for hours in a refrigeration room, half-frozen and with numbed hands as he teased the brownish powder from his Penicillium mould juice. McCorquodale had grown the first blue-green mould at Abbott's in 1941 from a sample obtained from Peoria and early in 1942 he had followed the Heatley-Chain process of capturing the elusive unstable molecules through a solvent process. In heavy clothing and thick boots, he had stood for hours in the cold-room winning the grains of concentrate which went to the Mayo Clinic in mid-summer 1942.

In the famous centre for healing at Rochester, Minnesota, Herrell had struggled with his own mould-growing problems, and, with the one hundred milligrams of extract given to him by Florey, had carried out tissue culture tests and assay work, but had been prevented from starting his first clinical trials. When he heard of the work McCorquodale and his colleagues were doing at the Abbott plant, he asked directly for a supply, and, to his delight, received a few of Abbott's first ampoules.

The arrival of the drug coincided with the battle for life that Rubin Steige was waging against staphylococcal invasion of his bloodstream. He was the same age as Mrs Ogden Miller—thirty-three—and in his high fever his heart was hammering and he was gasping in the air every two or three seconds through a closing throat. Herrell considered the man was suffering from cavernous sinus thrombosis, but referred to the case in his notes as facial cellulitis and staphylococcal septicaemia. The bacteria, untouched by massive doses of sulpha drugs of various types, was slowly killing Steige. His nasal passages were already closed, and then, in that same pattern which had struck Albert Alexander, the bacteria attacked his eyes, broke out in suppurations on his scalp and lodged colonies in the lining of his lungs. He could not see out of either eye and, as each day went by, he grew progressively worse.

Herrell obtained a total of 160 000 units from Abbott's and immediately started treatment with the intravenous drip method. In private communication, long afterwards, Herrell wrote,

'I can recall my reactions when he responded to treatment. Since he was obviously dying before he was changed from sul-phadiazine to penicillin, I regarded the response as a miracle. He got well, but he never recovered the vision in his right eye. I, personally, think he was as gravely ill as that Oxford policeman . . . but, fortunately, for us all, he recovered.'[8]

Herrell's second patient was four-year-old Carol Moen, of the south Minnesota village of Byron, who had a habit of chewing the inside of her cheeks. For several weeks in the summer of 1942, her father had admonished her, but the child persisted in the habit and one night she was taken, seriously ill, to the Kahler Hospital in Rochester, her pretty face bloated and swollen from the *Staphylococci aureus* swarming through her body. Her tongue had been forced up against a bacterially hardened palate and, to allow her to breathe, surgeons made a simple stab wound in her throat to pass a small air-tube into her windpipe below the swelling.

Herrell got to hear of the case late one evening and, with enough penicillin in hand to treat a child, he hurried to the Kahler Hospital. He found evidence of cyanosis, and pneumonia in her right lung, while his pathological tests showed a falling rate of leucocytes in her blood as the colonies of bacteria overwhelmed her immune response to the danger. She had no hope of life without penicillin, and Herrell spent the rest of the night and most of the following day by the little girl's bedside. In each cubic centimetre of the child's blood he found there were, on average, 25 colonies of the bacteria; and the staphylococci were identified as a haemolytic type that were breaking down the walls of her cells.

He used 12 000 units of penicillin dissolved into a litre of saline solution and allowed this to drip through a needle inserted into the child's arm. For the next five days he ranged the dose between 20 000 and 30 000 units; at the end of the first thirty-six hours, Carol Moen's blood samples were sterile, free of bacteria, and she was on the mend.

How Herrell felt about the case was perpetuated in the classic note at the end of the report on Carol to the Mayo Foundation, 'An infection of this type is almost universally fatal. She developed leukopenia at the height of the illness, and this is also usually considered of grave prognostic significance.' Yet in two weeks her temperature was normal and her appetite was back, and, with the wound in her throat healing, she was ready to go home.

These first cases were supplemented by others as the drug came into pilot scale production at the handful of industrial plants engaged in work on the new therapeutic agent. Keefer received supplies from Squibb's, a company which could have led the world but for classically faulty advice from their scientific adviser, in 1937, who killed a passing interest in the clinical potential of the Penicillium mould when he considered that 'lack of stability, slowness of the bactericidal action showed by penicillin make its production and marketing impracticable'. Upjohn's, too, soon began supplying the drug to Keefer's committee. Under the urging of Dr John Evans, the man who had been inspired by Florey's paper in the August 1940 issue of the *Lancet* to grow his own Penicillium mould, the plant was scaled up and the rush to produce the precious drug began.

Evans built rows of separating and refining columns and found, eventually, he could get his material close to 80% purity. 'But this reduced it to a mere pinch. I couldn't believe my eyes. The power against bacteria was quite unbelievable,' he said later.* He used the new data on corn steep liquor gained from Coghill and installed 120 000 two-quart milk bottles in which he grew the mould, and for the rest of the war years found himself in a restless flurry of nagging worry and work. 'We faced breakdowns and heartbreaks, boil-overs of material, stinking messes across the roof and the floor, and always trouble at week-ends and holidays. There was a Dantesque quality about life; but, in January 1943, we delivered 125 ampoules to Keefer, our first ampoules, with 100 000 units in each.'[9]

Towards the end of the first year of penicillin therapy in the United States, the tedious method of growing the drug in bottles of mould culture was in hand in many centres. The field of three firms, which had shown interest to Florey in 1941, had then expanded to a line-up of nearly two dozen runners, all ready to compete for the priority that government recognition would give their undertaking—and out of those first fumbling, low-yield operations, came the scraps of the drug that found their way through the hands of Keefer's committee to victims of one of America's greatest civil tragedies in which more than 500 persons lost their lives in a disastrous fire, in Boston.

A young physician, Dr Champ Lyons, obtained a small supply of penicillin and treated many of these people, winning the same dramatic results as those achieved by Dennis Bodenham in the

---

* The work in Oxford had shown that penicillin could be diluted 120 million times and still remain effective against bacteria.

burns of British airmen earlier that year. Lyons' work was dramatic, but tinged with qualification; there had been use of sulphapyridine and other sulphonamides, and those patients given penicillin recovered; but it could not be claimed for certain that penicillin saved these lives. For the first time, however, contaminated wounds healed naturally and this led to the Keefer committee sponsoring Lyons for the US Army's first mass trials—at the huge Bushnell General Hospital, a few miles from Salt Lake City. Appointed an Army major, Champ Lyons faced the proving tests of penicillin that had already been achieved in Britain by Florey's team. Dozens of men were at Bushnell, brought from the battle zones in the Pacific. Hopeless cases teemed with wounds that were infected within hours of infliction. Bacteraemia, blood poisoning, osteomyelitis, meningitis—they were all there.

Champ Lyons, who later worked on antibiotics in the Mediterranean area, wrote his report for the Committee on Medical Research and named it, *Penicillin Therapy for Compound Fractures in a Military Hospital*. This classic report was described by the National Co-ordinator of the Penicillin Programme, Mr A. L. (Larry) Elder, as 'the spark which triggered the accelerated program'.

The effect of penicillin on the hopeless cases at Bushnell led the cautious generals in the medical service to order more extensive tests of the same kind at other hospitals throughout the country.

Soon the penicillin project had mushroomed into one of the most extensive studies of a single biological substance in history.

In dozens of universities and industrial laboratories men, pledged to secrecy, collaborated with their colleagues across America and in Britain to attack the weaknesses and strengths of the penicillin molecule, ferreting out the mystery of its chemical structure and searching for clues to a path that could lead to the complete synthesis that never came. In laboratories on both sides of the Atlantic, the crystallographers and biochemists worked ceaselessly to reconstruct the molecule that was man's ally against disease, in an attempt to find the methods and techniques of achieving higher purity. Hundreds of new names joined the

confidential penicillin literature, among them many future
Nobel laureates. There was the spur to fame, and the sense of
contribution to the war effort among them all. Dr James Hinman,
who had left Wisconsin University to work at Upjohn's, found
himself involved in the bustle of finding the structure of penicillin.
'The amazing instability of the substance, the astonishing structure, was unique and outside our chemical experience,' he said.
'We worked twelve, sometimes fourteen, hours a day, filled
with tired excitement; and we had regular meetings with other
people across the country and were involved in an enormous
network and data pool which took in the mid-West group of
companies, the eastern drug houses and the whole complex of
the British industrial and academic research.'[10]

The realization on both sides of the Atlantic that penicillin had
strategic value led to a formal agreement between the two governments being negotiated on a diplomatic level. For a time this
caused delay in the exchange of data between the two nations,
but it in no way diminished the pace of the research. In Britain,
the name of the general committee was changed to the Penicillin
Producers' Conference, and co-ordinators on both sides were
appointed to see that the secret reports, known as the 'Pen'
reports, went only to the recognized working groups.

The experiment in Room 46 at the Dunn School with the
eight mice in May 1940 was turned, by the end of 1943, into a
full-scale operation involving scientists of many disciplines.
Technology of new kinds had given birth to the new profession
of biochemical engineering, and the more farsighted workers
were already on the frontiers of the microworld searching for
new antibiotics. Others, in a dozen research centres, were operating under government contract in a quest for the ideal strain of
penicillin mould on which industry could build mass economic
production of the drug, and, as had already happened once, the
answer was found in the most unexpected place. Good fortune
and brilliant research once again touched the penicillin project in
the mid-West wheat town of Peoria.

In the Northern Regional Research Laboratory, Dr Robert
Coghill had steadily expanded the work which had started with
Florey's visit in July 1941. When Heatley left to join Merck's at

the end of that year, Coghill and his colleagues—Dr Ward, his deputy, Dr Moyer, Dr Kenneth Raper and Dr Frank Stodola— carried the penicillin work beyond yield increase to studies of recovery processes, purification methods, the chemistry of the substance, and to the search for new strains which would be suitable for submerged culture in tank production. Kenneth Raper's global operation, in which pilots of Air Transport Command across the world sent back samples of soil, had produced hundreds of mould growths separated from the soil organisms, many of them showing activity against bacteria in Raper's dish colonies. This work was demanding and slow and, as the weeks and months went on, brought no significant advance, except to show that strains of moulds able to defend themselves against bacteria were of wide global distribution. In all this effort, Raper did not neglect the minor interest of local moulds, of the fungus growing down the street, or on damp shoes dropped into a dark cupboard, and he encouraged local people to bring him every scraping of mould they could find. Employees at the laboratories were assiduous in the hunt, and scraps of rotten fruit, vegetables, bread and cheese found their way to Raper's office. One Peoria woman, Miss Mary Hunt, was especially enthusiastic. She spent her days combing the shops and the back alleys. Dustbins, cartons of rubbish left for garbage collection, and especially fruit stores, were her prime targets. She brought many fungal colonies to Raper over the weeks until she earned the title among Peoria business people of 'Mouldy Mary'.

One summer day in 1943 she picked up a cantaloup, a mouldering melon on which grew a fungus which had what she called 'a pretty, golden look'. She brought it to Raper's office where it joined all the dark blue-greens and white, fluffy moulds from around the world. It was tested in the tight screening method which Raper had developed and was classified as *Penicillium chrysogenum Thom*—after the man Florey had consulted—and given the laboratory number of NRRL 1951. The first surface tests showed it produced slightly more than the currently-used NRRL 832, the offshoot of the Fleming mould. Then it showed part of its growth to contain a natural variant where the yield was higher. When this was cultured separately, the penicillin yield was more than doubled. This sub-strain was numbered NRRL 1951–B25. It was intensively studied and later made available to industry for submerged culture and became famous as the 'cantaloup strain'. It was seized on by the scientists working at the University of Wisconsin, Stanford University, Minnesota University, and the Carnegie Institute at Cold Spring Harbour, NY, and the strain 'Mouldy Mary' had picked up behind a Peoria fruit market was bombarded with X-rays and ultra-violet light, spores were separated out which showed higher yields, and the whole process repeated, again and again. Then, in the Carnegie centre, Dr Demerec induced a mutant of the canta-loup strain, tagged X–1612, which produced a mould with a yield of 500 units a millilitre of brew—a yield Florey described as 'fantastic by former standards'. The ultimate had not even then been reached. The group working in Wisconsin put Demerec's X–1612 among their range of ultraviolet light mutation tests and found another substrain that gave yields close to 1 000 units a millilitre. They christened their discovery Q–176.

'The effect of these discoveries on industrial production can hardly be exaggerated,' Florey wrote. Pfizer's, for instance, were able to expand their production of 416 000 units a month to more than 130 000 times that amount within two years. By 1944, they were producing penicillin at the annual rate of 1 200 billion units.

In the beginning, the cost of a million units, recognized in 1944 as a single treatment for a severe case of sepsis, was $200. The year following the discovery and development of the Peoria cantaloup strain the price dropped to $6·50 a million units, and, in the following years, underwent further transformation until pure crystalline penicillin was one ten-thousandth of its 1943 price—and, in many instances, bulk supply penicillin was costing less to produce than the packages in which it had originally been delivered for tablet manufacture.

Not only the patient work of scientists and the fluke of 'Mouldy Mary' and her mouldering melon were responsible for the drop in price of penicillin and the enormous output increase achieved by the American drug industry by D-Day—also responsible was a decision taken late one night at the coffee bar in the basement of the towering mass of Chicago's Palmer House Hotel.

Mr Larry Elder, who had been given the task of increasing penicillin production to keep the guarantee that Allied soldiers would have enough by D-Day was sipping his coffee with Dr Robert Coghill, talking of the bottle production plants that were steadily putting out penicillin.

'We know we can get the stuff with bottles and we know we can get it from 1 000 gallon tanks, but shall we go even bigger? Shall we go to 10 000 gallon tanks?' Larry Elder threw the questions at Coghill. He was the nation's penicillin production boss, but Coghill told him that there was no guarantee that the mould would go on working in fluid-nutrient of that volume. Coghill later remembered that talk over coffee in Chicago,

'The 1 000 gallon tanks would have required ten times as many tanks, ten times as many valves—for all the double valving most necessary in this production—ten times as much pipes, and all the other equipment; and, by this stage of the war, these things were enormously difficult to get. Larry had to make the decision one way or the other. He bet on the big equipment and time has shown how right he was.'[11]

The big tanks went into construction and Q–176 put to work— a union between a piece of mouldy fruit in the mid-West of America and a decision in an underground coffee bar in Chicago that transformed the prospects of the antibiotic industry.

It was not as difficult to obtain the supplies as Coghill imagined and the project was given a higher official rating. One of the US Army's senior procurement officers, Captain Richard E. Yates, recorded how, in October 1943, the first standard army contracts for penicillin were issued to eight contractors, marking 'the beginning of the real penicillin program which engrossed the efforts of many purchasing officers and which was granted the *highest priorities accorded to any military item, except the atomic bomb*'.[12]*

America had found the know-how of the antibiotic age, and when he visited the Pfizer plant in Brooklyn one winter morning early in 1944, Dr Robert Coghill had his moment of personal triumph for the years of toil which had followed the arrival of Florey and Heatley in Peoria in July 1941. He stood at Pfizer's with the huge tanks towering above him, each with their capacity

* Author's italics.

of 10 000 gallons of brew—each tank holding four and a half times the amount Florey had sought when he had asked for his 'kilo' of extract, and which he never did receive—and felt his personal goal had been reached.

'I stood at the end of the finishing line and saw the 100 000 unit vials coming out quicker than I could count them. It was then that I knew the battle had been won and that victory was ours. It had been a long road from Fleming's petri dish to the finished vials ready for the physician's hands.'[13]

In the onslaught leading to the defeat of Germany, penicillin produced in the amounts such as Coghill witnessed was used as a precaution against infection in wounds, and 95% of the wounded men treated with penicillin in the battle for Europe recovered. The attendant spectre of combat wounds, gas gangrene, was virtually banished. Where this disease had taken the lives of 150 men out of every 1 000 casualties in the Great War in Europe, between D-Day and the German surrender in May 1945, the case figures plummeted to nearly non-existent levels—'in a way' said one army report, 'that military surgeons of a previous age would have refused to believe'. The official records of the 21st Army Group say, 'The results were dramatic ... wounds which had taken many lives in previous campaigns were no longer dangerous. Open fractures had a recovery rate between 94 and 100%, and there was a startling reversal in the figures on war burns. For the first time in the history of war, burns, of one-fifth, or less, of the body surface showed a 100% recovery rate.'[14]

By this time, however, the determined action by American administrators, technologists, chemical engineers and research workers, had won what seemed to be a totally unexpected bonus from the increased flow of penicillin from industrial undertakings.

When Keefer's committee found the predicted annual flow of 40 000 million units being exceeded* they widened their range of clinical investigators to include Dr John F. Mahoney of the US Public Health Service. At the time, Mahoney and a group of colleagues were working at the venereal disease hospital at Staten

* Under the urgings of a new strong-man, Mr Fred J. Stock, who appeared on the penicillin scene for the War Production Board in May 1943.

14

Island where they used established practice of testing every new drug that came their way on the major forms of venereal affliction. Mahoney read the Oxford reports on culture tests on the lethal power of penicillin against the gonococcal organism, and knew how effective an agent it was. But in their glass dish culture tests with the deadly spirochaete of syphilis, as in Oxford three years before, the penicillin left the organism unharmed. When one of Mahoney's team, Dr Arnold, confirmed the Oxford findings that *in vitro* the coiled-spring organisms of syphilis were unharmed by doses of penicillin, Mahoney then asked Arnold to inject penicillin into a syphilitic rabbit and to test the reaction. The result was a revolution in venereal treatment and in those few hours, Dr Mahoney and his colleagues were drawn into medical history with a totally unexpected advance against this long-standing human affliction. They showed that penicillin, in the living system, could cure syphilis as certainly as it did gonorrhoea.

In that first experiment, the effect of penicillin in the living form was so catastrophic to the spirochaete population in the animal's blood that Mahoney and Arnold could not believe their eyes. Blood samples showed a total eradication of the infective agents, and a chancre of syphilis on the animal's ear proved sterile. The test was repeated on more diseased rabbits; penicillin left no doubt of its effect *in vivo*. Mahoney and Arnold showed the improbable to be possible. As Domagk's old prontosil had proved useless in the glass dish, but lethal against streptococci in the living system, so penicillin became effective in that different environment. It was, said Florey when the news reached him, 'a striking addition to our knowledge'. He observed that patients could harbour syphilis for years and that it was always difficult to state categorically that a cure had been attained. 'But these preliminary reports give every hope of more effective treatment by penicillin than by any other means available,' he said.

From the wooden building on Staten Island, off New York, Mahoney, with Arnold and another of his team Dr A. Harris, a serologist, went directly to human patients. With any other drug such a direct leap into human clinical application would have been unpardonable; with penicillin it was justified. At that time thousands of people had been treated for a variety of infections without a single report of toxicity. Florey had said in America, 'This drug can be administered in amounts one hundred times above the necessary dose without any toxic effect.'

Their first patient was a young sailor, desperate and sickened with the recent confirmation that he had contracted syphilis and who faced, at the best, a long and painful treatment calling for courage and endurance. He readily agreed to Mahoney's suggestion that he be used as a test case with penicillin. They started with doses of 25 000 units every four hours and went on to the end of a total dose of 1 000 000. The young man suffered, in all, forty-eight injections; but the beaming faces of his doctors as they came back from each blood test gave him assurance and a new future. After the first four injections they failed to find a single spirochaete in his blood samples; but they still went on with the treatment.

After this success they expanded their clinical trial by taking in three other early syphilis cases in the hospital, with the same results.

It was hard to accept that they had mastered this dreaded agent of ill-health and death, but the facts were indisputable. From the early records of exploration, syphilis had been known as a wild marauder that rode the seaways in the bodies of its sailor victims, paralysing and destroying its hosts with fearful penetration of their inner structure, and remorseless attack on brain, heart and nerve tissues that would leave a human being wrecked, if indeed it left at all; its common mark was *locomotor ataxia*, a shuffling, foot-flapping gait, perhaps blindness, or deafness, and a body racked with shooting pains and a mind empty of thought, or hope of a return to co-ordination.

When Mahoney and his colleagues opened the new era in treatment, the only chance for a sufferer from syphilis to return to a normal life was the long drawn-out agony of the Ehrlich legacy, the arsphenamine or salvarsan, which had been Ehrlich's limited answer to the dream of the magic bullet, the arsenic treatment that demanded great courage from the patient. At that time—June 1943—there were several thousand venereal disease clinics across the United States where the lapse in completion of syphilis treatments ranged as high as 80%. The reactions and the pain, the constant indignity and the stigma of secrecy imposed

by a bigoted society, stopped many patients from continuing
the year-long battles to conquer the terrible spirochaetes, with a
consequent spread of the debility and shame. In military circles,
however, the rigid disciplines made it possible to impose the long,
systemic application of the arsenic and the heavy metals of injection, and success against the disease of above 80% was recorded
by army doctors.

Penicillin changed this whole picture and Mahoney, Arnold
and Harris wrote a brief preliminary report in that month of
June that moved the chairman of the Committee on Medical
Research, Florey's friend, A. Newton Richards, in a phrase,
tightened to suppress too much excitement, to comment, 'The
discovery gave a new and highly important turn to the examination and treatment of this disease . . . it can be considered as the
beginning of a revolution in the treatment of syphilis.'[15]

Richards acted very promptly, realizing the strategic importance of the pathological fact which Mahoney had stressed in his
report. 'The patient promptly becomes non-infectious at the
start of treatment and the necessary period of his hospitalization is
greatly shortened.' A great saving of manpower in the Armed
Forces was in sight, Richards observed. He called together the
heads of eight civilian venereal clinics, representatives of the
British and the Canadian scientific groups and informed them of
the discovery and his intention to make 40 million penicillin units
available for a rapid trial of about 350 syphilitic patients. This he
later expanded to sixty different centres in the United States
within a few months.

The United States Army adopted penicillin as the routine
treatment for syphilis on 26th June the following year, three
weeks after the start of the Normandy landings.

Richards later took pride in the comment which Florey wrote
on the mass production of penicillin in America. 'Too high a
tribute cannot be paid to the enterprise and energy with which
the American manufacturing firms tackled the large-scale production of the drug. Had it not been for their efforts, there would
certainly not have been sufficient penicillin by D-Day in Normandy, in 1944, to treat all severe casualties, both British and
American.'[16]

THE PRIZE
AND THE PRICE

THE FIRST PENICILLIN ADMINISTERED IN A WAR ZONE WAS used at the 15th Scottish General Hospital, Cairo, on 17th August 1942, by Major R. J. V. Pulvertaft. In the heat of an Egyptian summer, penicillin's application in the war fulfilled that role of a surface antiseptic which Fleming had sought for it. 'It may be an efficient antiseptic for application to, or injection into, areas infected with penicillin-sensitive microbes.'

Penicillin had been sent to war before Florey and Ethel had completed the bulk of the systemic cases in the second series of human clinical trials, and Florey had denuded his stock to make the move. But he sent the drug for a proving run in the heat, sand and flies of the Middle East, because he already had his eye on the eventual use of penicillin in the bigger continental battles that were to come. Once again, the poverty of supply limited his ambitions, and the tiny amount he handed to the War Office—into the hands of Major-General L. T. Poole, the Director of Pathology—had necessarily to be restricted to surface use—and Major Pulvertaft had received his instructions to this effect.

In the report he sent home for secret circulation—but which was published the following year, with some additions—Pulvertaft listed his first case of treatment as penicillin's first success in a war zone. This case, however, was not a battle casualty—nor in fact was it really Pulvertaft's first. The case he listed—a young New Zealand sergeant whose name, Pulvertaft believed, was Newton—had had his legs broken in a road accident and had spent two weeks on a treatment of solid doses of sulphanilamide which had left the bacteria in the pus of his infected injuries untouched. His bandages and bed were soaked with the foul suppuration. In its exciting and dramatic fashion the washings of penicillin powder swept away the disease and, in the terse language of his case notes, Pulvertaft wrote, 'Complete recovery. Streps disappeared from injuries twenty-four hours after start of treatment.' But the first soldier on active service to be dosed with penicillin was a thirty-one-year-old fighting man of the British Eighth Army into whose pelvis the flying metal fragments of a German shrapnel shell had ploughed their way. Pulvertaft did not record the name of this first battle casualty to be treated with penicillin, nor did he record whether the man lived or not. He was critically ill, and Pulvertaft could do no more than use him as his initial *in vivo* test. The notes read, '17th August, 1942: Not suitable for treatment since probable duration of illness would absorb all available penicillin; case used as test of action on organisms.'

That day, and on the following one, Pulvertaft washed the wounds with a penicillin solution containing one hundred milligrams which if the activity was as high as when this material left Oxford, would have contained 4 000 units.

The effect was noticeable immediately, and the case notes read, 'Patient, and his friends commented on alteration of smell. Discharge less; smell less offensive.' Pulvertaft allowed a lapse of two days, and the discharge and smell resumed. Then he applied a further one hundred milligrams and again there was a diminution of the pus. The test was then discontinued with the wounds showing signs of improvement.

The third man to receive the drug in the Middle East did die. This was a case of multiple bomb wounds, one of which had penetrated and exposed part of the soldier's brain. Four cubic centimetres of penicillin solution were applied when the cerebral tissue was seen to be infected. This cleared the bacteria, but the man died from other causes.[1]

By the end of his first few cases, Pulvertaft was intrigued, 'Penicillin is of real value in the control of gram-positive organisms. It does not always eliminate them, perhaps because it cannot always get to their hiding places when externally applied.' He received two more batches of penicillin from ICI in the following November and in March 1943, but this was not enough for him and his colleague, Colonel J. S. K. Boyd. Convinced that penicillin offered the best known prospect of cleaning up the continuous flow of septic wounds in the base hospital, they started their own culture. Pulvertaft obtained 'through unofficial channels' a sample of Fleming's old mould, and they grew a small farm of fungus in the cellars of the Citadel in Cairo, as it was the coolest place they could find. This particular use of the basement in an old Khedive Palace by British officers must have caused a few eyebrows to be raised.

When they had their mould growing well, they made simple filtrates of the mould juice. No attempts were made to concentrate the drug and, in the same way as Fleming had injected his rabbit and mice in 1928, they treated infected soldiers with the yellow nutrient on which the *Penicillium notatum* had grown. They also dressed the wounds and recorded their successes with comments, 'No discharge; wound healing,' or, 'No discharge; patient regaining feeling in hip.'[2]

Pulvertaft and Boyd did not publish details of this work for the reason, Pulvertaft later attested, that they did not think it was very reliable. When he heard of these experiments, Florey was savagely critical, regarding the use of crude filtrate on wounded men as retrograde and unnecessary. 'It was only used in local treatment,' Pulvertaft commented after the war, 'but Florey strongly—perhaps rightly—disapproved of this.'[3]

When he read Pulvertaft's first report from the Middle East, Florey knew nothing of the mould-growing enterprise in Cairo and he assessed the war zone results as moderately successful and debated with his friend Hugh Cairns, on the steps by which penicillin could be used experimentally on a wider range of cases. Florey said he wanted to go to North Africa where the Allied forces were then trapping the Afrika Corps in Tunisia in a pincer operation. In the discussions he resisted suggestions that he should, if he went to the war zone, take on military rank and insisted he should remain a civilian. He laid his plans, held discussions in Whitehall, and gradually built up the stock of penicillin available. To the supplies his own team were providing he was able to add the production of the pilot-plant operations by ICI and the Therapeutic Research Corporation. It was a lengthy process and the weeks slipped by as the pile of penicillin built up to proportions on which a battle zone trial of the substance could be staged.

It was during this time that Florey gave the American Army's medical services their first direct contact with penicillin and its healing power when Lieutenant-Colonel Rudolph Schullinger brought the 2nd US General Hospital to Britain in July 1942.* The Colonel and his staff were given a reception by the university medical staff at Oxford and jokingly welcomed as the 'invaders who had taken over Headington'. Schullinger, a warm and pleasant man, soon made friends with Florey and his wife—whom he insisted on calling 'Mildred' for some reason—and was invited to visit the Dunn Building to see the Oxford penicillin 'factory'. He wrote a report on his experience which went back to Washington, and into the files, without making any great impact there.

'Once inside,' he wrote, 'the visitor could sense an atmosphere of considerable activity. As one passed the various research units, it was apparent that doctors and technicians were busy and intent on their work. It became apparent that here was a great project in full play. Professor Florey was at the helm, directing the technical aspects of all the production and refinement of penicillin, and consulting with his wife who was carrying out clinical applications.'[4]

Schullinger also made one of the very few tributes paid, by the American services, to Florey and his workers, for their contributions to the development of penicillin. 'It would be impossible to express to them adequately the gratitude due to their selfless expenditure of time and effort in counselling and encouraging me during this stirring period of study in our medical service,' he stated, in one of a whole series of speeches made by senior members of the US Army's medical service. In one of the more important of these, made by the Surgeon-General, General Kirk,

---

* The same month as Dr Chester S. Keefer's committee had acquired sufficient penicillin to treat no more than ten civilian trial cases. The United States Army, at that time, was almost totally unaware of what penicillin was, or what it could achieve, although the Surgeon-General of the Army, General Norman T. Kirk, was to claim, just before D-Day that the services had had 'their eye on penicillin from the time of the civil trials'.

to the American Pharmaceutical Manufacturers' Association—
six months before the Normandy landings—he reviewed the
history of the development of penicillin, praised it as a tremendous
agent in military service, said it had great potential as an eradicator
of dread diseases of war, but did not mention the existence of the
British scientists, who, with the secrets they had won by their
sweat at Oxford, had set the wheels in motion. The Surgeon-
General spoke to an association which contained members who
made tens of millions of dollars of profit from penicillin, and who,
when the war was finished, presented a cheque for $100 000 to
Alexander Fleming, to devote to research as he saw fit.

In the late summer of 1942, Schullinger was the first senior
American medical officer to witness the dramatic results of
penicillin therapy when he was taken to the wards of the RAF
hospital at Halton where he saw 'the wonderful results in burns'
achieved by Bodenham, and to civilian hospitals where Ethel was
conducting her systemic and topical treatments. In his report he
declared, 'The results were entirely dramatic. Here is an agent
that could be used with great and enormous benefit to both
civilian and military purposes.'

Schullinger consulted Colonel Elliott Cutler, the US Army's
senior surgical expert in the European theatre and then decided
to seek an urgent supply of penicillin.

But Schullinger was asking Washington for penicillin which it
did not possess and could not obtain. His requisition was allowed
to lie unanswered.

As the weeks went by, Schullinger's enthusiasm expanded with
experience and his request reached his superiors at a time when
there was a mounting demand in America for the new 'miracle
drug' for civilian use. But the Army was still months away from
its own decision to open mass studies of the capabilities of the
mould product as a therapeutic, and it first had to satisfy itself
that all the British scientists had claimed for penicillin was, in
fact, true.

Schullinger repeated his request for penicillin supplies, with the
same negative result. There was no hope of obtaining any from
British sources where every grain was precious, but he did enlist
the support of Mellanby and the British Medical Research Council

in a third appeal to Washington and, when the winter had gone
and the first hospital study had opened at two military hospitals
in America, a supply of penicillin—the first of a constantly
increasing amount—reached him at his hospital just outside
Oxford.

The day the penicillin came to Schullinger was 8th May 1943.
He called in Florey, Cutler, and two other officers, to help him
plan how the drug would be used. The instructions from Washington were explicit, 'This was to be regarded as a clinical trial
and not an experiment. The penicillin is to be used only by, and
on, United States service personnel.' By Florey's Oxford standards the supplies were an Eldorado, a total of 18 million units—
more than his total production so far at Oxford. So precious was
it that Schullinger had it taken, under escort, to the hospital
kitchen where it was locked into the ice box and a guard set
over it.[5]

'The orders were quite clear,' Schullinger recalled, 'but it was
very difficult to resist or deny the urgent requests from neigh-
bouring British hospitals', and he saved the life of a British soldier
dying in a hospital at Shaftesbury with septicaemia by allocating
five million of the precious units.

Schullinger began to travel the countryside to address and
badger both American and British hospital workers on the new
'revolution in healing'. But he was well behind. The day he
called on Florey for advice and guidance on the use of his first
supplies, the two leading members of Florey's team of ten surgeons, taking penicillin into the battle areas, had arrived in
Algiers and were preparing for the initial war zone survey.
They were Lieutenant-Colonel Ian Fraser, a surgeon, and Major
Scott Thomson, a bacteriologist, and they opened their study
of wounds to determine the types of injury that should be dealt
with by penicillin, and the strains of bacteria that would be most
commonly met in the North African theatre.

Thus North Africa became the nursery of the use of penicillin
in military surgery; and in that vast, dusty, heated arena the
wounds of 300 fighting men were used in a tight and comprehen-
sive clinical exercise which shaped the pattern of antibiotic

treatment in war. Before the work began, however, the rapid victory of the Allied Forces in North Africa caused necessary readjustment in the plans of the penicillin mission. When Fraser and Thomson arrived in Algiers, at the beginning of May, the remnants of Rommel's Afrika Corps and the fragmented Italian forces were being crushed between the armour of Montgomery's Eighth Army and Eisenhower's forces which met in Tunis.

When Florey arrived with Cairns two weeks later, in mid-May 1943, there were no fresh battle wounds on which to try out penicillin. There were men by the thousands in hospitals in conditions that filled many hearts with despair. There the two scientists found infections, weeks old, and some with months of bacterial history; men whose shattered, broken limbs had micro-flora, unchecked by the sulpha drugs, growing in the ends of bones; men afflicted with bed sores and deep-rooted, persistent abscesses; and everywhere, the flies, the sand, the heat beating off the rocky country. The conditions shocked Florey and Cairns, but they had to face the fact that to apply their limited supply of penicillin on these battle casualties would be to repeat that same old uphill fight for penicillin; to prove again that it would reclaim health when all else had failed. Many of the cases were near hopeless, but it was also hopeless to prove what was already known. Penicillin had to be shown as an agent that would usher in a new age of surgery and healing, and its use had to be reserved for that purpose. Florey and Cairns made this objective plain in the joint report which was afterwards hailed by Major-General Poole, in London, as an 'historic document'.

They said,

It should be clearly understood that the object was not primarily to ascertain whether penicillin was capable of dealing with gram-positive organisms in septic conditions; this we consider had been amply shown in England already. The main problem was to learn to employ the small quantities of penicillin likely to be available for service use to the best advantage. The work, then, had been designed to give an answer to the question,

'Can penicillin be used effectively in the field at all?' and 'If so, how much is required and at what place in the Army organization can it be used to best advantage?'⁶

They sought quick answers, compressing the study into three hectic, work-filled months, for very soon the tide of war gave them a stage on which to operate—the invasion of Sicily, on 10th July 1943. Their surgical team was spread across North Africa at different centres, with Florey and Cairns going backwards and forwards between Sousse, Algiers and Philipville.

When the Sicily campaign opened, the hospital ship, the *Somersetshire*, started to bring back the British wounded to base hospitals on the African mainland with Colonel Fraser aboard using his small ration of penicillin on selected cases. The American soldiers still depended on the range of sulpha drugs but some Canadians were treated in the British penicillin programme.

The results of the first few cases quickly confirmed the opinion of the British team, and Florey and Cairns wrote into their report, 'One strong impression conveyed to all who followed these cases was that it was far too late to start penicillin treatment weeks or months after wounding, at a Rear Base Hospital, and that its use should be tried much earlier, before the establishment of serious infection.'

On the basis of this report, the drug was moved to the frontline hospitals, 'One of the main preoccupations of the fighting portion of an army is the conservation of its manpower,' their report went on, 'and a great deal of the activity of the medical services is directed towards this end . . . it would be of considerable importance to improve on the present method of treating large flesh wounds so that infection could be prevented . . . with a consequent earlier return to duty.'⁷

They proposed to fly in the face of traditional military surgery which was to leave the wounds open for debriding and incising of flesh at some later date when it was apparently safe to sew up a wound—for, there had been, Florey recorded, some catastrophes in suturing wounds which held the seeds of bacterial poisoning. Instead he suffused wounds with penicillin and then stitched them together, often leaving tiny rubber catheters—or tubes—inserted so that penicillin could be applied in solution until the healing was healthy and clean. This new technique was not always readily accepted by the experienced army surgeons whom he was teaching. He ruefully recalled one case, when an army doctor became red-faced with anger and exploded, 'It's murder—bloody murder!'

The work, said Florey, had the active support of senior army medical men in Britain, but 'not everyone shared that view'. He later quoted one opinion expressed at that time in North Africa, 'There is no doubt that even after viewing the wonderful results that penicillin can achieve most surgeons and most administrators, if forced to choose between penicillin and sulphonamides, would say, *Give us sulphonamides every time.*'[8]

Despite the wonderful and dramatic results in both civil and military trials, the resistance to antibiotics treatment in the middle of 1943, was still strong—especially in the high echelons of the American army medical services. To those minds the proof had to be large-scale and the American army staged its own tests against gonorrhoea, taking a total of fifty men in each of sixteen military hospitals—a grand overall case list of 800 cases of venereal disease—to satisfy themselves that Florey's and Cairns' findings that penicillin acted against the gonococcus *in vivo* were valid. In the North Africa survey, on the other hand, the point was made in a matter of a few days. In Tunis a British army specialist in venereal disease, Major W. H. D. Priest, had found a worrying increase in the cases of sulpha-resistant gonorrhoea, especially among the élite troops—the paratroops and the commandos— who, for some unknown reason, seemed more open to this infection. Priest registered the suspicion that French doctors, whose task it was to supervise the brothels in Tunis, were to blame for the spread of the sulpha-resistant types of gonorrhoea, by issuing prostitutes with small doses of sulpha drugs which were used to mask their condition at the times when the compulsory smear tests came around. 'This meant that the women were able to go on distributing this disease among their clients,' Priest alleged. 'That this practice is common among the French doctors is not freely admitted, but, in this area, the French doctor-in-charge has actually asked my assistant if he could spare some sulphapyridine for this very purpose.'

When Florey handed him his first supplies of penicillin, Major
Priest chose nine of his most difficult cases. These were soldiers
infected with gonorrhoea that had resisted several courses with
different types of sulpha drugs. He also included a 'fresh' case,
chosen at random. They were all injected with moderate doses of
penicillin and were all back on duty in forty-eight hours.

Priest reported, 'In all cases, the improvement was dramatic; it
was just like turning off a tap.'9

Florey's comment was that the treatment was so simple, 'there
would appear now to be no reason why it should not be carried
out in forward areas with no more than two days' absence from
duty.'

As with gonorrhoea, so it was with the more legitimate
afflictions of war. As the cases passing through Fraser's hands
aboard the *Somersetshire* flowed into the North African hospitals
the changing pattern became more and more obvious. One
hospital, in particular, from which penicillin patients were returned quickly to duty, was the 3rd New Zealand Hospital where
Lieutenant-Colonel Eardley Button commanded the surgical
unit. This hospital was no more than a collection of tents swelter-
ing under the broiling African sun. For sick and wounded men
the conditions were near to inhuman with Button himself complaining, 'During this period under review the temperature in
the tented wards has been above 100°F on eleven days, above
110°F on three or more days, and, on one day, reached 118°F—
on 18th July. Only on ten days did the temperature drop below
100°F.' In amelioration of these discouraging and heartless
conditions, Button reported, 'The operating theatre has, however,
been sited in an adjoining building, thus allowing greater control
of the dust problems.'10 The conditions for wounded men
suffering from uncontrolled infection and suppurations of their
injuries belonged to a past age and strongly contrasted with the
cases of recovery when penicillin was used.

To conserve the penicillin supply to cover as wide a range as
possible, Florey concentrated on 'soft tissue wounds'. Only in a
few cases did he inject; on the more difficult and demanding of
injuries where bones had been shattered and infected or deep
cavities of the body were involved. In the flesh wounds catheters

were inserted for feeding the penicillin, and the wounds were
stitched. They healed in nearly all cases by what surgeons call
'first intention', and so revolutionary were the results that they
caught the attention of Eisenhower and Montgomery, and were
reported back to Britain.

Venereal cases apart—which at any one time could be reckoned
to keep up to three divisions of men from duty—the rapid defeat
of disease and the speedy healing and return to duty of fighting
men was remarkable. At times, said Florey, recovery was so
quick that the question of how soon a man could face war again
after injury became more psychological than physical.

The case lists emphasized the rapid healing, with instance after
instance of men badly hit in the heat of battle being back in
action within a few weeks. For instance: Lieutenant R. was making a reconnaissance of a hill-top position in eastern Sicily when
he crawled into the sights of a German sniper and was shot
through the thigh of one leg. He was just able to crawl back to
the first aid post and was taken to the casualty clearing station
where they failed to find the bullet. Aboard the *Somersetshire*
the bullet was located and removed, the deep wounds sufflated
with penicillin and sewn up. Within a month of being wounded,
the officer was back fighting with the Dorset Regiment in the
final quelling of the Axis forces in Sicily.

Another example was Private O. of the Royal Scots Fusiliers
who was two miles inland on the day of landing in Sicily when
he was hit by shellfire. Several men were killed and he was hit in
both legs, but he still went to the aid of some comrades and then
lay for two hours in the shade of olive trees until the stretcher
bearers found him. They got him back to the general hospital
by ship in three days and the wounds which had penetrated the
backs of both thighs were treated with penicillin. The notes read,
'25th July; stitches out. Wounds dry and united at first intention.'
On 10th August, one month after the invasion started, this case
note stated, 'Firmly healed; good scar and little disability.'

But Florey and Cairns were eager to push penicillin even
further into the front line and to see it in action as an injectible
which would kill infection at the outset. Although this practice
was not introduced till the American forces landed in Normandy

15

the following year, with ample supplies of the antibiotic, the results gained in North Africa had delighted Florey and his team. Both in treatment and as a prophylactic agent, it was unchallenged and Major-General Poole later wrote of Florey's preliminary report on the antibiotic, 'Publication of this historic report marked the second milestone of progress towards establishing penicillin in the treatment of war wounds . . . it set forth many lessons in a very short time; these had to be made widely and quickly known so that the use of penicillin could be extended.'[11]

The War Office organized lectures and demonstrations, and set up courses of penicillin training for nearly 200 pathologists and 500 clinicians at Woolwich. While he was in North Africa, Florey had put his flair for photography to work by making a colour film of the three-month clinical trial of the antibiotic in a war zone, and this film was used at Woolwich to instruct the men who would take penicillin into the field in Italy and during the Normandy landings.

At this time the American army authorities were beginning to support Schullinger's efforts in Britain more strongly. An army record in Washington reveals,

The opportunity to study the efficacy of penicillin in the European theatre of operations was unparalleled, for, in the United Kingdom were some of the persons at the forefront of its development. A beginning in this direction has been made by the studies which Lt-Col. Rudolph N. Schullinger was conducting at the 2nd General Hospital at Headington, with the help and advice of Professor Howard W. Florey and Dr Mildred E. Florey, his wife. By the opportune arrival of more penicillin in September 1943, Colonel Schullinger was able to continue his work and bring it to a conclusion in March 1944. There were indications that it might prove to be the greatest bacteriological agent yet produced.

Even these indications failed to break down completely the caution that pervaded the minds of senior American army medical officers and it was not until penicillin had proved itself during and after D-Day that they abandoned the attitude mentioned by

Florey of opting for sulphonamides 'every time'. The Florey and Cairns report was freely handed around among the American medical officers and, again and again, they engaged in their own trials to prove the experience of the British. The carpet had been laid for penicillin therapy in war, but the American officers were still unwilling to tread on it, and, a bare six months before the Normandy landings in June 1944, General Norman T. Kirk proclaimed,

> We were in touch with the civilian trials, and as the promising results began to appear so our interest grew. It seemed evident that penicillin had great possibilities. But lengthy testing was needed, in our view, before this could be confirmed as fact ... we knew it would be useful, but it had only been studied where the sulphas had failed and we did now know to what extent it would replace, rather than supplement, those other drugs.

Even when the European-based American officers began preparation of the directives on where, when and how the increasing penicillin supplies were to be used, their orders still showed some residual caution. In March 1944, after Schullinger, Cutler and others had held a series of meetings, their reports on these discussions described the available data on penicillin as 'tentative and in some cases even contradictory'.[12]

These reports displayed their doubts about the effectiveness of the drug on gas gangrene. Cutler, especially, hesitated, in drawing up precise instructions for the American medical officers who would apply penicillin in the field after D-Day. As late as 10th April 1944, he was writing to a Colonel Morton, 'I have sent you a copy of the Florey-Cairns report. There is no one here much to help you with gas gangrene, though if we can arrange some kind of meeting with MacLennan, who is back from the Mediterranean now, I will see you are implicated.'

Eventually, as the US Army's senior surgical expert in the European theatre, Cutler, in May 1944, wrote a directive to his fellow senior officers,

We will begin the parenteral (injection) use of penicillin as far forward in battle as possible, and we will also place powder in the wounds.

Each soft part injury requires 420 000 units; each compound fracture requires 580 000 units, and both these amounts are doubled in wounds in the peritoneum or the buttocks. If we take 6 000 injuries per day—which one might say is one thousand from each of six divisions—then the requirements would be . . . a total of 2 840 million units. If 10% of wounds are of the type needing double doses, then we will need a total daily supply of 3 140 million units. This, for one month, would mean 94 200 million units which would mean 940 000 vials. I recommend that you transmit a demand for at least 75 000 million units each month once operations commence.

As enormous as these amounts would have seemed to the Oxford workers the previous year, they were even greater than had been dreamed of by Cutler himself only weeks before, when, in March, he had considered what he would need to have for the Allied troops to storm the Normandy beaches in June. 'The shipment to the European Theatre for the month of March was 500 million units and there are indications that this will be increased soon to 3 000 million units. Other sources say the supply is now unlimited.' Colonel Silas B. Hays, the new theatre medical supply officer, said at a conference on 13th March 1944, 'In fact, I would not be surprised if by the summer time we don't get too much penicillin!'[13]

There was a series of meetings throughout March and April which formed the directives on how treatment for gas gangrene was to proceed in all the field stations and hospitals. These were included in a circular from the Office of the Chief Surgeon, ETOUSA, dealing with the treatment of battle casualties in the combat zones.

The instructions were published on 15th May, three weeks before D-Day, and roughly a week before the fourth anniversary of that sunny Saturday morning when Florey had walked across the University Parks in Oxford to where Kent was waiting with the eight Swiss albino mice.

When the battle for Europe was over, Florey commented, while delivering the Lister Memorial Lecture at the Royal College of Surgeons in London,

In the use of penicillin in war surgery there has been an evolution. The really important point ... is the recognition that there exists an antiseptic beyond the dreams of Lister—an antiseptic which can be applied through the blood stream as well as by appropriate local means, one immensely powerful against many pathogenic organisms, but, at the same time, harmless even to very delicate tissues, and one fully active in surroundings where the sulphonamides fail.

DURING THE THREE MONTHS FLOREY SPENT IN THE NORTH African war zone, the notion of the wonder drug had gripped public imagination and had won high development priority in industrial, academic, government and military circles. When he and Cairns returned to England early in September 1943 weary from the months of travel and work in the heat of the African summer, he found a new surge of urgency breaking over his life like a tidal wave, flooding every waking hour with demands on his time, his energy and his experience. No one else could take his place for a while, not Raistrick, Fleming nor any single person in his own team; his position as a scientist was such that the burden of power rested on him as it had never done before, and he found himself swept into the most strenuous period of his life.

The pressures were remorseless; reports and meetings with the War Office on battle surgery; meetings with hospital and medical authorities, and with the Medical Research Council to discuss its plans to establish new research units; talks with the people inside his own department on whom he came to depend so heavily: Chain, urgently seeking the crystallization of pure penicillin and searching for other substances on the new frontier of antibiosis to broaden the attack on disease. Heatley, Sanders, Abraham and Dr Margaret Jennings were all carrying extra burdens to keep the penicillin work moving, to maintain the teaching function of the Sir William Dunn School, and to share the search for new materials from moulds, plants and bacteria. The snail's pace of the British industrial effort brought Florey disappointment and dismayed him, and there were many meetings of the penicillin committee with little sign of hope that large supplies would soon be flowing. It soon became plain to Florey and his colleagues that the country would have to depend on American generosity when the great battles began in northern France. The progress was so poor that Winston Churchill was urging that 'as big a supply as possible should be obtained from America', and then, still later, voicing his disappointment that 'we are to get only about one-tenth of the expected output this year'.

Late in September 1943, the British Prime Minister, President Roosevelt and Premier Stalin met in Teheran for their last meeting before the invasion of Europe. There, the three leaders gave their final approval to arrangements made by the Joint Allied Commission for a visit of an Anglo-American mission to Russia. These plans included the visit of a group of four scientists who would give the Russians the benefit of new advances made in Britain and America in a number of scientific fields. One of the main subjects to be passed to the Russians was the development of techniques and the clinical application of penicillin. The selection of Florey as the leader of the two British members of the team placed a new strain on him and led to his suffering his first bout of pneumonia since leaving Adelaide in 1921 and which put him into a Middle East Hospital for several weeks.

The secret journey to Russia commenced on 23rd December 1943—three years from the day when Norman Heatley had coaxed the small service van over the hundred miles of black ice to Oxford with the crude ceramic pots clinking behind him.

Florey had been told by the Medical Research Council, via Mellanby, that he could 'take one other person with him' on this confidential mission to Russia, and he chose Dr Gordon Sanders as his companion. Dr Sanders recalled, 'He asked me if I would like to go and told me that he had been very busily gathering material on about ten different matters of medical science, other than penicillin, and that we would be carrying mould samples and also some of our best purified penicillin extract.'[1]

The diplomatic negotiations which had preceded Florey's selection of Sanders as his companion necessitated approval on the highest level and were conducted with the strictest war-time secrecy. Their documents were prepared and diplomatic arrangements were made for the handling of the baggage and the valuable written research reports and penicillin samples.

Florey and Sanders slipped out of Oxford in the early hours of 23rd December, and boarded a train for London at 2.30 a.m. The carriages were packed with hundreds of soldiers who were all merry—drinking, smoking and happy to be going home for Christmas leave. The two medical scientists felt outsiders in their civilian clothes and they sat on their suitcases in the cold, draughty corridor, unable to find a seat. It was foggy and still dark when they disembarked in London at half past six. The car sent by the Foreign Office to meet them carried them off to the Air Transport Command office in North Audley Street. Without further rest they were rushed through the formalities, and then were sent on their way to Hendon where a service aircraft waited to carry them north to Prestwick in Scotland. But Hendon, when they arrived, was fogbound. Cold and tired, they kicked their heels for an hour or so and then, with no sign of the thick fog lifting, returned to London. They booked in at a London hotel, while the Foreign Office made alternative arrangements for their journey to Prestwick, and in the late afternoon went to a cinema to see a Korda film, which neither of them liked, and a documentary on the islands of the South Pacific, which they both enjoyed.

At half past eight that evening they boarded a train at Euston station. After spending the night in warm, comfortable sleeping compartments, they reached Kilmarnock in Scotland just before eight in the morning on Christmas Eve 1943. It was a day of cutting cold wind and mists, and they spent it waiting at Prestwick airport—from just before nine in the morning until they eventually took off into a winter night in a big, four-engined bomber, heading out over the Atlantic in an enormous dog-leg flight to avoid contact with German fighter aircraft stationed in north-west France. It was Sanders' first flight and was a grim, uncomfortable introduction to air travel, with the coarse-sounding propeller engines roaring through the night until they reached North Africa more than ten hours later, landing at Marrakesh soon after four in the morning. As they climbed down on to the runway in the dark, Florey muttered a tired 'Happy Christmas' and they fell into the seats of a waiting car which took them to a nearby hotel, to hot water and a splendid breakfast. 'All those wonderful things to eat again,' wrote Sanders. 'Eggs and bacon, and sausages, butter and rolls. Then, alas, it was over and we had Christmas dinner that day in a hot barn of a place at Algiers. It consisted of sandwiches and coffee, paid for by an American because we had not been provided with suitable money. We were at the airfield at Algiers because we had to take off again in a different aircraft at three in the afternoon and there was no time to go to the local military mess.'[2] They flew across the vast North African battlefield—over Tunis and Libya and south of Tobruk, now all quiet after the great battles and the remarkable siege—and landed at Cairo, at twenty minutes after midnight.

The local security authorities would not risk installing them in an hotel. Instead they were taken to a guarded military barracks and slept there for eight hours while their luggage and documents, and the precious mould samples, were in safe keeping at the British Embassy. On their one day in Cairo, Florey made contact with Pulvertaft to ask about recent results in the battle casualty testing of penicillin. Pulvertaft, then just back from tending Churchill during his illness at Carthage two weeks earlier, at first suspected that Florey was present in the Middle East to pursue the question of penicillin having reputedly saved the life of the great war leader.* Pulvertaft suggested to Florey that he might lecture on his penicillin work while in the Middle East and Florey asked Sanders to write to Dr Margaret Jennings for films and illustrative material to be sent out.

In the evening of that day, Florey and Sanders went out to the military airfield and took off on their journey to Teheran by the

---

* Recounting his story many years later Pulvertaft said he had been called to Carthage when Churchill returned from the Teheran conference suffering from a sore throat and chest pains which turned into a severe bout of pneumonia. Pulvertaft had been called to make the pathological tests for Lord Moran, Churchill's private physician who was also, coincidentally, a former dean of the medical school at St Mary's where Fleming worked. Pulvertaft said, 'When I learned that Churchill had pneumonia I suggested to Lord Moran that he should use penicillin, but he had never had experience with its administration, and was quite adamant. It was never true that penicillin saved Churchill's life on that occasion. He was saved by sulphonamides, and fortunately so, because I had no penicillin on hand which I could be sure was non-toxic.'

indirect way via Abadan in the Persian Gulf, refuelling at the air-force centre at Habbaniya. Diplomatic officials explained to Florey that the diversion was being made to avoid flying over the mountainous regions to the north. They spent the day in Abadan and in the evening linked up with the two members of the American half of their mission—Professor Baird Hastings, who had attended the historic meeting on penicillin called by Newton Richards in December 1941, and his companion, Dr Michael Shimkin, an American-born son of Russian parents who spoke Russian fluently and so proved invaluable in the weeks ahead.

They travelled to Teheran where they were told they would have to wait for the Russians to make the decision on their flight into Soviet territory. 'They told us that the Russians would only allow their own planes to cross the border and that civilians would only be flown if the weather was suitable,' said Sanders. They had to wait several days. It was very cold in Teheran and Florey became ill. He complained of breathing trouble and pressure on his chest, and he told Sanders if necessary Hastings and Shimkin would have to go ahead. The American Hospital at Teheran was well provided with equipment and highly qualified staff, and Florey's chest trouble was soon diagnosed as bronchopneumonia; it meant they could not leave Teheran for some weeks but Florey was determined not to face a heavy schedule in mid-winter in Moscow until he felt he could stand the rigours of the tour.

At the end of January, Florey said he was able to travel and he and Sanders were put into the hands of the Russians who treated them as very important people. They climbed into a DC3 (which their escort proudly claimed was built in Russia) and set off for their first fuelling stop at the Baku oilfields. They then flew to Stalingrad, and on to a snow-bound Moscow airport where the British Ambassador's car was waiting to take them to the National Hotel where they were installed in a big suite with bedroom cubicles and a bathroom.

The four weeks they spent in Moscow were packed with events and entertainment. Their escort was Professor V. V. Parin who held some power as a Party commissar and spoke excellent

English. There were formal opening occasions. On one of these, a visit to the Soviet Academy of Sciences, Florey handed over a letter of greeting from Sir Henry Dale, president of the Royal Society, and presented the Academy with a valuable old book. Along with these official functions there were the visits to the Bolshoi ballet and the opera—all a delight to Florey.

Much of their time was spent at the Institute for the Bio-chemistry of Microbes and Immunology (known to the Russians as VIEM), a centre of advanced studies under the stern discipline of a woman scientist, Professor Yermolieva, who proudly showed them cultures of a Penicillium mould, which she identified as *P. crustosum*, but which was later identified as *P. notatum*. Florey recorded that, following the interest aroused at VIEM by the Oxford papers, and by the reports in *Lancet*, a young woman biologist, Dr Kaplan, had noticed the mould growing on the wall of an air-raid shelter during a German attack on Moscow. She had cultured this mould and had shown, before the British and American scientists arrived, that it had antibacterial activity but that—as Sanders recorded in the notes for the Royal Society and the Medical Research Council—the activity was slight and the Soviet workers had been unable to extract the active substance. What Dr Kaplan had found was a poor relation to Fleming's old mould, and a very distant cousin to Mouldy Mary's cantaloup strain in Peoria; but it was enough for Russian pride and earned the Stalin Prize for Dr Kaplan.

Sanders said, 'We often went to Yermolieva's laboratory and worked with her and Dr Kaplan, and helped them get the work on penicillin moving ahead. It was all new to them in the sense that they had never ever got a method of extraction going, so had not obtained effective supplies for tests.'[3]

Florey presented the Institute with samples of the dried mould he had brought with him and spent many days teaching them the principles of extraction, while Sanders taught the method of assay which Heatley had devised. Then, one day, Florey was asked to go to a Soviet military medical clinic to demonstrate the use of penicillin against infected wounds. Among the cases he selected was a young Russian officer whose left leg had become infected after amputation. He taught the principles of the approach to

surgery, the culture and identification of the infecting organism
and proof of its sensitivity to penicillin, and then demonstrated
the two methods of attack—topical and systemic. He spent several
days treating the young soldier, taking part at one stage in the
surgical procedures in the operating theatre, and when the time
came to leave Moscow to return to the West, Florey claimed a
'very solid improvement in the young man's condition'. The
septicaemia had been overcome and the wound was healing and,
although the chief Russian surgeon, Professor Rufanov, said he
would inform him—and he did receive some notes on his way
back to Teheran—the final outcome of this first Russian penicillin
treatment was never made known to Florey.

The crowded visit to Moscow absorbed Florey's energy but,
in Sanders' view, he stood the 'solid pace set by the Russian's
hospitality' with fortitude, despite his recent illness. He felt he was
rendering a service that was valuable to both Britain and America,
countries the Russians then loved to call their 'glorious allies'.
More than that, he seemed to revel again in the role of teacher and
instructor, and enjoyed the task of giving the Soviet scientists the
fruits of work done in the West. The British Ambassador, who
was a close friend of Hugh Cairns, rated the visit highly. Besides
the all-important discussions on penicillin, he reported that the
passing over to Russian sources of the details of work on blood
transfusions and substitute plasmas—in which Sanders was the
expert—and the data on the anti-malarial compounds—including
atabrine which had been developed because of the lack of quinine,
due to Japanese occupation of the East Indies—had made the
Anglo-American mission to Moscow a valuable contribution to
friendship between the allies.

But when it was over, Florey thankfully turned his back on
Moscow, glad to be going back to Teheran and to some days of
relaxation. But in Teheran he found a full itinerary had been
arranged by local academics and medical workers. Among these
was Dr Zoriassatein, of the Pasteur Institute, who produced a
mould culture which he had under study and which, like that
given to Florey from the Moscow air-raid shelter, was cultured
later by Pulvertaft and identified as *Penicillium notatum*. Florey
prepared a script for lecturing with the films and slides which

Margaret Jennings had sent him, and this was framed so that translations could be given by interpreters after each sentence and illustration. He delivered the lecture and then flew to Cairo where, again, he spoke to audiences in several centres, including the Anglo-Egyptian Society and Pulvertaft's colleagues at the Scottish General Hospital. At the urging of the British Council representative, Professor Boaze, who was also president of Magdalen College, Oxford, they travelled on to Beirut to lecture, and then went back to instruct the members of the Jerusalem Medical Society and to lectures at the Hadassah Hospital.

Florey was also enticed to go to the Weitzman Institute, as a very honoured guest, and spent some time there talking on penicillin and the development of antibiotics. From there, the two scientists returned to Tel Aviv and flew over the Sinai Desert, back to Cairo and to warmer weather. They talked with Pulvertaft again and Sanders worked on the reports of the mission to Russia at the Mena House Hotel, praising the 'deep and wide knowledge Florey had shown on medical matters and his unfailing kindness and friendliness'.

The work done, the two took a tourist's holiday. They caught a train to Luxor and went sightseeing, studying the treasures and the ancient Egyptian relics, Florey employing his camera on every occasion and relishing his break like a schoolboy. It lasted exactly three days and then he became anxious to get back to Oxford. They flew from Cairo to Casablanca, and after a day lolling about in the sun, boarded a military aircraft for the return to England. They had left on Christmas Eve and were away exactly three months, one of which Florey had spent in hospital and recuperating in Teheran.

As the spring of 1944 unfolded across Britain bringing the prospect of the invasion of Europe close, Florey returned to his laboratories to find thrilling news from America of the development of the investigation into the nature of the penicillin molecule and of the drug's effectiveness against the scourge of syphilis.

In the laboratories in South Parks Road, Chain and Abraham had pushed on with the purification, vital to their work on the

chemical structure of penicillin. This work was done in close
collaboration with Robert Robinson and his colleague, W. Baker,
at the Dyson-Perrins laboratory, and with the crystallographers
along the street led by Dr Dorothy Crowfoot.* Because of the
critical importance of this study, and since it could lead to synthesis of the drug, the Lord President of the Council had imposed
a ban on publication of reports in 1943, so the results were
circulated privately. Other workers had joined the files, notably
those at the Imperial College of Science, and, soon afterwards,
the first clues on the nature of the wonder drug appeared. Then
came word that rapid progress had been achieved in purification
by teams in America; and Coghill, who was in Oxford as the
American 'co-ordinator without portfolio', brought news to
Chain at Oxford that Drs H. B. MacPhillamy and O. Winteres-
teiner, working at Squibb's, had isolated the first pure sodium
salts of penicillin. Coghill recorded that meeting with Chain in
the Dunn Laboratories,

> Chain took the news with good grace. He was, however,
> completely unable to understand the data which came with the
> information. The elementary analysis was quite different from
> his best preparations, which he considered to be essentially
> pure. Furthermore, the Squibb ultra-violet spectrum de-
> finitely indicated an aromatic ring, this absorption being
> completely absent in Chain's preparation. Chain placed his
> amorphous preparation on a microscope slide and we each had
> a good look at it. No crystals: we discussed the whole perplex-
> ing situation for the better part of the afternoon with Chain
> pacing his laboratory. Every once in a while he would stop
> and look through the microscope. At one of these stops he took
> a mere glance, and shouted, 'It's crystalline!' We each took
> another look, and, sure enough, long, beautiful needle crystals
> had taken the place of the powder of an hour or two ago.
> Chain was excited and elated—and justifiably so. In retrospect,
> we know the answers to what happened that day.[4]

* Later to be Dr Dorothy Hodgkin, who won the Nobel Prize for Chemistry
in 1964.

Penicillin had been induced to reveal itself—not as a single type of molecule, but one with several faces and each face with a slightly different nature. What Chain and Coghill puzzled over was solved when it was shown that the British and American penicillins were different—not all that much different, but not quite the same; and the apparent differentiation came from the growth of the mould on American corn steep liquor. The central feature of the molecule, as it appeared, was called by Coghill 'a four-member ring which had never before been found in natural compounds, a structure which explained why it was so unstable'. Twelve years before these events, the molecular brittleness of this ring had defeated Raistrick's attempts to extract the salts of penicillin ... 'it was labile and did the chemically impossible of vanishing into thin air', he had recorded. But, in the different penicillins which emerged in America and in Britain, the ring remained the central unchanging feature; it was the side-chain which was different.

This was the beginning of the exciting prospect of fashioning the molecules by changing basic nutrient ratios. It opened the way to broadening penicillin's action against disease organisms as well as to changing the side-chain so that it could avoid defeat by the enzyme, penicillinase, which some offending bacteria were able to produce to destroy the activity of penicillin. It was the dawn of the semi-synthetic penicillins, and the so-called 'tailor-made' antibiotics. The wide range of antibiotics which Florey had mentioned in his letter to old Sir Charles Sherrington two years before, was suddenly beginning to emerge.

Within penicillin itself the field was also beginning to widen and new types of penicillins turned up in both countries—one of them, known as Penicillin X, was discovered by Dr Frank Stodola at Peoria—each with a slightly different action, some more stable and resistant to acid, and some excreted more slowly from the body. Alongside these new and exciting advances Florey and his team were probing further into the new country of antibiotics. Heatley summed up this period of work by his chief, 'Florey continued to work personally on biological aspects of penicillin and other antibiotics and to supervise clinical trials of various kinds. He extracted, and crystallized claviformin, and took a hand in the detection, extraction, and assessment of several others . . .'5 It was the building of a vast new edifice of science and it sprang from the demonstration that the first antibiotic was not a simple antiseptic, as had been supposed by the pioneers, but a chemotherapeutic in the real meaning of the term. Florey noted at the time that a great outburst of research had followed penicillin's discovery, and he commented,

> Workers who had abandoned the field years ago again became interested; and it was not long before the air was filled with the cries of those wishing to join the new experimental 'Gold Rush' and to secure what had previously been abandoned . . . I cannot help feeling that Lister would be mightily amused to see the army of eager enthusiasts now stretching out suppliant petri dishes in the hope that they will receive some miraculous therapeutic manna![6]

Florey maintained that this situation had not been reached by any flash of insight on anyone's part, but from the conscious choice at Oxford of penicillin, from among a number of known antibacterials, plus the 'good fortune that this was the first substance to be shown to be non-toxic to man'.

In the 'gold rush' that followed the discovery of penicillin's true nature, the pure crystals allowed scientists to view the structure of this wonderful substance. The 'yellow magic' of the imaginative writers had gone. It was shown to be a mere yellow pigment and was as useless as prontosil's red colouring. By the grace of fortune, it was also a pigment so harmless to man that it did not hide the bland face of the first and greatest, antibiotic behind a shield of poison. The power of penicillin therapy lay in those crystals which were looked at for the first time in America and Britain almost simultaneously. They showed a beauty of regularity surpassing most crystals which, when penicillin was produced in quantity, lent it the now characteristic pure white, luminous glow.

The prospect of penicillin becoming available for general medical practice was drawing closer as American and British factories pressed their production figures higher under the stimulus of the pending invasion of north-west Europe. In America, the War Production Board had formed a Penicillin Producers Industry Advisory Board to organize the supply of the drug to civilians and had posted to the job of committee chairman the same energetic Mr Fred Stock who had driven drug industry executives frantic with his demands in the previous two years. Mr Stock devised a plan taking in one thousand hospitals in which the first civilian penicillin would be available. In London, in that month of May 1944, the *Lancet* was also forecasting similar moves in England. But not until after 1945 would the domestic doctor, the general practitioner in both Britain and America attain the wizardry that penicillin brought to his profession.

In May, the same month as the *Lancet* article, Florey was given an indication that his new eminence in the profession had been marked elsewhere and that, with his concurrence, the 1944 recommendations from Winston Churchill to King George VI would include that of Professor Howard Walter Florey. He was to be knighted.*

Congratulations came to him from many people both in high, and obscure, places. Some came from academics who had smiled at 'Florey's Follies'—growing moulds in the Oxford laboratory in 1940—and to one of them was attributed a remark made during dinner in college at the time when the first clinical trials were under way and the urine was being carried, bottle by bottle, back to the laboratory for re-extraction processing. Tongue in cheek, the academic had observed, 'My fellows, you should learn about Florey's penicillin. It is a remarkable substance. It is grown in bed-pans and is purified by passage through the Oxford Police Force.'[7]

Now the don was congratulating Florey on an honour which no scientist achieves without being one of the outstanding minds in the profession. Outlandish Florey's experiments may have appeared to outsiders at the time, but the makeshift penicillin-growing factory in the Sir William Dunn laboratory solved, in the end, one of the most vital problems in science.

* The publicity this caused inspired a farmer in Scotland, convinced of the antibacterial value of his oat-bran to send Florey a raw herring wrapped in the bran to prove it would kill the bacteria and allow the fish to stay fresh.
16

But the days of the world's first penicillin factory, established in Florey's laboratories in Oxford, were now numbered. The struggle to produce the few thousand litres of mould broth, the few million units of penicillin activity sought since the effort began in 1940, was ended and commercial production was under way.

The drug industry was churning out a torrent of penicillin and the Medical Research Council had set up its own penicillin centres to deepen and broaden the knowledge of how the drug could be used in medical practice; in Oxford, Edinburgh and other centres, groups of leading minds had been turned to the chase for the chemical structure and possibilities of synthesis—a citadel that was gradually receding as the superb technical ability of the American engineers turned Mouldy Mary's cantaloup strain, and its derivatives, to full account and the product steadily fell in price. The time had come to dismantle the ingenious devices contrived by the Oxford team.

In the former animal room and the other accommodation which the penicillin paraphernalia had occupied, the apparatus, the equipment and the makeshift extraction units were all pulled out. Piping, bottles, wooden frames and the hundreds of valves and receptacles were thrown on a junk heap to lie disregarded for their place in historical medicine, at the back of the Dunn building near where, five years earlier, the scientists and technicians had dug their own air-raid shelter.

The hundreds of precious ceramic rectangular bottles which Heatley had transported so gingerly on the icy roads were dumped into a private garden, and that first galvanized tin bath, used in the frantic early days, was filled with soil. The laboratory-cum-factory turned again to its original task of concentrating on the search for undiscovered territory in the microworld where there might lie hidden substances that would extend the fight against disease.

For Florey it was a change in pace; a time of pause; a time that might have been given to reassessment of the kind he had practised with Chain in 1938. But, instead of this, the pace became more hectic and the pressures continued to grow with demands for his service. He grew tense and irritable and little events disturbed him more. In his forty-sixth year, his sixth year since he started the penicillin project, with all its pressures, he was feeling the strain of constant effort.

To some of his colleagues he appeared not to have recovered completely from the illness he suffered in Teheran followed by the rigours of the winter schedule in Moscow—despite the three days' holiday in Luxor. He also seemed, suddenly to some of them, to be a lonely man. Ethel was entirely engrossed with her dedication to the application of antibiotics to healing, building a formidable card index that was to be the foundation of her own book on this subject.

Despite his inclination to irritability, he took a possessive pride in his team and what they had accomplished; and he did not hesitate to record their place in the history of the development of medical science techniques. He said, publicly, in that year of 1944,

> To work on the metabolic products of moulds from biological to chemical aspects needs a team of specialized workers . . . and it was most fortunate that such a team was available in Oxford. I should like to stress—so that there can be no doubt on the subject—that this work would not have been carried through so quickly had it not been for the unremitting labours of the following people:
>
> Dr Chain, Dr Abraham, Professor Gardner, Dr Heatley, Dr Jennings, Dr Sanders, Dr Fletcher, and Mrs Florey. Nor could we have got far without the work of . . . Mr Glister and his 'penicillin girls', Mr Kent and, for some chemical work, Mr Callow and Mr Burtt.
>
> The body of work done by this team . . . produced a single end result—penicillin as a proved chemotherapeutic drug.[8]

When he learned one day that Heatley had been considering the offer of a post with a prominent drug firm in Britain, he became annoyed and, confronting the quiet scientist in the corridor, he rasped out, 'What's wrong with you, Heatley? Aren't you satisfied with us here anymore? Why did you consider taking this job?' Heatley tried to explain that he thought his days of useful application in the penicillin task were over and that there would not be much else for him to do at the Dunn School, but Florey would not have that. 'There will be plenty to do here for a long time to come. You know how hard it is for me to get good people these days. You can stay on—but only if you want to!' Heatley saw the emotion in him and sensed the feeling he had for his group. Another who saw that same emotion was Dr Fletcher. Walking through a hospital in Hammersmith he met Florey unexpectedly. Florey's face lit up with friendly recognition, and he said, 'Those days were wonderful days, Fletcher. We none of us can expect to know that kind of excitement again. That sort of thing can only happen once in anybody's lifetime.'

Many years later, Fletcher remembered the words when it had happened to Florey the second time—when a new antibiotic came out of his laboratories to counter the growing resistance building up among bacteria.

Almost simultaneously with the confidential notice that he would be named a knight in the King's honours list that would precede the invasion, Florey received the first summons to his native land. In London, where he had been attending a meeting of Commonwealth leaders to discuss with Churchill the coming strategy of war and the problems of peace, the Australian Prime Minister, Mr John Curtin, asked Florey if he would visit Australia as soon as possible to advise military and civilian doctors on the latest developments and uses of penicillin. If he would please come, Curtin's message said, Australia would be privileged and proud; arrangements would be made with General MacArthur, the Pacific commander, for his transportation.

Florey had thought his war journeys were ended; but he could not refuse, although he had already spent six months of the past year abroad and knew that another long journey—across the world in military aircraft—would certainly be strenuous. He informed Curtin, through Dr Evatt, the Australian foreign minister, that he would come as soon as he could.

But first there were important meetings of the research groups; and he wanted to be in England for the start of the Second Front, to hear the first reports of penicillin used in massive doses in prevention of disease in wounds. He had administrative tasks still to attend to in his office in South Parks Road, Oxford, several research projects operating on a collaborative basis with members of his team, and papers to be written for publication.

In the midst of his preparations for the Australia journey, he was informed that the Americans had asked that he should visit some of the military hospitals in the Pacific and lecture on penicillin, and he agreed. Because of this there were only two days left in August when an American bomber flew him over the scars that Japanese air attacks had left in Darwin, Australia's northernmost town. Howard Florey was back in Australia after an absence of eight years and a month of rocking and bumping in an aircraft from post to post in the Pacific, a long schedule of talks, and demonstration and film showings, all of which had ended in a tour of hospitals along the recently reoccupied north coast of New Guinea.

He had been to Madang, to Alexishafen and to Lae, and there he saw for himself the results of penicillin application to wounds in a jungle war theatre. He saw the results of penicillin produced in Australia and heard for the first time the rough details of one of the outstanding achievements in the world story of penicillin. He also learnt that his visit to the Pacific had originally stemmed from the strong urging of the Australian commander-in-chief, General Sir Thomas Blamey, who had been pressed by his army medical advisers to ask the world's greatest authority on penicillin to revisit his homeland to give them his advice and guidance. 'He will be asked to give Australian authorities the most recent information on the subject,' said Curtin. 'Sir Howard Florey's visit will be of inestimable value and will lead to the saving of many lives in a period when Australian treatment is to a certain extent still experimental.' The politician framed the words, but it was the Australian Army's medical administration talking, and it was from there that had come the action which led to Australia —and by the time Florey arrived this had been achieved—becoming the first nation to produce sufficient penicillin for all its military and civil requirements, and still have some left over for American soldiers fighting in the south-west Pacific.

CHAPTER 16

AUSTRALIA'S ACHIEVEMENT IN GAINING AN INDEPENDENT supply of penicillin is one of the outstanding stories in the history of the development of the drug.

The first step in this direction was taken in October 1943 when Major Percival Bazeley, sitting in an armoured tank in northern New Guinea, was brought a message from army headquarters in Melbourne. For two years he had trained with the tank squadron which he now commanded and, as the Australian 5th Division moved through the heavy terrain of the Huon Peninsula, and the 9th Division—of Alamein fame—operated on the heights overlooking the Markham Valley, Bazeley felt the strong urge to take part in his first tank battle.

The army message did not bring the order to move into action; instead, it asked him to return to headquarters to begin preparations to investigate the possibilities of penicillin production. They did not want him to go into battle; they asked him to go to America instead—and he demurred. 'So they had to order me to go,' Bazeley recalled. 'They hustled me out of the north and down to Port Moresby in an old Lockheed bomber and, after spending the night in a hangar there, we took off at dawn for Brisbane.'[1] There, the army's sense of urgency came to a brief halt because someone had failed to order priority on travel and Bazeley spent the next two days in a train covering the twelve hundred miles to Melbourne.

In Melbourne he met his assistant, Lieutenant H. H. Kretchmar, a chemist, and the two were immediately dispatched back to Brisbane. They boarded an American bomber which was returning to the United States and flew out over the Pacific Ocean to

224

open their investigation into the possible production of penicillin
in Australia.

The man who decided to remove Bazeley from the pending
battle in the Huon Peninsula was Colonel E. V. Keogh. Later
an eminent figure in Australian medicine, Dr Keogh gave his
reason for selecting Bazeley,

I knew Val Bazeley from the time he had worked in the
Commonwealth Serum Laboratories. He was a veterinary man.
Not a doctor, nor a medical scientist, although he later took a
medical degree. But I knew he had courage and was a determined man and that he had a great flair for organization on a
large scale. Bazeley was the man to whom Australia owed its
penicillin, and after, when he became director of CSL, to whom
it owed its polio vaccine; but for neither of these things did he
get much credit, either from the public or the government.[2]

Early in November, Bazeley and Kretchmar arrived in San
Francisco, having flown a nerve-racking journey by way of
Samoa, Christmas Island and Hawaii. 'The Americans were
wonderful to us and helped us in the most open fashion and in an
entirely free-handed way,' said Bazeley. He and Kretchmar went
to the big firms—Merck's, Squibb's, Abbott's, Pfizer's—and
travelled to Peoria to talk with Coghill and his team, and then
on to Washington to confer with the Australian scientific attaché,
Mr Neville Whiffen, who arranged further visits to penicillin
production centres.

It was the high tide of bottle production in the United States
and Larry Elder had yet to force the decision to go to the huge
deep fermentation tank method. Bazeley and his companion
were sent off by Whiffen to see the bottle production plant at
Wyeth which was run by the Reichel Laboratories Company—
at that time America's largest producer of the drug. Bazeley
recalled the visit.

It was a strange thing, but it turned out that the successful
man in this organization was Mr G. Raymond Rettew who
operated the plant because he had acquired a lot of knowledge

of fungus from his personal interest in mushroom production.
He had adapted these mushroom methods for growing the
Penicillium fungus on the surface of an arrangement of glassware, and his system of extraction was very simple and very
effective. As soon as I saw this, I said that this was the method
we should use in Australia. Kretchmar had his doubts about
this, but I felt sure it was right and this was what we used.
I took full notes of all that Rettew did, and then went back to
Peoria and obtained samples of the strain of mould which had
been found in the Peoria market place. When I saw all this, and
what we had, I knew what we could do. I knew the potential
at the Serum Laboratories and I knew what was possible. We
turned for home and got back to Melbourne early in December.
There was no question of anyone leaning on me and I had good
collaboration. I knew that there were big shows being planned
for battles against the Japanese in the north and that penicillin
would be wanted badly for our soldiers, especially when the
attack on Borneo got under way.

Bazeley calculated all that would have to be done, and then,
after a precise review of his calculations, set a target date of full-
scale penicillin production at the CSL. The date was a mere six
weeks ahead.

'We simply worked like beavers to get this system going,
growing the mould in sufficient amounts, and extracting, and
then improving the purification techniques. One man, Harold
Cochran, was of great help, but everybody there worked hard,'
Bazeley said. Dr Keogh did not use the analogy of a beaver for
Bazeley. 'He was much more like a tiger, and only his drive and
his bite drove it all through in the allotted time.'

In the feverish atmosphere that filled the Commonwealth
Serum Laboratories in December 1943, each hour was stretched
to its limit and every day saw a distinct advance; not a worker
faltered in the knowledge that their product would save the lives
of men then fighting in New Guinea, under conditions which
Winston Churchill recorded as 'the worst faced by any troops in
the Second World War'.

In these first few weeks, the initial experimental batches of

Penicillin being cultured for clinical use in ceramic pots at Oxford, early 1941 (*Sir William Dunn School, Oxford*)

Heatley's Heath-Robinson apparatus for counter-current penicillin. When the level of crude penicillin broth fell in the gallon-sized lemonade jars at the top of the former Bodleian Library bookcases the bell on the right sounded, and the electric light showed (*Sir William Dunn School, Oxford*)

Surface culture of penicillin in 120,000 bottles at Abbots, Chicago, 1943 (*Ward C. Morgan Studio, Kalamazoo*)

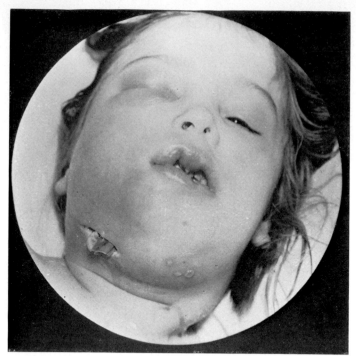

The first child to be treated with penicillin by Dr Wallace Herrell of the Mayo Clinic. The first (above) was taken on 10th January, 1943; the second (below), after treatment, was taken on 4th February, 1943 (*Abbots, Chicago*)

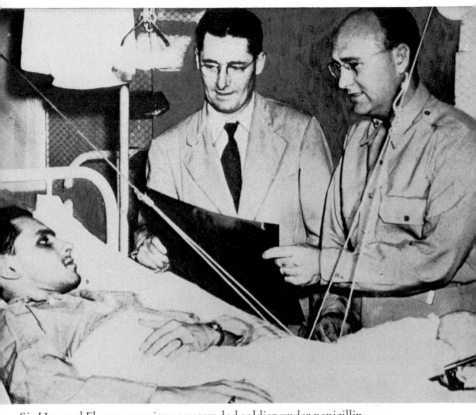

Sir Howard Florey examines a wounded soldier under penicillin
treatment in an American military hospital, near New York, 1944
(*Keystone, London*)

The Nobel Prize Festival, Stockholm, 10th December, 1945: Sir
Alexander Fleming (second from left), Dr Ernst Chain (centre), and
Sir Howard Florey (right) (*Keystone, London*)

Sir Howard Florey receiving the Royal Society's Gold Medal from Lord Adrian, President of the Royal Society, 1951 (*Keystone, London*)

Declaring open the John Curtin Medical Research School,
Canberra, 27th March, 1958. Front row, from Florey's right: Dr H. C.
Coombs, Sir Robert Menzies (Australian Prime Minister), Sir Hugh
Ennor (Dean of the School). To Florey's left: Dr Clive Evatt (Leader of
the opposition) (*Sir Hugh Ennor*)

powder came out of the production system and, after bacteriological sampling, the vials were flown northward to test the behaviour of the Australian penicillin in a tropical zone, and its performance under conditions as rigorous as any yet faced.

Savagery from endemic difference in race, behaviour and temperament marked the bitter conflict of the Pacific war; and hatred born out of the cruelty of the Japanese left no room for chivalry, with almost entire garrisons being destroyed with little talk of surrender. Yet, in the steaming jungles, and in the squelching mud of the Kokoda Trail, the real enemies of the allied forces were the teeming bacteria which fastened on to any exposed flesh, from a scratch to a gaping shell wound.

Incredible suffering was encountered in the super-heated, tented casualty stations, and there the skilled surgeons and those dedicated women who nursed the wounded so close to the firing lines were always fighting a desperate battle against infection.

Colonel Charles Littlejohn, later to be knighted, was the commanding surgical officer for the area and he came through the jungle one day to the forward casualty station, the 2/3rd, which was treating soldiers from the 5th Division. It was close to Christmas 1943, and the colonel carried a few of the first vials won by Bazeley's work in Melbourne. In that casualty station Colonel J. Ellis Gillespie was in charge, and the nursing sister was Miss J. M. Langham; but the central figure was a young soldier whose wounded left arm nourished an enormous colony of *Staphylococcus aureus*. The man's arm was as big as his thigh and was bursting with the infection that threatened his whole system with septicaemia. Under those conditions he would have soon been a dead man.

I can remember our deep concern at this first penicillin patient. His left arm was so very tender and discoloured, and his pulse was very rapid and his temperature was high. Under Colonel Littlejohn's instruction we administered the penicillin in conditions as aseptic as we could make them. We all wore masks, there in the jungle, and I sterilized the instruments by boiling them over a primus stove. I remember clearly the dramatic result from the injections of that first day. The swelling subsided, and all other symptoms faded away to normal as the toxaemia quickly decreased. I think it was in another four or five days that all danger had gone.[3]

Miss Langham could recall it all three decades later; so, too, could the people in other stations to which Littlejohn carried those first vials from Melbourne—at Guy's Post, where the Red Cross installed a kerosene refrigerator to keep the drug as cold as possible; at the base hospitals where one surgeon was Dr Hugh Barry from Sydney, a former Rhodes scholar who had worked with Florey in the Dunn building in Oxford seven years earlier.

Barry was attached to the 2/5th Australian General Hospital as a surgical major. 'It was there I saw for the first time the clinical application of penicillin on which Florey had worked after I had left the Dunn School,' he said. 'I was working with the late Colonel Renou and Colonel Buchanan, both from Melbourne, and we were all staggered when we saw the effect of penicillin on war wounds. I remember in particular an enormous wound of a buttock which was sewn back into place and several tubes were inserted into which penicillin could be instilled. This wound healed by first intention which we regarded as quite miraculous.'

With Bazeley meeting his self-imposed schedule by the beginning of February, Colonel Keogh was able to arrange for three doctors, with extensive campaign experience in surgery and treatment, to open a wide-ranging study of 140 different types of cases at the Heidelberg military hospital in Melbourne, which provided the guideline for regular army medical practice. He chose Major R. Officer, who had been a senior surgeon in civilian life, Major John Lowenthal, later to be Professor of Surgery at Sydney University and Dean of the Medical School, and Captain J. W. Perry, who handled the bacteriological and chemical work.[4] More than a quarter of a century later, Professor John Lowenthal—the only surviving member of that original team—vividly recalled the first military trials of penicillin therapy in Australia.

We had been on the lookout for a really suitable case to try this new drug on and we found him this winter day in Heidelberg Hospital. He was a subaltern, quite a young fellow and I don't know that I ever knew his name. He was down on leave from New Guinea, which was excuse enough for anybody, and he probably had been on a bit of revelry and had slept out on the grass in Albert Park in Melbourne, and it was winter, remember.

He was sick, very sick with pneumonia, and we gave him about 15 000 units every four hours, and within a day he was better! We couldn't believe it! We simply couldn't accept that this could happen. I had used sulphapyridine and other sulphas and I knew what they could do, but this was different. It seemed unbelievable. But we went on to try the drug out elsewhere. We had to do it quickly and thoroughly because we knew this big Borneo campaign was coming up. I knew from experience in New Guinea that you could be wounded up there and not get help for days, and we wanted to work out some way that we could protect these men while they were being brought back through the mountains and along the jungle tracks; we had to know how, and what, and at which levels they were to be given penicillin protection. We did 'wicked things'—to ourselves, as well as to about 140 of our patients—to find out what we wanted to know![5]

The Australian army medical authorities had acted with speed and without hesitation; and, ten months before Florey arrived, civilian clinical workers in a Brisbane hospital acted with the same characteristic decisiveness. In October, when the army medical authorities were taking the first steps to initiate penicillin production by sending Bazeley and Kretchmar to the United States, Queensland University's Professor of Pathology, J. V. Duhigg, and his assistant, Dr David Grey, began growing their own Penicillium mould in large amounts, and, refusing to be baulked by the total lack of purified penicillin, had decided to inject the crude mould brew, roughly filtered, into a human being.

It was a step Fleming had not taken in 1928 at the height of his faith in the mould juice, and one which could have transformed medicine a decade earlier.*

In Brisbane, Duhigg and Grey took this step. It was one for which Florey had condemned Pulvertaft in the Middle East, but it was one which, while taken in desperation at the absence of supply of properly purified drug, was eminently successful. The Brisbane scientists were courageous men; but not fool-hardy, nor were they blind to the value of life. Their first patient was a woman dying of septicaemia. She had no other hope and was close to death when they pumped a massive injection of 300 cubic centimetres—near to half a pint of the mould broth—into her faltering bloodstream in November 1943. The hospital physician, Dr M. Greany, worked with them and later presented a little-known paper on the case. On some occasions they injected as much as 600 cubic centimetres of the mould brew and each time her temperature fell. They had no control over dosage in terms of Oxford units, but they estimated each injection ranged from about one thousand units upwards. In all, they injected about two thousand five hundred cubic centimetres of the yellow mould juice filtrate—which Fleming had initially called penicillin—into the veins of the forty-two-year-old Brisbane woman. Although this could not have amounted to more than twelve thousand units, they saved her life and weeks later she was sent home to her family. In all, the Brisbane doctors treated a total of thirty-two cases with this crude substance, losing a few lives, but saving many. But then, so fast was the Australian action to reach production, it was no longer necessary to resort to the use of this crude material.

It was against this background that Florey, nervous and dark-eyed with exhaustion, reached Melbourne in August 1944 to find

* The second Lady Fleming herself hinted at what this could have meant, when, in a letter to a United States Senate hearing in December 1961, she wrote, in her contention that money and lack of support prevented Fleming from proving the value of penicillin in the late 1920s, '... Yet, in spite of these repeated efforts, some fourteen years had elapsed before it could be used for treatment of human beings, years during which thousands of patients, who could have been saved, died. Why? ...' Why, indeed?

a crowded itinerary arranged for him. He was intensely proud to be back in his homeland, honoured and successful; but he was a little dismayed at the pressures of public life which suddenly confronted him, and impulsively he stated that he would make no public appearances.

Reporters who recorded the statement noted the way he 'continuously twirled a cigarette in his slim fingers and replied with the precision of a practised lecturer'. He told them, 'My time here is very limited and it is important that I devote it to lecturing medical people on the correct use of penicillin.'

One correspondent at that brief confrontation with the press, wrote,

'Little of the publicity which has been turned on the new drug has fallen on Sir Howard Florey, the man directly responsible for its development. Until his arrival here few Australians realized that he was born in Adelaide.' Noting that Florey made little effort to change this state of things, the reporter added, 'An innate reserve makes him vague on personal matters. Asked about his young son and daughter, he could not recall their ages and said they "were about ten years old".'

His meetings with the press were thereafter avoided as far as possible, but his lectures attracted doctors from across the continent. When he talked in Sydney, doctors who had travelled many miles to hear him lodged a severe criticism that they could not get into the Union Hall. The organizers replied that this was a monthly meeting which normally drew attendances of about thirty doctors; on this occasion all 500 seats were filled and the aisles packed to overflowing. Florey also went to Melbourne to talk with Keogh and Bazeley on their penicillin operation, and, while full of praise for their speedy accomplishment, and acknowledging their product to be of high standard, his feeling of nationalism led him to protest.

As Keogh remembers, he was quite explicit, saying, 'Why the hell did you go running off to the Americans; am I not Australian? Have I not had some leading role in this thing? Why was I not asked, or even approached for help or advice?' He could not easily accept their reasons that they had little time to spare in the full flush of the war in the north. He believed he had been slighted by his own countrymen, but, as the tour went on, the hurt faded away into new friendships. He had meetings with his former colleague, Professor 'Pansy' Wright, and meals with Bazeley, at one of which he was suffering from a sore throat which he treated with his own penicillin preparation. He had vials of the drug with him, he said, which he had taken to Russia; nine months later its activity was quite undiminished.

At the end of September he flew to Adelaide, and the visit gained a more personal flavour. His sisters, Hilda and Valetta, waited to greet him and attended the ceremony at which the university conferred on him the degree of M.D., 'in recognition of his distinguished contributions to medical science'. He stood again where he had stood as a graduate in 1921 to take his M.B., B.S., and he was cheered to the echo when speaking on the development of medical science. He mentioned the lack of opportunity which had driven many young Australian scientists to work overseas.

The time has come to mention whether Australia can afford to lose its bright young people; whether it is not time to take a leap forward in scientific research. I note that Dr F. M. Burnet, of the Walter and Eliza Hall Institute, has called the amount of work done here 'insignificant' because young men go to England to work. I have the greatest confidence that the leap can be taken here, and that, within a few years, Australia will have centres that compare favourably with those overseas. Then Dr Burnet's remarks will be out of place.[6]

It was a brief speech, but soon afterwards it bore fruit and stimulated official action.

The students and the women's organizations fêted him, and his sisters were especially proud. They had evenings at which it was forbidden to mention the word 'penicillin', and he called on Molly Bowen and went again to look at 'Coreega'.

While in Adelaide he was delighted to hear that a local firm of manufacturing chemists had taken the plunge into penicillin production of its own volition, without any urging or prompting from either government or military.

The firm, F. H. Faulding and Co. Ltd, had become interested in the Oxford reports and in 1943, obtained a sample of Penicillium mould from Dr Nancy Atkinson, a lecturer in bacteriology at Adelaide University, who had been experimenting with the growth of the mould for some time, having obtained a transfer of the fungus from England. She had supplied the firm with the data on mould growth, on corn steep liquor, and on the method of extraction, using amyl acetate and a high speed centrifuge to produce a sodium salt by resorting to the use of low temperature in high vacuum.

Florey was met by an executive of the firm, Mr E. H. Phillips, and he spent an entire morning talking to the staff on production methods and clinical application. 'I suppose it will make me sound a little parochial,' he told Phillips, 'but it is a thrill for me to find the drug being produced commercially for the first time outside of Britain and America right here in the city where I grew up and went to school.'[7]

The firm had had its *Penicillium notatum* mould growing before Bazeley came back to Australia with the Peoria cantaloup strain; but the claim to growing the first mould in Australia for production of penicillin broth rested with the Brisbane workers, Duhigg and Grey, who had opened their pioneer clinical work in November 1943.

When his time in Adelaide was finished, Florey went back to Melbourne to talk with university people. Whilst there, he was asked to meet Dr H. C. Coombs,* an emissary from the Prime Minister, who sent a request that was to figure largely in Florey's activities for the rest of his life.

Coombs asked Florey if he would consider writing a memorandum for the Prime Minister, Mr Curtin, giving his views on the establishment of a medical research centre of high calibre in Australia. Could it be done with the success needed for its continuation and could it be sited in the national territory at Canberra where the national parliament was located? Florey promised

---

* Dr Coombs, a small man with cool blue eyes, was destined to hold a prominent place in Australian affairs and eventually to succeed Florey as Chancellor of the National University which had then, in 1944, not yet been envisaged.

that it would be done when he returned to Oxford, saying that he felt privileged and honoured.

Later in the year he wrote the memorandum to the Prime Minister, stating emphatically that Australian graduates were as talented as any in the world and that, therefore, there could be no question but that a research institution of the highest calibre would be of value to the nation. He also said he saw no reason why such a centre should not be based in the small capital city of Canberra, which had every prospect of growing to a large metropolis. His proposals for the institution advanced the concept of departments dealing with basic medical science subjects, and this was eventually followed in the establishment of the John Curtin School of Medical Research. He wrote his views, and why he held them, not seeing the pattern that would develop from them. But, as always, he made the point that such an undertaking must be funded adequately or it would be best left alone.

EARLY IN OCTOBER FLOREY BOARDED AN ARMY BOMBER and endured the long flight across the Pacific. He stayed briefly in the United States for fact-finding visits and courtesy calls and then crossed the Atlantic in an uncomfortable clipper flight to Lisbon and on to Bristol, along that corridor which had been so dangerous when he and Heatley had travelled to America in 1941.

Exhausted from his long travels, Florey immediately found himself the centre of a controversy which had arisen out of the tidal wave of penicillin publicity. The name of the drug had by then entered everyday language across the earth, its slim syllables being fitted into thousands of newspaper columns and Florey, despite his deep aversion to publicity, found himself caught in the limelight which was already transforming the life of Alexander Fleming. He was flooded with requests to appear on platforms to explain the development of penicillin.

In America, too, public debate surrounded Florey's name and his activities, and Chain's former doctoral assistant, Epstein— now a serving medical officer with the adopted name of Falk— entered the lists to dispute the misconception, widespread in America, that the work of Dr René Dubos on soil organisms at the Rockefeller Medical Institute in 1939 had stimulated the Oxford group into their penicillin undertaking. Falk was affronted by this impression since he had worked on the early penicillin research while a student of Florey's (who, in 1938, had assigned him his doctoral thesis under the title of, *The actions of certain bacteriolytic principles*). Florey himself was too busy to bother with this misconception, though he found the inference hurtful that he had known all along of the wonderful power in

the Penicillium mould and had only tackled its development
because of competition with Dubos and the needs of war.

Falk wrote about his objections to the *American Journal of
Medicine*. He stated that the penicillin work had started in Oxford
a year before the lysozyme project was closed down and a year
before Dubos announced his gramacidin results. 'With Professor
Florey's permission we (with Chain) cultivated the mould and
made a few preliminary tests, but as is often the way with these,
they were not very impressive.' Both he and Dr Chain had begun
to 'share Professor Florey's interest in antibacterial substances in
1937', he declared, and that it was lysozyme which had led to
penicillin—not Dubos, nor war. He also stated that when they
came on the little-known paper by Fleming and were impressed
with its potential they found 'it difficult to understand why the
study of penicillin had lapsed for nine years'.

Then, among all the civil clamour for release of penicillin
supplies for individual treatment in the United States, came the
Fosdick statement. This comment by the President of the Rockefeller Foundation, Dr. Raymond B. Fosdick, placed Florey in the
centre of a controversy that lack of faith and foresight had given
away to American industry the greatest single discovery in the
history of medicine.

Fosdick's comment in the Foundation's 1944 annual report was
that the grant of $1 280 made to Florey for chemical work in
1936 had led to the discovery of therapeutic penicillin. In a thin
parody of Churchill's Battle of Britain phrase he said, 'seldom has
so small a contribution led to such momentous results'. He
continued, 'Professor Florey later asked for $5 000 for a year's
support—a sum immediately put at his disposal—and by the end
of 1940 he was able to write to this Foundation, "There is good
ground for hoping that this substance will be much more effective
than the sulphonamides, hence the prosecution of the work is of
the utmost urgency and importance." A second grant of $5 000
was made.'

By itself, the Rockefeller Foundation annual report did not
cause more than minor comment, but it was picked up by a
London newspaper, *The Evening News*, and John Wynden told
the story of 'how the Americans gave us the wonder drug,

penicillin, which we, in our ignorance of the truth, claim as an entirely British discovery.' In his review of Fosdick's report, Wynden stated,

> Here, I say, we have a clear statement on the manner of how penicillin was made ready for public use. Have you noticed the absurdly small sum which Dr Florey first asked for and received? Now, I cannot help thinking that research in this country must be shamefully starved if an Oxford professor, for a paltry sum of less than £500 for sensational research work, has to go to the United States with a request for aid. I have read in various organs of the Press complaints about the way penicillin has been taken over by the Americans. But, if I am to take the facts as stated by the Rockefeller Foundation report, our allies have a perfect moral right to exploit the discovery which only their financial support made a practicable affair . . . Why was it necessary, however, to wait for an American body to come and do the research? Money again. But look . . . at our immense loss of prestige?

Wynden, along with others who were critical, did not know that when Florey had asked urgently for £100 in September 1939, for chemicals to open the work on penicillin growth and extraction, the Medical Research Council had told him he 'could assume he would get £25'. Instead, the outspoken head of the MRC, Sir Edward Mellanby, attacked Fosdick's claims in unvarnished terms. 'It is grotesque—simply grotesque to claim that a grant worth little more than £320 in 1936 should have led to penicillin,' he fumed. At once he was receiving telephone calls from both government sources and media, and he soon had officials preparing figures to show that support of Florey's activities over the years ran to many thousands of pounds.[1]

This led to Mr John Dugdale rising in the House of Commons to ask if it were true that an American grant to Florey in 1936 had led to the research on penicillin. This question enabled the government to tell the House that since 1927 Florey had received a total of £7 000 to aid his researches. Again, no mention was made of the bitterness Florey had expressed in 1939 when he came close to throwing up his post at Oxford, angry at being termed a 'bushranger of research' and an 'academic highway robber'. Nor was any mention made of the fact that he had only turned to American sources after full consultation, and with the agreement of scientific authority in the persons of Sir Edward Mellanby and Sir Henry Dale—both confidential advisers to the British government. The fact that he had been given official permission to go and seek help in America was ignored; nor was much attention paid to the fact that British soldiers in Europe had been highly dependent upon American penicillin supplies.*

At about the same time as this controversy was being discussed on both sides of the Atlantic, Florey became involved in another when British interests collaborating in the joint penicillin project found many of the processes were the subject of patents lodged with the United Kingdom Patents Office in London. Among the names making these applications, disclosed on 31st May 1945, was that of a scientist who had been researching on problems of the agricultural industry until Florey and Heatley had arrived at Peoria, Illinois, in the summer of 1941, with the fundamental data on penicillin. They had handed it over with the proviso that any benefit that accrued should be shared between the Peoria establishment and the Rockefeller Foundation.

The name of the scientist who lodged patent application numbers 13674–6 was Dr Andrew Moyer. He sought to claim the rights for the use of additions to the penicillin growth media, covering corn steep liquor, lactose, phenyl acetate and other chemicals.

This revelation was seized upon by critics of the decision which had led Florey and Heatley to take their penicillin discoveries to the United States in 1941; and Florey became the centre of a rising tide of recrimination, which roused the anger of many people, that British industry should pay royalties for the developmental processes of a British discovery. Both pride and profit were involved; and it became easy, in the absence of evidence

* In the last year of the war US factories poured out 20 times the amount of penicillin produced in Britain. US production for 1945 was 587 698 million Oxford units against 26 000 million in Britain.

that the Medical Research Council had been consulted and had concurred on both the question of patents and the need to enlist American resources, to berate Florey and to allege that 'he took penicillin to the Americans and handed it to them on a platter'.

Disclosure of Moyer's hand in the London patents came as a shock to the Oxford team, but it did not surprise Dr Norman Heatley. He had spent six months in close association with Moyer in Peoria and had seen at first-hand the secretive behaviour of the American scientist. Even disregarding Moyer's reputation among his colleagues at Peoria, Heatley had experienced an unfortunate incident with Moyer. Before he had left Peoria, when the extensive work that led to industrial production was over, Heatley had agreed to author a joint paper summarizing the experiments and the results, and, when this was completed, he had handed it to Moyer who said he would go over it and then arrange for a copy of the corrected version to go to Heatley at Merck's at Rahway. The draft never arrived and Heatley saw the details he had compiled two years later in a published report which did not mention his name. The British scientist had no interest in personal gain from his work, so did not take up the issue.

With the staff working under Dr Coghill in Peoria, Moyer had a reputation for toughness, for being devious and a 'most difficult character'. A senior member of that staff said of him,

He was exceedingly suspicious and difficult to work with. However, Andy was a product of his background. He was driven from his farm home in Indiana at the age of fifteen by his stepfather. On his own he worked his way through high school, college, and on to take a Ph.D.—and that takes guts! Those years of privation and mistreatment made him what he was. So—when he had a chance to make money on penicillin— he did it ... the work on which his patents were based was done very early, historically, before the rest of the Fermentation Division at Peoria was involved; so Moyer owed nothing to anyone except Heatley who was working there in his lab at the time. But, knowing Moyer, I am certain he never let Heatley know exactly what was going into the media. I don't want to be his judge, and it should be emphasized that he had every legal right to those patents. Steep liquor was his idea and he tried it first. The government regulations required that all patents made by employees should revert to the people, through the Secretary, but the right to seek foreign patents was left with the employee, to be undertaken at his own expense. Moyer did this and, I believe, became quite rich. Others of the staff did not and remained quite poor.[2]

At the dinner given in his honour by the drug industry in New York in 1945, at which he received the cheque for $100 000 to use in support of research, Fleming expressed his distaste that a great discovery, freely given to the world, should be traduced by people seeking personal profit from patents; and Dr Charles Thom, the mycologist who had helped set the trail to Peoria, reportedly stated, 'It is doubtful to my mind whether any of the patents applied for represent valid claims to originality.'

Also, in the wrangling which these events produced among British scientists and administrators, it was almost forgotten that had Florey and Heatley not gone to Peoria, there almost certainly would not have been ample penicillin on the battlefields in the last year of war.

Florey withdrew into a noncommittal posture. He said nothing in public but privately he confessed to friends at having learned a lasting lesson.* The stricture of Mellanby and Sir Henry Dale early in the war that 'the people have paid for this work and should have the benefits made freely available to them' no longer applied.[3]

Despite Florey's reputation for blunt and forthright speech there were elements of shyness deep in his character, and the publicity bandwaggon, which rolled along with penicillin, rubbed a raw nerve. On this aspect of Florey's disposition, Dr Norman Heatley wrote, 'It is paradoxical that behind the easy and outgoing personality that made him such a genial companion there lay extreme modesty, the very existence of which might not

---

* This lesson, in the end, was to earn Britain tens of millions of dollars annually with the later discovery of a wide-spectrum antibiotic from Florey's Oxford laboratories.

have been suspected. It showed itself in his horror of the Press or of any kind of personal publicity and his avoidance of personal topics in conversation, even with those he knew quite well.'[4]

In Florey's mind it was quite wrong for any scientist to seek the limelight; the researcher's place was in research; and the offence was compounded when it was accompanied by ill-judged statements and claims which had no basis in fact. On these grounds he was bound to be annoyed and exasperated by Fleming's performance as a public figure. Fleming's careless claiming of Mrs Anne Ogden Miller in America as his 'most important patient', and his airy treatment of the gap of neglect between 1932 and the later Oxford work, offended him. But, while he was caustic and sardonic to associates about Fleming, he did not indulge in public disparagement.[5]

At first he agreed to making several joint public appearances with Fleming and he used these to lay his own claims to truth while in Fleming's presence. Hence his words when he spoke of holding out suppliant petri dishes to catch therapeutic manna; and, at the Royal Society of Arts in London, he stated bluntly, 'In 1940, the first observations on penicillin were published . . . up to this time the real nature of penicillin had escaped detection.'[6]

The legend that Fleming realized and foresaw the importance of penicillin as a systemic chemotherapeutic agent was also discounted by Professor E. P. Abraham in a biographical memoir on Florey written in 1971 for the Royal Society. He also rejected the claims that Fleming had been frustrated by the lack of chemical support and by Sir Almroth Wright's opposition. Abraham wrote, 'This supposed explanation of his inactivity is scarcely credible.'

In his analysis and review of the events Abraham went on,

. . . Fleming was deterred by the difficulties of isolating penicillin and quickly lost faith in the idea that it might find a place in medicine, since he said in 1940 with reference to its earlier use as a local antiseptic, that 'the trouble of making it seemed not worth while'. Five years later he remarked 'and now after various ups and downs we have penicillin'. This summary of the work of others in a short and somewhat infelicitous phrase served to strengthen Florey's belief that little attempt was being made to present the story in its true perspective.

Indeed, Abraham noted, the publicity relating to penicillin caused Florey considerable agitation at the time and he remained sensitive to this even after he became more tranquil in his later years. And when, after the end of the war, Florey was asked to write a review of the penicillin phenomenon for the now-defunct *Oxford Magazine*, he wrote,

In 1929 Fleming published his observations on a mould subsequently identified as *Penicillium notatum* which had the power to stop the growth of a number of bacteria which cause disease in man. The substance responsible for this action was present in the broth on which the mould grew and it was suggested that this crude broth—to which the name penicillin was given—might be of value to apply locally to septic infections much in the same way as chemical products and antiseptics such as pyocyanase had been used before, and, indeed, a few patients were so treated without, however, any very striking results.

No experiments on animals infected with susceptible organisms were performed, and as the activity of the substance appeared to be easily destroyed, Fleming did no more towards its introduction into medicine.

Attempts made in 1929 and in 1932 to extract the active substance failed and the experiments were not pursued as at that time penicillin's remarkable combination of properties and its real potentialities were not appreciated.[7]

The differences in the character and the strengths of the two men were wide, and while Florey rebuked the media for gross distortion, dramatization and disregard of the truth, Fleming tolerated fallacy without much protest. He was often the victim of total misrepresentation. On one occasion this man of small stature with a large head and an unimpressive style of speech was described as a man of tall imposing presence with a voice of distinction. He was even credited with saving a boy in a lake in Scotland from drowning—a boy who grew up to fame as

Winston Churchill—a tale still given currency despite the fact that Churchill was much older than Fleming. The victim of a publicity campaign organized by a British government anxious to capitalize on the discovery, the bacteriologist smiled and shook his head but did not protest.

Later in his life when speaking with the one-time member of the Oxford team, Dr C. M. Fletcher, he gave the doctor the impression of a 'scholarly little man who was rather hurt at the lack of recognition for his work among his fellow scientists'.[8]

In the public image which Fleming adopted, however, an historical summary in the reports of the British Medical Research Council shows him revelling in the public gaze,

> When the work of Florey and his colleagues eventually brought penicillin as a boon to mankind, Fleming rightly received his share of public acclaim and the many honours this brought—Nobel Prize, knighthood and much else. He thoroughly enjoyed—and why not?—this late phase of his working life; and he travelled widely to receive honorary degrees and other awards. Once, in Spain, when he was walking in procession from the graduation ceremony to a bullfight, members of the crowd fell to their knees and kissed the hem of his latest colourful robe—he later resented a cynical suggestion that he had been mistaken for a new cardinal! There was, in fact, a tribute, reaching the Council through diplomatic channels, to Fleming's value from the public relations angle.[9]

Fleming's predicament should have been revealed to Florey when a letter dropped on to his desk in Oxford, soon after the end of the war, from the Appeals Committee of St Mary's Hospital. However, instead of exposing to Florey Fleming's position as a victim of the modern machinery of publicity, the letter left him tight-lipped with indignant anger.

He showed the letter to many of his associates as an example of the distortion of the story behind penicillin development. Dr Fletcher, calling into the office in South Parks Road, was handed the letter to read. He later said of this occasion,

I don't recall the exact wording, but it went something along
the lines that everyone had heard of the benefaction that had
come from the discovery of penicillin and that this wonderful
gift had been made possible by Professor Sir Alexander Fleming
at St Mary's Hospital, Paddington. The organizers had no
doubt that Professor Florey would like to pay his own tribute,
along with other people, and so a theatre première had been
arranged and seats would cost two guineas each. After I had
read it, Florey told me that he intended to put the letter on
display.

Professor Brian Maegraith was also shown the letter. It was
thrown across the desk to him as Florey growled, 'And what do
you think of that piece of impertinence?'

'I told him without hesitation what I would do with it, but he
told me he was having it framed and that it would hang in the
foyer of the Dunn building. I understand that he did this and it
was hanging there for some time for everyone to see—with no
comment attached at all.'

It was in this atmosphere, when they appeared together on a
platform in London, that Fleming told an audience,

'It seems to me that the fates have willed it that Professor
Florey and I shall be associated, although we have never worked
together.'[10]

Soon, however, they were thrust together, along with Ernst
Chain, into the full glare that came with the Nobel Prize for
Medicine, a shared award that not only failed to bring amity but
which, in fact, widened the rift between them.

So extensive had been the promotion of Fleming, that in the
early stages of the examination of credentials for the first prize to
be awarded for medicine after the war—and there was no challenge to penicillin—it was widely forecast that it would be
awarded solely to Alexander Fleming. The selection of the
awards followed the usual rigid pattern. Institutions and a few
unimpeachable people around the world made their nominations
—and these all went through the process of argument by the
appointed people from Sweden's centres of learning. By October
1945, the main papers were in for discussion, and the final recom-

mendations to the *Nobelstiftelsen* and the General Committee were being made, when a news leak said, in effect, that strong pressure had been exerted for a single award to Fleming.

A later president of the Nobel Institute, Professor Arne Tiselius, in a comment on the sharing of the Nobel Prize, made this observation, 'This often calls for much inside information which is always difficult to obtain—and there is, of course, always the danger of injustice in sharing a prize equally between two or more candidates. It is all done secretly, of course, but there sometimes are leaks of information . . .'

This particular leak went even further; it reported that there was a question of a compromise and it had been suggested that Fleming should receive one-half of the prize and that Florey and Chain should each receive a quarter share. None of these reports or implications, were ever confirmed or denied, since this was against Nobel practice. In the end, the general committee ruled for an equal sharing of the prize between the three men.

In Stockholm, on the days preceding the presentation, the ritual of press conferences saw Fleming holding the limelight, and it was plain that the legend of Fleming being vindicated in the end after ten years of crying alone to the world was accepted, even in Sweden. While Fleming held several conferences, Florey and Ethel drove out to Uppsala University and spent the time at luncheons or lecturing to the students at the medical school.

Following the awards, the banquet at the Palace, and the Ball in the huge gold mosaic room in Stockholm's *Stadhuset*, the laureates gathered on 11th December at the University to deliver their Nobel orations. In his address, Fleming looked back to the discovery of the mould and spoke of his observations and the long period of inactivity that followed.

Had I been an active clinician I would doubtless have used it more extensively that I did therapeutically. The work started as a chance observation, and it was a fortunate occurrence; and my only merit is that I did not neglect that chance observation and pursued it as a bacteriologist. The first practical use was to sort out bacteria that were sensitive from those that were not. We tried to concentrate it but found, as others did later, that it was easily destroyed—and to all intents and purposes, we failed.[11]

Florey, on the other hand, spent little of his time looking over his shoulder at the past, but, in a masterly treatise, held open the door for his audience to glimpse the unfolding of the age of antibiotics and the revolution they promised in medicine. Penicillin, shown to be a systemic agent, had stimulated an outburst of investigation across the world, he said, and great interest was centred on the action by which the moulds and the other organisms produced the substances active against bacteria.

A thorough knowledge of this may bring with it the ability to construct—as it were—tailor-made chemotherapeutic agents for use against every type of infection. From a still wider point of view, the clear definition of these antibacterial substances may help us to understand the ceaseless struggle for existence which is waged by micro-organisms everywhere.

Referring to the outcome of his struggles in the mid-1930s, Florey said, 'These investigations were characterized by successful collaboration between chemists and those with biological training and knowledge. That, to my mind, was the crucial point and explains why up to that time so little had resulted from examination of a multitude of inhibitors.'[12]

His recognition of the credit due to his team was thus expressed in the full light of the Nobel assembly, and for the rest of his days he acknowledged the debt to others and to the fortune which fell on them all in this project; but among that team were men and women who also recognized that the concept he had determined to follow, the leadership he had given, and the problems he had overcome, had been the essentials to success.

Florey and Ethel returned to Oxford to spend their first Christmas with their children for five years, and he found an awkward gap with a boy rising eleven whom he had hardly known since he was five, and a strong-minded, teenage daughter of fifteen replacing the little girl who had gone to America at the start of the war. Ethel followed her usual ritual of driving in her small car with presents for the children of the staff members of the Dunn School, and then, when the holiday was over, returned immediately to her tasks as a clinical worker at the penicillin centre which the Medical Research Council had installed at the Radcliffe Infirmary. Two professional people bent on their own careers, they went into the post-war years acutely aware that the new age of medicine had only just opened and that they were, both of them, leaders with a place to maintain and challenges to meet.

FLOREY'S FIRST YEARS AFTER THE WAR WERE IN SOME WAYS his best years—busy, bustling and full of incident. There was nothing soft about these times, and there was little that was reflective—these qualities did not come until age and failing health slowed him down. In this post-war period he filled out as a man of power and influence and quiet assurance while still at an age where he could remember clearly the years of angry frustration.

He accepted membership of the Medical Research Council, became an adviser to the Minister of Supply, and was attached to the Nuffield Medical Research Committee. All these appointments gave him more influence on the various funding and academic organizations to sway opinion on how money should be spent.

With the new posts and appointments came the spate of honours, some of which he prized; others he took, or rejected, as a matter of form. The gold medals and honorary medallions he received were formed into a collection and later sent to the Ashmolean Museum in Oxford—and there were the many doctorates and honorary degrees recognizing his scientific work and its outcome for humanity.

These stemmed from many centres, in many countries, so that when he chose to accept he was obliged once again to go on his travels; often his staff would know nothing of a new award until he was missing from his place in the office or at the bench. Very few of the recognitions seemed worthy of comment to him. The French made him a Commander of the Legion of Honour and he was thus able to see his friends again in the Pasteur Institute; the American Congress awarded him the US

THE PRIZE AND THE PRICE

Medal of Merit; and the British Royal College of Surgeons in its annual selection of the outstanding scientist in the world at the time selected him to receive the famed Lister Medal and to deliver the Lister memorial lecture. The gowns, and the scientific acknowledgements, were draped round his shoulders, but he insisted constantly that enormous luck had attended the discovery of therapeutic penicillin and that only the co-operative dedication of a team of combined skills had made its application a reality.

He took the honours as they came and tried in every way possible to share them with the men and women at the Oxford laboratories with whose efforts his own work was irrevocably interwoven. At the height of the flurry of appreciation he would still not leave his Oxford tower for long. There, for all the members of the team, for Ethel, as well as Florey himself, the years of the new peace demanded considerable adjustment. When the veils of war secrecy were eventually drawn away from their work, and the true extent of the science that had been employed became apparent, the scientific community was able to see the brilliance of the whole project—in which, said one commentator, 'not a single experiment was wasted, so perfect had been Florey's planning'. Much of the Oxford team's work was hidden from the public eye by Florey's reticence and aversion to personal publicity—and by the glaring spotlight that fell on Fleming—but their feats became bywords in the world of science.

Yet at a time when the possibilities that lay ahead in antibiotic therapy were sensational, and the pharmaceutical monoliths were hungry for the brains and the skills that would push their ventures ahead further and faster than their competitors, the Oxford team remained together. Some of the names at the heart of the penicillin story, for instance, Robert D. Coghill and A. N. Richards in America, found themselves heading commercial projects and undertaking, but, in the Dunn School at Oxford, the break-up did not come until Chain moved away, in high dissatisfaction, to a new fermentation pilot plant centre in Rome in 1948.

In the face of the flow of tempting offers that came to different members at various times, the resulting unity under Florey's leadership was astounding; and thirty years after their monumental task the names of the majority of leading participants still showed on the indicator board in the entrance hall of the Dunn building . . . Sanders, Heatley, Abraham, the former Dr Margaret Jennings, while the faithful James Kent was still engaged in his laboratory duties. The flair for leadership and the sense of obligation that was deep-rooted in Florey showed in this unity, as it did in other ways during the post-war years.

In the early days the atmosphere of 'we band of brothers' at the Dunn School might have been expected, yet the spirit was the same two decades later when Florey still argued and campaigned for the people whom he felt he represented. He led them, guided them and saw that justice was done, so that they all came to look on him as a champion; and in the early post-war years he was accessible, ready to listen and to be an advocate, and to break tension with a wry joke; and they knew when he tried to hide kindness behind a gruff manner as he had with Chain in the difficult days in the mid-1930s.

This period of his life brought him some relief from personal financial problems, but did not change his careful attitude towards money. He would often take pleasure in showing some member of his group how to cut costs in some way, and Heatley recalled him holding him to one side at a meeting and saying in a confidential manner, 'Something you'll be interested in, Heatley. I've found a shop in London where you can get three pairs of socks for the price of one—I'll write the address down for you.' Heatley said, 'To the end, he lived only on his salary of a few thousand a year and most of his journeys were made on funds provided by some organization or foundation.' Professor Wright recalled, 'He could have earned quite a few thousand every year from National Health Service consultation fees, but he never could spare the time.'

However, soon after the end of the war, when penicillin was still held in an aura of wonderment in the public mind, Florey was given the opportunity of acquiring a fortune which he could have used as he wished; but he refused this without hesitation because he felt the tributes should go to the whole team. The great British philanthropist, Lord Nuffield, attempting to express a public debt, wanted to hand over £50 000 to Florey as a personal gift with no strings attached. Professor E. P. Abraham described Florey's reaction,

'He did not hesitate. He declined the gift and suggested that the money should be used instead to set up a fund to make several research fellowships—not tutorial—available at the Dunn School. It was used to do just this, and several fellowships were started paying a few hundred pounds a year for workers here.' They went, in fact, to Abraham himself, until he became a professor, and to Heatley, Sanders and others.[1]

This same sense of obligation to his associates motivated him when the Lasker Foundation of New York sought to reward him as it had the staff of the Peoria laboratories for their part in the penicillin development. He referred the question to Magdalen College and, after some debate and differences, a commemorative rose garden was planted in front of that college, with a stone tablet engraved to announce that it was presented by the Albert and Mary Lasker Foundation of New York. The inscription reads,

> This rose garden was given in honour of the research workers in this university who discovered the clinical importance of penicillin.
> FOR SAVING OF LIFE, RELIEF OF SUFFERING, AND INSPIRATION TO FURTHER RESEARCH, ALL MANKIND IS IN THEIR DEBT.
> Those who did the work were: E. P. Abraham, E. Chain, C. M. Fletcher, H. W. Florey, M. E. Florey, A. D. Gardner, M. A. Jennings, J. Orr-Ewing, A. G. Sanders.

Yet even as the fame of penicillin reached its height, deaths by reaction to the drug, and an increasing number of reports from around the world of patients failing to respond to treatment, began to shake the confidence of the medical profession in the drug, and to raise new issues and doubts about its use.

As these isolated incidences appeared more frequently and doctors in different countries commented on puzzling cases which failed to respond to even the most massive doses of penicillin, so the apprehension and fears which Florey had expressed in the war years—'penicillin is no cure-all . . . its use has to be carefully controlled . . . there is no reason to assume that penicillin will work in cases in which we have had no experience . . .'—took root and grew into deep concern among medical scientists.

In the very early work in Oxford, Professor Gardner had shown that under-dosing with penicillin had a startling effect on the size of the pathogenic agents, although Florey had maintained that with adequate dosage in living forms there was no chance of bacteria developing a protective system against penicillin's molecular attack. The disturbing reports increased until there was no longer any doubt that bacteria had evolved which had the ability to avoid the drug's action of breaking down their walls.

Over thousands of culture plates and test tubes the worried medical scientists sought the answers, and among many reports came one from the American workers, C. M. McKee and G. Rake, that the pneumococcus could build resistance to doses of penicillin up to thirty-two times as strong as the original application.

As the picture began to take shape, it brought the frightening possibility that a strain of *Staphylococcus aureus* could riot through patient after patient in hospital cross-infections, growing in savagery and virulence in the same way as had the bacteria passing through the bodies of batches of experimental animals in the early penicillin experiments in Florey's laboratories.

More than any of the other strains which emerged as immune to penicillin, the staphylococcal germ became dominant until the common name of 'Golden Staph' took on the same ominous ring which the fatal infectious illnesses had held in the days before penicillin. It was reasonable to assume that the bacteria were learning to live with the new substance and that this had been brought about by the vast numbers of penicillin units injected by tens of thousands of doctors around the earth in a joyous display of new power over a wide range of common sepsis and other ailments.

This picture was soon shown to be an illusion. The cause was, in fact, due to the extreme effectiveness of the widely used penicillin G substance, the commonly produced type of penicillin which had been derived from Mouldy Mary's rotting cantaloup.

It had been so proficient, so effective, that it had defeated the teeming bacteria with no inherent resistance to the penicillin molecule and had left enormously extended living room, fields without competition, for the odd mutant strains able to reverse the chemical warfare and destroy the penicillin structure. This they did with the ability to produce the enzyme, penicillinase, which, in effect, cleaved the central ring structure of the penicillin molecule from its side-chain making it inactive.

With the public warnings he had uttered as early as 1944, Florey had recognized there were holes in the penicillin shield and that its use should not be indiscriminate. But it was still a discouraging shock to him, so soon after the revolution which had been achieved with war wounds, to find medicine was again facing the threat of an enormous problem of infection from pathogens which defied the strongest penicillin—and not only defied it, but destroyed its ability to act against other sensitive agents in the same living system.

At the time of this developing anxiety, he spoke to groups of doctors and to medical gatherings in Britain and North America of the concern the new situation had brought; and these were the days when clinical centres were the main focus of the infections, before the untouchable bandit bacteria spilled out into domestic medical practice.

He told a group of Canadians,

Hospitals are bacteriologically dirty places. This is one of the reasons for the spread of the kind of diseases which are now giving us great concern. There can be little doubt that the prevalence of bacteria resistant to antibiotics is due primarily to the fact that surgeons, nursing staff, and practically every one who attends the patients, may be carriers of these organisms. These people pick up the resistant strains of organisms and transfer them to other patients, and it now becomes very clear that we must tighten up the precautions against cross-infection.[2]

The final solution, however, could only come from the development of antibiotics with new and broader striking power, and, he told his audiences, even when this was achieved, there would still be need of wise and carefully controlled use of the drugs. It should never be possible that the individual patient could go to the chemist and buy his antibiotics as he would a packet of aspirin.

But, even given new antibiotics, there was a further complication in the growing recognition that, while penicillin was non-toxic and hundreds of times the necessary dose could be given without severe reaction, this did not apply to all human beings. This was the new, nagging worry, the recognition of allergic reactions to penicillin which could range from skin blemishes to severe shock, and, in very rare cases, to death. In keeping with the recurrent pattern of scientific discovery, the new knowledge had revealed further problems beyond those solved, problems of greater depth and complexity. There was no ready and easy explanation to this situation as there had been when the first person injected with a partially purified penicillin injection in the Radcliffe Infirmary in January 1940, had reacted with a sudden and severe rigor. This puzzling situation appeared world-wide and one in about every million patients, in India as well as Australia and America, could succumb to the biological breakdown which the profession called 'anaphylactoid shock'.

In America, the anxiety was strengthened when a survey showed that one in every two hospitals had experienced a reaction to penicillin, and among sixty severe reactions one in three had been lethal. It was soon established that as many as 10% of people treated with penicillin G showed reactions, ranging from the very slight to that of shock ending in death.

The problem of reaction was most serious in America. This was due not to a local epidemic or use of penicillin containing toxic impurities but entirely to the volume of supply available and the readiness of physicians to use penicillin G which was the most stable, the easiest to handle, and the type that maintained a blood level longer than any other penicillin.

It soon became clear that penicillin G, as well as the less common earlier types, imposed limitations. The drug had shown what American scientists termed 'fantastic capability . . . and had brought unprecedented control over the diseases of pneumonia, pharyngitis, staphylococcal infections, syphilis, gonorrhoea; but, with continued use, it became apparent there were drawbacks to even this miracle drug'. The drawbacks rested in the configuration of the side-chain that was attached to the fused ring system, the central feature of the molecule.

The discovery made by Moyer in Peoria that an addition of phenylacetic acid to the nutrient medium would alter the side-chains grown by the mould to that of the benzyl group, or penicillin G, not only led to marked improvement in the production of penicillin G, it also indicated a direction by which the apparent vulnerability of penicillin could be avoided by further changes in the structure of the side-chain. There was a possibility of changing the character of the drug by manipulation of the nutrient broth—the key substance on which Ernst Chain had dwelt nearly ten years before—and it was a trail that later was marked with brilliant feats in biochemistry and biological engineering such as the achievement by the scientists at Beecham Research Laboratories in Britain when methicillin was introduced and quickly reversed the situation.

All these things were forerunners to a new power and new control that came out of a substance in a fungus called Cephalosporium discovered by Professor Brotzu, one of the thousands of scientists involved in the biological panning of Florey's 'experimental gold rush' which followed the discovery of penicillin as a therapeutic agent.

The first single spore of the Cephalosporium was hauled up in a bucket from the sea off the coast of Sardinia. Since the water in the bucket was taken near a sewer outlet, it was assumed the spore came from the sewer—but there never could be any certainty that it had not travelled from some other area of the Mediterranean Sea. When Professor Giuseppe Brotzu, a former Rector in Cagliari University, pulled up the bucket of water, the eyes behind the thick spectacles could not detect the presence of the spore, and proof of its existence had to wait until it revealed itself among the various cultures which the Italian scientist grew from the organisms floating in his bucket of water.

When it was taken into custody in 1945, the Cephalosporium gave no hint of the latent power held in its genetic blueprint. It gave no sign, even as it grew into the first colony of the

Brotzu strain, that it would enormously expand and amplify the antibiotic armament, nor that it held the key to a second triumph for Florey and his team. The minute fragment of its self-creation, which finally emerged into medical use, was so low in activity, so small a part of the whole, that for years its presence escaped the skilled searching and the most advanced techniques available, and there was not the slightest hint of the powerful weapon which eventually eased the concern and anxiety aroused by the spread of the bacteria resistant to penicillin.

Within two years—following the pattern set by the penicillin development—Brotzu grew the Cephalosporium mould, showed it to have some activity against bacteria, and discovered an added bonus in its potential usefulness against typhoid fever. He then went on and prepared a rough extract which he used in a brief clinical trial, with success, against the usual staphylococcal and streptococcal infections, as well as against typhoid and several other diseases. When he tried to interest the Italian drug industry he evoked little response, but he wrote a short paper on his work which was printed in a publication by Cagliari University's Institute of Hygiene. The implications in the paper were noted by Dr Blyth Brook, a British medical officer who served on the Sardinian Health Council with Brotzu. Brook advised Brotzu to write to the British Medical Research Council about the fungus, and, from there, Sir Edward Mellanby referred the matter to Florey in Oxford. Thus, in August 1948, three years after the spore had been lifted from the sea, the Cephalosporium cultures were thriving in the same laboratories where, ten years before, penicillin had first come under organized and co-ordinated scientific study. Sewer moulds were not unusual and one of Florey's workers, Dr T. L. Su, had cultured a number of growths from sewers in Oxford, from which he later isolated a substance known as micrococcin which attracted Florey's interest because it offered some prospect of useful activity against tubercle organisms under certain conditions.[3]

The prospect aroused in this field, and the confirmation of his view that many new substances awaited detection, both of which came out of the discovery of streptomycin by Waksman and his colleagues at Rutgers University, in America, led Florey to engage in many experiments which he thought might offer an advance in the treatment of tuberculosis.

He found that, in fine form, micrococcin could be used to strengthen the action of blood cells, known as phagocytes, against tubercle bacilli which were shielded by membranes from antibiotic substances, such as streptomycin. He spent a considerable effort and time on the work to which someone gave the amusing title of 'Florey's Fortified Phagocytes'. It was both an engrossing and entertaining idea, but, in the end, it was shown not to work.

As with micrococcin, so the Cephalosporium mould was another of the many antibiotic paths which the workers in his laboratories followed in the post-war years. But chemical brilliance and an extension of team work far beyond the scale started at the Dunn were necessary for its completion; and, as with penicillin, the broad spectrum cephalosporin antibiotic family was close to being shelved before the final picture of its considerable value was disclosed.

At first, the Brotzu mould aroused little more than curiosity among the many projects under way at Florey's establishment; yet, as the growing problem of the bandit bacteria gripped his mind, he took a day-by-day interest in the studies, although he had placed the major responsibility on Dr E. P. Abraham and a co-worker, Dr G. G. F. Newton. The joint work of these two men became a monument to the healing of human beings.

Six years of culturing the mould and identifying the substances it produced in the nutrient media, led them to a point in 1954 where they uncovered a new penicillin—they called it penicillin N—along with a number of other substances active against bacteria. Out of this came their biggest discovery which, at first sight, seemed a trivial and minute thing. Abraham explained it in this way,

We had worked on this project for a long time and we had found and named this new cousin to the penicillins. Then we were working on a partially purified sample of this penicillin and found, when we removed the contamination, that it held

another active substance. Until that moment it had been hidden
from man. It had nothing to do with the activity which Brotzu
had noted and it had escaped us for nearly six years because
its activity was so low it would not be detected until it was
removed from the rest of the material.[4]

We called it cephalosporin C, and although it was related to
penicillin, it was somehow different, and we found we could
get it easily into a crystalline sodium salt. But it was low in
activity and I began to feel that I should consult Florey. I
wrote to him to suggest he might feel that we had taken this
far enough not to waste any more time, or money, and that
we might then hand it over to some commercial interest.

Abraham's letter reached Florey in Canberra, where he was
working on a project that had consumed his interest as much as
Cephalosporium and his other research during the post-war years,
and, from 13 000 miles away, he considered the implications of
the work being done in Oxford. Once more, his insight—a kind
of scientific sixth-sense—came into play and he made a vital
decision. He told Abraham that, rather than hand it over half-
completed to industry, the Oxford team should seek the whole
truth: that the potential should not be ignored so long as the
work could go ahead. For Florey found—just as he had with
penicillin in 1938—the problem of the Brotzu mould an intellectual challenge and he wanted to know the biochemical answers.

It was his wish, rather than a command, but Abraham and
Newton pushed their investigation deeper into the nature of
cephalosporin C, and Abraham afterwards commented,

'We found it to have properties that were powerful stimuli to
further investigations. It killed bacteria rapidly. It had a very low
toxicity in mice. And it was resistant to the penicillinase enzyme
which was then causing all the worry in world medicine.'

The tiny fraction in Brotzu's mould was shown to have a
different chemical nature to the classic penicillins, although the
structure of the molecule was similar in that it had a central ring
feature with a side-chain. When they tried this antibiotic material
against the bandit strains of bacteria which had defied all penicillins they melted away like shadows. On the surface, it appeared

that the answer to resistant bacteria had been found. But the material was obtainable only in the smallest amounts. Extensive chemical manipulation and many years of patience were still needed before the drug was brought into intensive commercial production, but when that was achieved, it was also shown to be useful for patients who were allergic to penicillin.

Bringing cephalosporin C into commercial production was the achievement of the Eli Lilly research centre in Indiana but, in the view of some leading American workers, it was the action of patenting the cephalosporin discovery that made certain the eventual successful development and production of the new family of semi-synthetic antibiotics; so much effort by so many people and so many millions of dollars would never have been invested without exclusive protection. But before the stage of high interest in the new drug had been reached, both in the Oxford laboratories and among certain well-informed drug houses, Florey had taken just this precaution and the full rights to Cephalosporium had been made over to the National Research and Development Corporation, a government body set up in Britain to handle such matters for the public good.

This meant that when the commercial possibilities became manifest, the drug industry dealt not with two scientists in mid-war, anxious to get a life-saving drug into production, but with an organized and specialized corporation designed to negotiate the complex issues of royalties and licences under which the work might be extended.

In the mid-1950s the Eli Lilly research centre noted the patent protection, and interest in Cephalosporium was aroused when a number of companies advanced on the problem of the semi-synthetic penicillins. Lilly chemists had worked on the project of devising methods for changing the nature of penicillin by dislodging the side-chain and substituting another. When they had achieved the removal of the side-chains of the penicillin molecules, they were left with a material known as 6-APA (6-aminopenicillanic acid). Similar work was being done elsewhere, too, notably by workers at the Beecham Laboratories in Britain where the path was being opened to literally thousands of new semi-synthetic penicillins which could be designed to give great therapeutic advantages.

At the Indiana centre, this research had the effect of intensifying interest in the nucleus of the substance which had been discovered in Florey's laboratories. The central ring feature of the cephalosporin C molecule had been identified by this time as 7-APA, slightly different from the normal ring but still capable of isolation and molecular manipulation. Rather than chase interests who were already ahead with the semi-synthetic penicillins, the Lilly chemists sought the rights to work on the cephalosporin material, and the company's director of the patents division, Dr Arthur M. Van Arendonk, wrote to the British NRDC to negotiate for an option to obtain a licence.

The effort mounted in the Lilly centre was of major proportions. In climbing the chemical barriers which nature had erected between them and their prize, hundreds of chemists, bacteriologists, toxicologists and a host of other specialists and technologists were employed, year after year, in many thousands of experiments until, in the end, the solutions fell into place.[5] The molecular manipulation of the gifted Lilly chemists stripped the unwanted side-chains from the central rings of the cephalosporin, and, in chemical conjuring of the highest order, they found methods of attaching the new side-chains, running through thousands of experiments, looking for one, then two, then four special effects that were the advances they sought in medicine.

In the first kilograms of 7-APA the Lilly chemists accumulated, were trillions upon trillions of tiny rings, like microscopic chariot wheels, to which they could attach chemical knives of specific shape and action, and then send them, Boadicea-like, racing into action against the invading bacteria. From this work—described by one American authority as of 'epic proportions'—came the new horizon in healing which Florey had glimpsed in his Nobel oration in Stockholm in 1945 when he spoke of the prospects of achieving tailor-made antibiotics.[6]

In the end, it brought him the satisfaction of learning that, such was the success of the new family of cephalosporin antibiotics, the royalties accruing to the National Research and Develop-

ment Corporation eventually amounted to more than a half of
the corporation's total income, worth many millions of dollars a
year to the British people; a late reward for the initial launching
of the antibiotic era.

CHAPTER 19

RUNNING PARALLEL WITH HIS INTEREST IN CEPHALO-
sporium and the wide field of research that was being pursued in
Oxford Florey, during the post-war years, became closely
involved in a project which appealed both to his latent nationalism and his enthusiasm to promote the cause of scientific research.
The project was an expansion of the one put to him in Melbourne
by Dr Coombs; and it was Coombs who, in the autumn of 1946,
came to the Dunn building in Oxford as an emissary of Australia's
new Prime Minister, Ben Chifley.

Florey and Coombs were two men of a kind, and Coombs
did not beat about the bush. He recalled the discussions thus,

> I told him frankly that we had gone far beyond the ideas he
> had expressed in his memorandum written, at my request, in
> 1944. I told him, 'We are now proposing that this medical
> centre idea of yours should be one of four such institutions;
> that these four research schools would form the nucleus of a
> university of higher learning, equal to any in the world. And
> one of the purposes of my coming here to see you and tell you
> this—and I am approaching other distinguished Australians
> abroad—is to tell you that, if you will give your service and
> help us to create this establishment, we intend to invite you all
> home to fill the key chairs at this university.' I told him that and
> I told the others the same thing, and explained we were still,
> then, selling the idea to Mr Chifley on the basis that a national
> centre of learning in Canberra would help to attract some of
> our best native brains back home and keep people there who
> would otherwise go overseas. We wanted Florey, and we

wanted Oliphant, and others of highly respected standing around whom this thing could be built. It was made very plain from the start that this was the idea.

He didn't leap at the prospect by any means, but I saw his eyes light up and he said in that quietly powerful way of his, 'This is a really exciting idea. I think it's a wonderful thing. I am certainly going to think very carefully about it.' That was that; nothing more. He welcomed me, made a fuss of me, took me off to dinner at college, and then put me on the train back to London.[1]

The appeal was to the mind and the heart; and Florey could not resist the pull of service to his homeland and the prospect that he could create something new to obviate the situation which a quarter of a century before had made him feel he would never return home. There was also the prospect that the task, properly undertaken, would mean journeys back to his birthplace and being associated with a chapter of its national history. Being Florey and being Australian, he gave himself to the task so that, in the end, Norman Heatley wrote of his efforts, 'This Australian work alone would have formed a considerable part of an above-average man's creative activity.'[2]

He led the formation of the first Advisory Committee and, as convener, called meetings in his office in South Parks Road, his fellow committeemen coming from Cambridge and London, as well as Oxford. The project renewed his acquaintance with the shock-haired physicist who had taken a final drink with him at Adelaide University when he had left to take up the Rhodes scholarship at the end of 1921—Mark Oliphant. Oliphant had worked with Lord Rutherford and blazed a distinguished trail in physics at the Cavendish Laboratory in Cambridge in the great days of the nuclear discoveries that led to the development of the Manhattan Project to which he had led a British team. He had also been a pioneer in British radar work and a member of the team at Birmingham which had provided essential equipment for the defence of the country in the first days of the blitz.

Florey and Oliphant firmed their friendship and remained close for the rest of their lives. The other two members of the

committee were the historian, Sir Keith Hancock and Professor
Raymond Firth from London University, while the Secretary
of the Commonwealth Universities Association, Dr J. F. Foster,
who had been Registrar at Melbourne University, provided the
secretarial services.

As they discussed the prospects of the Australian National
University at one of their first meetings, Florey observed, 'If
they mean what they say out there—and they are able to keep to
their promises—it could be a very good thing indeed.' In the
words was an underlying doubt, which tugged at his mind
frequently in the succeeding years as the work progressed and the
moment of decision—to leave Oxford and to return to Australia—
came closer and closer.

They lavished their time and their thought on the task and the
meetings in Oxford were enjoyed by them all, usually ending
with Florey producing a decanter of sherry and enquiring whether
his guests were 'in need of anaesthetic'. In this way the simple
request, made by Coombs in 1944, grew into a commitment
which at times dominated Florey's activities and his thoughts;
he took pride in the fact that he could plunge into the task of
preparing a great new university in Australia at postgraduate
level, and he called in many of his Oxford friends and members
of his staff to help with the detailed planning which the scheme
entailed. He had Dr Gordon Sanders give much of his time to the
undertaking and involved him later in three or four separate
journeys to Australia to advise on the spot how the work of
construction should go; and, little by little, he came gradually
towards the time when he had to consider whether he would
return home to lead the new medical centre—afterwards named
the John Curtin School of Medical Research—to which he endowed so much of his energy and ambition. He began to ease his
mind of the probable wrench with dreams of taking his whole
Oxford team, as a unit, back to Australia, to the capital—lifting
them lock, stock and barrel, from the Oxford setting to the fast-
growing bush town four hundred miles from Melbourne and two
hundred from Sydney. In fact, he became so deeply involved
with the wholesale move that he proposed it as a condition to the
Australian university authorities and spent some time sounding

out members of his staff on their readiness to follow him there. In these years he was, at times, like a big fish on a line tugging him across the seas to Canberra, one moment wanting to yield, and the next fighting away and resisting the pull with his doubts and his apprehensions strong within him.

After four years of planning, they made an exploratory visit to the site which the Government had set aside for the new campus and, at the same time, conferred with the university Interim Council. The four academics were then formally invited to return to head the four separate research schools which had been set up under a new act of parliament. Sir Mark Oliphant recollected, when the site which they had visited had been transformed from bushland into parklands holding a series of modern school buildings and research laboratories,

> We were talking about this thing back in Oxford and Florey and I were with Sir Robert Robinson, the distinguished chemist who worked on the chemical structure of penicillin. Robinson said that for both Florey and I to return to Australia and work would be tantamount to committing scientific hara-kiri! I think this view had some effect on Florey, and when I left England in 1950 to return to lead the School of Physical Sciences, Florey's parting words were, 'I hope you find more out there than a hole in the ground and a lot of promises.' His words were prophetic for that was exactly what greeted me when I reached Canberra.[3]

Nothing that took place afterwards ever erased the doubts that were in his mind from the time of his first discussion with Dr Coombs. Since the money for the work at the national centre would come from political sources, he questioned whether there would be freedom from control, and whether strings would be pulled to shape the direction of the work nearer to political desire.

One man who did not share Florey's doubts was Sir Edward Mellanby, the secretary of the British Medical Research Council. He told Oliphant on one occasion after Florey had discussed the matter, 'I will not be at all disturbed if Florey decides to go to

Australia. Wherever he is, good work will be done, and my concern is that he should have the best of opportunities and support.'[4]
Dr Coombs said of Florey's doubts,

> I think there was a good deal of truth in the belief held by
> many that he was looking for excuses not to return to Aus-
> tralia. He really could not bring himself to leave what he had
> ... this feeling of standing, and permanence; and when it
> came to the push he made this request that we take his whole
> team over on a year's provisional basis, and, of course, there
> were arguments about that with the different emissaries that
> went to see him. But I feel the truth was that, while he was
> always Australian and felt the pull home, he just couldn't
> bring himself to make the break.

Two of the emissaries from Australia who tried to entice him
home were Sir Hugh Ennor and Sir Roland Wilson. Wilson
spoke afterwards of the strong doubt and suspicion he had found
in Florey,

> I had several meetings with him, but found him quite un-
> wordly in his approach to the hard facts of life. He had fears
> and apprehensions about the role of government and its effect
> on his intellectual freedom. I told him, 'I have come to wipe a
> few of the scales from your eyes.' But I'm afraid this did no
> good. He hedged, and dithered, despite argument and assur-
> ances of the high esteem in which he was held, and the power
> that would be used to safeguard his position. I felt his mind
> had been sharpened by others against making the final decision.[5]

Ennor made no more progress when, some years later, he was
sent with a definite proposal for Florey to return and assume
leadership of the John Curtin School. They spent a torrid day in
argument in Florey's office. The main issue was the moving of
key members of his Oxford team to Canberra, on the basis of a
year of trial, but this was flatly refused. Dr Coombs said afterwards, 'We could not do this—it was not within our terms of
reference.'

On another occasion, when Florey went to Canberra to present his views on the structure of the staff for the John Curtin School and was asked to vacate the meeting while it voted on the appointment of the vice-chancellor, he took umbrage and vowed that, as a founder and director of the university, he had been insulted. Wilson said, 'We told him money was no problem. We gave assurances and undertakings for housing, and security, and general comfort; but, though we tried for years, there seemed always some cause for disruption, some reason to halt the negotiations.'

It fell to the lot of his friend, Professor Oliphant, as acting vice-chancellor of the young university, to announce in June 1953, that Florey had finally declined the invitation to become director of the John Curtin School although he would be happy to continue as adviser.

It became clear as time went on that he was an expatriate who had been away too long to return without trauma; but he was a man who was still influenced by the sight and the sound of his country. In the end, he satisfied himself with frequent visits to Australia. The line pulled, and he played it carefully without ever being reeled in. He went back to his homeland, year after year, until a journey there almost became an annual sojourn from the power and position he held in Britain, Europe and America. But, despite the nostalgia he must have felt, the pull was not strong enough to break the link with Britain; the appeal of the sun on the yellowstone of 'Coreega' in the Adelaide hills, was replaced by the ancient wall of a college library in Oxford; the banks of oleanders and high-rising eucalypts were finally supplanted by his rose garden, the chestnuts and the oaks.

During one of his visits to Australia, in 1950, he heard of an outstanding young graduate who had won a university prize for bacteriology and he asked to meet him. Dr Henry Harris was then working as a resident at the Royal Prince Alfred Hospital and a telephone call invited him to go to the university to meet Florey. He leapt at the chance, but was a little disappointed at the sight of the man who stood in front of him; quiet, of medium build and greying at the temples.

It was a meeting that affected both their lives. Florey asked if Harris would like to study at the Dunn School in Oxford, but

19

said he would first have to spend a preparatory period under
Professor R. D. Wright in Melbourne. Harris agreed to this and
eventually arrived at Florey's school in April 1952, destined to
step into his master's shoes when Florey retired ten years later.

The cephalosporin work and the Australian National University
project were in their early stages, and Florey was in his mid-
fifties, when he was struck two personal blows. His old mentor
and guide, the man with the bird-like mannerisms, Professor
Sir Charles Sherrington, died at the age of 94, and in the same
year Florey faced the reality that his heart was damaged and would
remain defective.

Sherrington's death in March 1952 roused in Florey all his
memories of the first years at Oxford and the guidance and shaping of his professional approach by a teacher who was described
in his obituary in the *British Medical Journal* as a 'man of genius'.
Sherrington's death left an indelible mark on Florey and it touched
him deeply, despite Sherrington's advanced age. The eyes peer-
ing down the beak-like nose, the voice which had said that nature
would give intelligible answers to intelligent questions, were
stilled, and Florey felt that a light which had always been looking
on appreciatively at his own work had been extinguished.

Florey's first heart attack—its severity and its duration, even
the date—he kept a secret. He told no one, and not until many
years had passed did those close to him learn he had nursed a
heart condition of increasing seriousness for over sixteen active
years.

His daughter learned about it from him following her mother's
death in 1966, and, as with others close to him, he spoke of its
beginning as a slow process which increased in severity as the
years went on; others in Australia had memories of him saying
that the trouble hit him in the chest 'like the kick of a mule'.[6]
However it began, he could not fail, with his experience and his
knowledge of physiology, to recognize the onset of angina
pectoris, the transitory pain of the strangling cramp in the centre
of the chest, the extension into the left arm and hand. That he
kept it secret from those close to him until less than two years

before his death was part of the iron control which helped him reshape his living from the early 1950s. Only his medical attendant knew that the reason for the slow change in the vigorous and often explosive professor was that the years of work and stress, and the long years of travel, had laid the foundations of arteriosclerosis in his main blood vessels.

Where, in earlier times, he was accessible to his staff, he later had erected at his office door an installation which came to be known as the 'Florey traffic lights'. It was a signal device with a green, amber and red light to indicate his availability to his secretary. Amber was a caution that interruption was to be only on urgent grounds; red was a barrier never to be breached, and the red light was used more frequently as the years went by and the days of pain and distress occurred more often.

Senior academics from overseas, in Oxford specifically to talk with him, would sometimes be affronted that a long-standing appointment could not be kept. The red light was showing and another day had to be designated. One incensed professor, due to see Florey on a Thursday, came back three times to find the red 'traffic light' showing, not knowing that the pull-out bed in the oaken panelling was probably in use as a couch of recovery. When the meeting finally occurred on the following Monday, Florey was charming and deeply apologetic, but breathed not a word of the reasons for the delayed consultation. His illness brought him face to face with the final banishment from his life of cigarettes; he accepted the warning of his medical attendant and broke free of the habit. Kent remembered him tying a cigarette packet on a piece of string and hanging it in his office, calling it his 'tempter'.

As the 1950s came to a close, it became commonplace to say at the Dunn School that 'the professor had mellowed a lot in recent years'. Those who knew him very well saw, later, how he had imposed on his life a new tranquillity enforced only by stern will-power. At times the exasperation of wordy meetings and interminable committees eating into his time, was very hard for him to bear.

The softening hand of indisposition coincided with the more reflective years of his life, and the philosophical aspects of the

effects of his work took a larger share of his thoughts as he saw
limited time ahead of him. In his research work he slowly lost the
driving interest in antibiotics, and, with a burning interest in the
deterioration of his own heart, he opened his studies on arteriosclerosis, work that reflected his very early engrossment with
blood vessels and the process of inflammation. He had many
willing collaborators and one man whom he brought into exploratory discussions was an old friend from his days at Cambridge, the man who had sent him Dr Margaret Jennings in 1936
—Professor Robert Webb.

In this final stage of his life in research his sense of obligation
made Florey choose people from America and Australia to work
in his laboratories, especially the younger workers.

'I rested a lot on Australians and Americans and other nationa-
lities. I didn't like taking too many British people into this research; in fact, I made quite a point not to—if I could avoid it.
There were so few jobs to be had in experimental pathology that
it became an embarrassment, because once you help to train
people, you are always left with the personal problem of what to
do with them, and this seemed to worry me at times. A few did
come to the School, but I never really encouraged them.'⁷

Though he still spent every available hour working at the
bench, he confessed openly during one visit to Canberra, 'I am
afraid I do so little these days. I am really nothing but a desk-
bound administrator.' It was an overstatement; he was still
engaged in investigation work centred on the blood vessels and
the flow of papers under his name showed little let-up. But, in
his lectures to the students at the Dunn School as the 1950s drew
to a close, he showed the introspection and examination from
which the outstanding statesman of science was to emerge.
Always a realist in the thought that research could not advance
without proper finance, now he began to see wider social and
community implications in his life's work which he had not concerned his mind with before. This thesis became a recurring one
for him. In front of his assembled staff and students in a lecture
room at the Dunn School he commented,

All our training has been to conserve life at any cost. And I cannot remember when I was a student, or a young man, giving much—if any—thought to the consequences of what I was doing in the wider context of things. I was quite happy to go on doing my experiments.

Medical schools will now have to bring before students some, at least, of the problems which previously have not been considered to be within the ambit of organized medicine. A danger besets us in these institutions—we tend to forget the social need that gave rise to them and which bestowed the privilege . . . and sometimes the community ends up with a poor bargain.[8]

On another occasion he made his thoughts clearer when he spoke of the responsibility in modern medicine.

Progress is now so very rapid in medical science and we are today so much more conscious than ever before of our debt to our predecessors—not only those of the immediate past, but to those also of more remote times. But we have failed to think clearly about our roles and our function in medicine and about the means and methods at our disposal.[9]

The sense of obligation had grown beyond the individual, past the well-being of single patients or groups of patients, to the whole community at large.

When he turned sixty Florey had to face the prospect of his coming retirement and the loss of the spacious university house he had occupied since 1935—nearly a quarter of a century. He also faced the loss of access to the laboratories so familiar to him and in which his life had centred for so long. Then one day he heard of a parcel of land for sale in the Oxford suburb of Marston and took for himself one of two blocks making sure of a congenial neighbour by mentioning the availability of the other to his colleague, Dr Gordon Sanders, who had been uncomfortably enduring life in a flat.

The planning and construction of his first, and only, house gave him much joy and he gained added pleasure when, during renovation of the Wren-built Sheldonian Theatre in Oxford, he was able to obtain two of the original heads in sandstone. The erosion of time on the stone faces appealed to him and he had them set into the wall which formed one side of a courtyard and garage.

While the house at Marston was being built, the Floreys finally vacated number 16 Parks Road and their former home was demolished to make way for a new school. Ethel went off to stay with friends and her daughter, but Florey stayed in Oxford, sleeping in the oak-framed pull-out bed in his office and eating in college.

He faced quiet years ahead; a chance to create his own rose garden, to relax from the interminable meetings and argument; to spend time on photography and the oil painting which he had recently taken up.

But as the moves for his first house went ahead, other events were shaping a new and totally unexpected future.

CHAPTER 20

AS THE NEW DECADE OPENED, FLOREY WAS IN HIS SIXTY-second year, and behind him lay a brilliant career studded with major scientific contributions, ranging from the penicillin discoveries and the opening of the true era of antibiotics to the new cephalosporins, the amassing of valuable and original data on the behaviour of human cells, and the mechanisms of defence against disease. He was still giving his time to a variety of boards, committees and academic groups, and was generally accounted as a valuable member for his common-sense approach and his ability to get to the heart of a problem. Sir Rudolph Peters wrote of him as, 'Always a powerful and dynamic member of a committee, often putting an original face on an old problem . . . though there were times, of course, when his destructive criticism outran his construction.' Sir Rudolph also recorded that Florey showed special attitudes to special groupings, 'He took a particularly firm line on the Nuffield Committee which was set up to develop medical research . . .'[1]

The coming of the 1960s brought five glorious years to Florey in which he was awarded his highest honours, and he obtained deep enjoyment and satisfaction from his last major achievement —The Presidency of the Royal Society. He was the tenth medical scientist to occupy the office and the first Australian to win this honour.

Within the rigid traditionalism of their establishment, the senior members of the Royal Society formed a deputation to approach him as they had for the agreement of the great names— Banks, Newton, Darwin, Faraday, Lister—through the previous three centuries. It was done to give him the right of rejection;

but there was little chance of that. It was a moment of triumph to
be invited to wear the crown of scientific leadership for five years,
but he had to keep his election secret until its formal announcement on the Society's traditional day, 30th November when,
each year, it holds its annual meeting and dinner.

Florey had already committed himself to visit Australia and the
United States, and both commitments he decided to keep. He
found it difficult to contain his excitement, however, and in the
friendly house at New Haven, Connecticut, he told Mrs Lucia
Fulton, 'You must not breathe a word to a living soul.' His eyes
were shining as she had never seen them before. 'I'm going to be
the next President of the Royal Society. Isn't it thrilling?'²

The formal election was held in the musty confines of the old
home of the Society, Burlington House. In the evening he pre-
sided over the annual dinner, his first function as president. The
choice of the annual guest of honour for the dinner, Viscount
Slim, was a kind thought and a recognition of his origins, for
Slim had recently returned from a successful term as Governor-
General of Australia.

Slim opened his address with personal congratulations to Florey
on the 'highest honour which the oldest and most famous
scientific body in the world can confer ... not only for your
outstanding contributions to knowledge and to the welfare of
mankind alone, but also for your integrity and your character'.³

At this great moment in his life, and facing an audience
holding several men who had preceded him in the office,
Florey began expounding the theme which had burned in his
mind since the difficult days of research before the Second World
War.

He did not gloss over his thoughts or his ideas, and his words
were to the point. A senior member of the Society's staff later
recalled how Florey had said to him, after looking at the office-
bearing members with whom he would work, 'You know, I've
got to be jolly careful or they will ask, "What's this bloody bushranger up to now?" ' On this first evening he showed the direct
and forthright style that marked his presidency to the end, and
he stated bluntly, 'The machinery for financing much research
in this country, and the relative paucity of resources in some

branches of science, place too great a burden on many of those whose business it is to make discoveries and to instruct young people.' It was time, he said, to campaign for the money to achieve the tasks, and it was also time to change the image of scientists in the public eye. 'Scientists are often portrayed as round-shouldered, myopic people muttering incomprehensible words and hiding themselves in backrooms. If they are young, they will be shown with dirty finger nails, and, of course, if they wear a beard, they will harbour evil designs; or they may be represented as supermen who pluck out the secrets of nature by methods denied to ordinary specimens of *Homo sapiens*.'[4]

Within weeks of the annual dinner, it was clear to many that a fresh breeze was blowing through the gloomy rooms of Burlington House. It had been argued that the Royal Society, in its centuries of existence, had changed with the times; but, in Florey's view, it had not changed very much at all. The Royal Society had been brought into being in the middle of the seventeenth century by a group of scholars whose objective it was to escape from the hand of politics, to shut themselves off from the outside world in order to devote their minds to their intellectual pursuits. Florey held the view that, because science had developed such enormous powers for good or evil, the time was on hand when they had to step back 'into the forum' and involve themselves with social and community matters.

He did it, not by commanding, said one observer, but by leadership. There had been many erudite leaders of the Royal Society, but never such a man of action and he left his mark upon this august body. One chronicler wrote,

Plans—tentative, unformed and faintly impractical, that had been born before his presidency—suddenly became firm, possible and urgent; things happened, committees of hoary venerability assumed new names and new vigour ... What was noticeable was the tempo of the change ... Florey, by his splendid presidency, his sage, bracing, always witty speeches and by his sound and balanced judgment in public affairs, gave the Society a new stature, a new weight in the affairs of the nation.

By any criterion, Florey is assured of his place among the greats who preceded him.[5]

The drive and vigour showed themselves in many ways; the work of committees and groups expanded and became enlivened; the number of new members elected each year increased to allow for better representation of the applied sciences; vice-presidents were no longer holders of honorary title, they became working vice-presidents; and then, in 1962—appalled by figures revealing the scope of the brain drain—Florey mounted pressure on the Government for allocation of more fellowships and scholarships.

He went further and moved to adjust the ancient face of the Society to the new age. He won recognition of the international organization, *PUGWASH*—formed to reflect scientific conscience—and not only induced the Royal Society to ignore the smear of Communist leanings, but also to give active aid to the movement.

In the flood of activity unleashed, it became obvious to Florey that the question of accommodation which had been hovering in the shadows for more than fifty years would soon have to be settled. He knew that in his term of office, Sir Henry Dale had made an attempt to fund the move, but had failed. Information came to him one day that three adjacent properties in Carlton House Terrace, sitting above the sweep of Pall Mall as it runs from Buckingham Palace to Admiralty Arch, might be obtainable under certain circumstances. One of the houses belonged to a millionaire from Argentina; one was the former German Embassy where, in pre-war days, Von Ribbentrop poured champagne and hatched his plots; the other was owned by the British Government. The magnificent façade of the Nash terrace fired his imagination and he became determined that the three buildings should become the new home of the Royal Society.

Persistence and determination pushed aside all objections and then he was faced with the shock of the cost of transformation of the three buildings into one. The Society asked for an estimate and were dismayed to be told that it would cost more than half a million pounds.

Florey plagued the Nuffield organization until he obtained an undertaking that they would meet half the cost, if the rest could be won from other sources. When they agreed he felt he had a lever to use on the Government, and so he was half-way home. A long campaign of pressure and influence was mounted and, one by one, the Government, various bodies and philanthropic organizations, were convinced and the cash total was reached. Occupation of the Nash terrace was obtained, and the work of conversion of the interiors was started. One contemporary wrote in an obituary, 'The full story of this splendid achievement is yet to be told, but there is no doubt at all that if Florey had not been President at the critical time, the project would never have been completed. His complete inability to accept defeat drove the Society gasping into its lovely new home.'

Yet, in his leadership, in his own abilities, he had doubts; and, in the beginning, some of his selectors held them, too. One of them said, when Florey expressed his lack of conviction that he could fulfil the office of President, 'Well, we have chosen you now, so we shall just have to keep our fingers crossed.'

Another colleague, more candid than the rest, told him, 'You are nowhere near as highbrow as your predecessors—but I like your trick of switching the lights on and off during lectures to keep the people awake.'[6]

The setting of Florey's life in Oxford in these years also changed. He had just moved into their new home in Marston when he was offered the appointment as Provost of Queen's College— and with it the Provost's lodgings, a spacious, period house with an outlook across green lawns and flower beds, to the ancient stone wall of the Queen's College library. He stood poised on the brink of decision for a time, but only briefly: later he explained his reasons for accepting the appointment.

'I was getting towards the end of my years as professor, and there were a number of reasons why this post was attractive. It had the advantage of my being able to stay there until the year 1971; it meant that I could live in one of the most beautiful of the old colleges and look out on to a beautiful garden with the façade of one of the loveliest college libraries in the world—well, in Oxford anyway.'[7] It also meant he inherited a professional housekeeper and a culinary standard which Ethel's lack of domesticity had never made possible.

He made his preparations for the move, with Ethel unhappy at leaving the house so recently acquired at Marston. He was adamant, and to help her overcome the difficulty of climbing stairs, he had a small lift installed in the Provost's lodgings—a facility which he later took to using himself to reach the upper-floor bedrooms.

At the Dunn School he tolerated no ideas of formal farewells. He spent the time finalizing his research which had commenced with the lysozyme and then the penicillin projects, and had ended with the cephalosporin triumph and a return to his studies of blood vessels.

He heard before his successor did that the appointment had been made. He took up the telephone and rang Dr Henry Harris, the young bacteriologist he had invited to join the Dunn School while in Sydney a decade before.

'I expect you have already received a letter from the Registrar,' he said. When Harris told him he had heard nothing, Florey replied, 'You will. You have been appointed to fill my Chair. Will you come and see me when you can? I would like to make an arrangement with you about using the electron microscope after I have left.'

There was no congratulation; no spontaneity—only an arrangement that would help to give him a continuing hand in science.

'When the day came for him to hand over to me,' said Professor Harris, 'he called me in as he was clearing a last few papers from his desk. He moved his hand round in a semi-sweep, encompassing the desk and the big bookcase with the pull-out bed kept underneath, and he said to me, rather brusquely, "You'll have no trouble here, Harris. It's a piece of cake, really." Then he was gone—no handshake, no goodbye, no wishing of luck. He just walked out.'[8]

Florey came back many times to the Dunn building; he could never desert the experiments and the challenges awaiting on the bench; but always, he went in and out by the basement door—to avoid impinging on Harris' authority in any way.

From the beginning money became the dominant theme of his leadership of the Royal Society but, in 1962, it reached a peak. Not only was he aghast at the amount of scientific talent leaving Britain for more attractive posts overseas, he was outraged by coming decisions, which he suspected had been leaked by government sources, on a retardation in the allowances for research and development.

He drove home his message in a quiet, but tense, voice at a Society dinner attended by government members and advisers, when he said,

The earning of the nation's living becomes increasingly difficult in a fiercely competitive world, and it would seem self-evident that the country should be straining every nerve to foster science and technology. We must, therefore, deplore the evident signs that some scientific activities, which depend to a large extent upon government aid, are to be curtailed, or, at least, not allowed to expand at the present time. Even if this is a temporary measure—as it is said to be—damage is being done to the confidence of our scientists and technologists in their future. They observe that those who control the situation have not yet recognized that the brains of the citizens are one of the greatest of the remaining national resources and that the country's future will be dictated largely by the use that is made of this asset.

In September 1964, he accepted an invitation to become Chancellor of the Australian National University on the retirement of Sir John Cockcroft the following July, and he found deep satisfaction in the offer.

When the Society's business did not claim his full attention, he paid visits to his beloved Spain where he painted landscapes or he returned to the Dunn School conducting experiments with the help of Kent—returning to his life-long interest in the behaviour of blood vessels—and always these experiments were objective and meticulous, progressively seeking new data. His successor Professor Harris, noting this aspect of Florey's professional approach, commented,

'The experiment was the overriding thing; and it was its technical elegance, its decisiveness, that counted.'[9]

His hands were now shaking with the imprint of hidden ill-health and advancing age, but he was still asking intelligent questions of nature and made his pilgrimages of inquiry to the laboratory bench in the Dunn building which James Kent always kept ready for him to use whenever the demands of Royal Society leadership allowed.

These halcyon days were spent in travel and on the careful composition of his more important addresses. His mornings were spent in thought looking out of his study window down along the path of paving stones he had laid through the rose-beds to the façade of the college library. The paving stones themselves were a memory of observation and action. He had been on his way to a meeting through Admiralty Arch one day when he saw workmen tearing up the stones for replacement and, struck by a sudden thought, he asked what would happen to them. Most likely, the foreman told him, they would be broken up as rubble for filling. So he bought them and arranged for their transport to Oxford where they were laid to join his study window to the historic wall of Queen's library.

It was along this path that he looked from his study window in November 1964 when he sat composing his address to be delivered at the anniversary dinner on the last day of the month. He wrote,

We should not conceive of applied scientists as being those associated particularly with the physical sciences. Perhaps it is the biologists and those dealing with human characteristics who will have to obtain and apply new knowledge if we are to have lives which will be really satisfactory and not an unendurable succession of frustrations. Calculations have been made that if the present rate of increase of population should continue, our descendants in 600 years' time will each have one square yard of land on which to conduct their affairs.

It is manifestly absurd and something is bound to happen before that time; but what?

It is all too easy for both politicians and scientists to leave a problem like this alone until the position is disastrous. More than frequent loud cries and metaphorical wringing of hands is now required. Ought we as a society to be considering how science and scientists can contribute to a solution of the great problem of bringing the human population into satisfactory, even if dynamic, equilibrium with its surroundings? Or should we wait for these matters to be tackled by people who may have little connection with us?

I have no doubt myself that we should try to lead scientific advances by positive action . . . scientists are perhaps becoming more self-conscious about their activities and their aspirations and how these can optimally be fitted into the social structure. It thus becomes of particular interest to examine what role the Royal Society can play specifically in the contemporary scene . . .

In his last year as President, Florey organized a mission to Russia to give expression to his belief that science was international in its character; with the invitation of the Soviet Academy secured, he led a successful deputation and the Russians greeted him warmly. He revisited the centres where he and Sanders had been in 1944 when they had administered the first penicillin to be used on a Russian soldier. In the room where, during that wartime visit, he had presented the gift from the Royal Society, he stood again to be awarded the Lomonossov Medal.*

He returned to Britain pleased with the visit. But, soon afterwards, he again gave expression to his growing concern on the plight the world was approaching through the unchecked population explosion. On a previous visit to Australia, in the Rivett Lecture, he had asked, 'How will the rapidly mounting population of the world be dealt with? What are we to do to foster the so-called social sciences—will their prosecution help us to understand man's behaviour . . . ?' It was the first of many statements showing his worry that uncontrolled procreation was the enemy of the quality of life.

Florey was raised to the peerage in the honours list which appeared on the first day of 1965, and, after consultation with the

* He was later made a foreign associate of the Soviet Academy.

Garter King-at-Arms, took the title Howard Walter, Baron Florey of Adelaide, in the Commonwealth of Australia, and Marston, in the County of Oxford. When the ritual of preparation had been fulfilled, he carried his Letters Patent to the House of Lords on 7th April—walking the chamber with his sponsors, deferring to the Lord Chancellor, smiling slightly to the cheers of his fellow peers, and then, outside, submitting to a posed photograph, in colour, of himself in his regalia.

He regarded the ritual as 'rather comic', pretentious and meaningless, and he never returned to the House of Lords. He immediately travelled north to see his daughter and grandchild; Paquita questioned his decision never to go back to Parliament. 'You can make your voice heard there on the things which concern you,' she said. 'It gives you a platform. Why not use it?'

He shrugged his shoulders. 'My voice would get lost among the torrent of nonsense in that place. I will do far more good working behind the scenes and making my views known where it really counts.'

When the coloured photograph reached him at his lodgings, he carried it across to the Dunn laboratories where Kent was preparing for an experiment. He threw it across the bench with a grin and said, 'Here you are, Kent. Here is a funny picture for your collection.'

Soon afterwards, he was offered and accepted, the award of the Order of Merit, and the letters O.M. were added to his growing list of distinctions. He also held honorary degrees from more than a dozen universities in three continents, along with college fellowships, membership of societies in America, Australia, Britain and Europe: the Royal Danish Academy of Sciences, the Swedish Medical Society, the American Philosophical Society and—of all things—honorary fellowship of the Royal College of Obstetricians and Gynaecologists. In all the coming and going which these honours represented in his life, he developed his flair for languages, speaking French tolerably well and being able to converse in Spanish and, with a little difficulty, in Italian.

The Presidency of the Royal Society gave Florey his captive audiences, and, in his final year, he hammered away at the threat of too many people in the world, the inaction of governments and the blind neglect by officialdom of the promise in science and technology. He told one gathering, 'The resources this country is prepared to devote to these fields is not enough to meet the demonstrated needs.'

He took public note of the immense technical and political prestige gained by the two super-powers with their space achievements. People in Britain were faced with questions, he said.

Is it now quite beyond the capacity of this nation to become mentally and physically stretched to the limit in cultivating some field of activity? Can not we canalize some great scientific adventure of which this country can be proud? Instead of the pathetic and inadequate effort to enter the space race against the great rocket powers, could not research into the sea be our pride and joy?

He spoke to an assembly of the top echelon of British scientific adminstration and seasoned brain power at the last address he was to make as President.

You may think I ask silly questions . . . I will make a statement instead. There is now overwhelming evidence that rapid population growth is bringing dire consequences to the human race. The effects will be felt, not only through food, but, also, through the action of overcrowding on social and mental adjustment. It is a task that will need more than biology and medicine to solve. It will need science on a broad front, from economics to psychology.[10]

He stood down, hoping his five years of work had achieved some progress in adapting the Society to the changing challenges and the environmental, scientific and technological futures. His five years of power had been a wonderful experience to him, as well as a personal triumph.

'I thoroughly enjoyed it all,' he said. 'They treated me handsomely and my British colleagues were extremely helpful. The time went by in a flash. We got on with the work; things were determined, and then done, and it was a pleasure to work with

20

absolutely first-class people. There was no quarrelling, and, you can take it from me, I had a very good time.'[11]

He ended his term of office, however, visibly aged, as against the vigorous man who had filled the chair in his early sixties, still able to hide the heart trouble that afflicted him.

His hair was now whiter, his step slower and there were the lines of pain and tiredness in his face. But he still filled a full calendar with engagements throughout the country, and almost immediately, on the death of Lord Brain, he accepted the presidency of the British Family Planning Association, and was soon advocating in-depth research into questions of birth control and legalized abortion.

For Ethel, it was a much different story, and, by the end of his term as President of the Royal Society, she was a near-physical wreck. The breakdown of her vascular system and the creeping infirmity of the years fastened her to an invalid chair propelled by a battery. She could still walk, but only just, and her progress was painful and laboured and was achieved only with the aid of a stick.

The previous year, defiant of stern medical advice, she had embarked on an overseas voyage, travelling to America to lecture, only to be laid low by a coronary attack from which she was rescued by the loving care of friends. She had then gone to Australia, by invitation, to give several lectures and to pay a last visit to her relatives in Adelaide.

It was a heart-rending visit for her sister, Mrs Emmeline Brebner, who had spent some months living in the Florey home in Oxford five years earlier. The changed appearance of her sister, although two years her junior, shocked her, and the desperate unhappiness she saw in Ethel aroused deep pity. Faced with her obvious ill health and exhaustion from travel, she begged her sister not to return to Britain.

Ethel refused and said, sadly, 'I could never desert those wonderful people over there. I worked with them all through the war and to leave them forever would be deserting.' She had made up her mind to resume her place in Oxford and her position as a clinical pioneer of the antibiotic age. Her resolute will dragged her from the comfort of her sister's home and Emmeline last saw her inching her way along the railway platform to the sleeper carriages at the far end, holding her plastic-covered asthmatic's pillow under her arm. Her hearing-aid was switched off, and her face showed the agony of each step as she shuffled the length of the platform.

Emmeline said, 'She was in such pain and so unhappy; but, I could do nothing. Both she and Floss were difficult people to influence. They were both a special kind of people—different to us—and it was useless to argue or try to persuade them.'[12]

Ethel met her obligations in Melbourne and moved on to Canberra, but there broke down and was rushed to Sydney where she was cared for by the one surviving member of the team which had conducted the first mass trials of penicillin in Australia, Professor John Lowenthal. He nursed her to a recovery which allowed her to travel home to Oxford, amazed at her progress. He said, 'She was a woman of immense will-power and courage. There was every reason why she should be dead; but her strength of mind kept her clinging to what was left of life.'[13]

She lived the winter through in Oxford, refusing to stay at Queen's, and seeing out her days alone in the house at Marston. Then, at the end of winter, she learned that her son was planning to marry and that the wedding would be held at the home of Mrs Lucia Fulton, in New Haven, Connecticut, where he had been sheltered for five years during the war. She was determined to see her son before he married, but Florey refused to meet the cost of her air fare. He told Professor Webb, 'I can't agree to her making that journey in her state. If she breaks down again and has to go into an American hospital, it will cost a fortune. In her condition it is madness to think of it.' Ethel defied him.[14]

Professor Robert Webb had always been very fond of her. He yielded to her pleading for help and arranged an insurance cover of $5 000, through the influence of his son who had a travel agency in Florida. He also provided her with dollar currency, and, by borrowing from her relatives she managed to journey to the wedding, arriving unexpectedly at New Haven and installing herself in a local hotel where, so infirm was she then, she had to be helped to dress and undress.

It was her last journey out of England. Soon after she returned to Marston Florey left for Australia and his installation in Canberra as the Chancellor of the Australian National University. He was thrilled and moved by the ceremony and felt welcomed back to his people when, at a lunch with the students, they dressed him in an old sacking cloak and a bush hat with corks dangling on strings to keep the flies from his eyes.

He was back in Oxford after two months away when, on 10th October he was called to Marston and told that Ethel had collapsed and died suddenly.

She was sixty-six years old and her death had come nine days from the fortieth anniversary of the day they had married at Trinity Church, Paddington, near Fleming's old laboratory.

Throughout their married life his inability to express emotion created a chasm which Ethel could never bridge. But in the shock of her death he suddenly opened his mind to his children, pouring out his recollections of his life, especially to his daughter, Paquita. He spoke of his work and strivings also to his son. Ethel's death unlocked his feelings which had always been hidden, and there was a sudden closeness between the three of them. All too soon, however, it disappeared and he withdrew again into his emotional solitude.

His son said,

He rarely spoke about himself at any time; his approach to his children was an intellectual one, his interest in us coming principally during our university years.

I think we both felt the lack of the love which he might have given, which I am fairly sure he felt but could not express.

His concern with our welfare and, I remember particularly, in helping me during my medical training were probably his substitutes. Quite simply, it is almost impossible to express an opinion about him from a child's point of view without having it clouded by a not very happy home life, and, in addition, spending a large part of my life elsewhere than at home.

Although he mellowed, my final impression when I saw him last in December 1967, was that he really hadn't changed so very much, because, despite feeling, just after my mother's death, the need to talk to us of his life, his closeness evaporated . . .[15]

The habits of the years took over and the withdrawal from any personal demonstration—which had cost his penicillin team their full public honour—was again in control and his scientific professionalism dominated his thoughts and actions.

The death of his wife also seemed to drive Florey into deeper reflection upon what he had achieved and its effect upon the world. Not only did he speak often at public functions on the population explosion and its effect upon the quality of life, he also sounded gloomy warnings on the changes in modern medicine on attitudes to living and on pollution and damage to the environment.

Within weeks of Ethel's death, he was in Edinburgh to lecture to the Royal College of Physicians, and, whilst in that city, he called on his daughter. He told her of his condition and his feeling that time was running out, and then commented,

'We now have a certain control of death, and I begin to wonder whether that was meant to be. The world is growing full of people—too full—and I suppose, along with the sanitary engineers, I am as responsible for that as any other man.'

On that visit he faced the members of the Royal College and spoke to them on how he saw the responsibilities of medicine in the modern world.

It is, I suppose, a common experience as we get older, and especially when we have retired from teaching posts and have time to think, that we are shocked—and bewildered—by what we do not know of the modern world, and, worse still, by what we have no means of comprehending. I have managed to keep a tiny field of scientific activity cultivated during recent years, not in the expectation of discovering something significant, but in the hope that I might remain relatively sane amidst the organizational complexity of modern life.

Again and again during these last years of his life he referred to what he called 'modern jargon' and so-called sophistication, and showed an extreme distaste for the 'horrible conception' of describing a scientific advance as a 'breakthrough'. In a rare confrontation with the Press in Canberra, when he faced the National Press Club, he was adamant that science did not advance by sudden leaps or a series of brilliant sorties. 'That does not bear serious examination,' he proclaimed.

He reiterated, too, his theme that enormous luck had blessed the penicillin undertaking and said,

> The great strides in understanding natural phenomena are the result of the labours of thousands of people, some of whom are good scientists—and some not so good. Their combined labours might be likened to the Pointillists who applied little dabs of colour to the canvas and built up a beautiful picture. Scientists can, with luck, from time to time, put a nice dab of colour on a metaphorical canvas; but, for the elaboration of the finished work, they are dependent on the activities of thousands of colleagues.[16]

He continued to cultivate his 'little field' of science during the early months of 1967, concentrating his interest on the blood vessels and investigating the degenerative disease of arteriosclerosis and its threatening sequel, coronary thrombosis, then hanging over his own life. The processes of this condition absorbed him and he sought for clues and answers to the 'spreading menace of this killer disease'.

In that year of 1967, he published his last joint paper, sharing the authorship with Dr Margaret Jennings. The subject was a study of the action of the capillaries, the tiny blood vessels on which he had first centred his interest more than forty years before.

Just before Easter 1967, he made another air journey to Australia. He had been elected for a second term as Chancellor of the Australian National University and when he reached his destination, he gave every sign of knowing that this would be his final visit to his homeland. He was no sooner in Canberra than he told his closest friends, 'I regret to admit to you that I am living on borrowed time. There is very little future left in me now, I'm afraid.'

When he climbed the rostrum in a packed theatre at the Australian National University one Thursday morning for a degree-conferring ceremony he was pale and shaky beneath the rich finery of the striped robes, and his hair showed white beneath the colourful hat.

Conferring a total of 282 degrees—then a record for the growing university—he brightened into pleasure when he threw the gown of doctor of science over the shoulders of Professor R. D. Wright, the old friend and collaborator who had sat one dark evening with him at the Dunn School in Oxford during 1938 and listened to the plans to investigate the mysterious substance in the juice of the Penicillium mould.

He praised Dr Wright's long service on the university council and said he hoped that he had not drifted too much out of touch with the young. But in his address to the assembled graduates, Asians among the Australians, he sounded apologetic.

I will be quite frank. I find it a frightful bore trying to run to keep up with the nimble minds of the young. Perhaps this is beyond the capacity of those who have passed forty years of age. Maybe I am slightly pessimistic here.

It was his last public address as Chancellor and again he showed the concern in his mind at the population explosion and the drift in society and again he looked back to the past, an old man repeating the words which sat on his conscience.

You are today joining a world community of scholars . . . but do not let us overestimate our position for there are some, I regret to say, who think that it is almost axiomatic that all academics if not positively stupid, are asses. It is conceived that we live in what is constantly referred to as the ivory tower . . . it is becoming less so of most who have had a university education. I think we are all much more self-conscious now than we once were.

I do not remember as a young man worrying for five minutes about whether what I was doing was desirable socially, or in any other way, except that in so far as it was likely to afford me a decent living. I enjoyed very much what I did and I do not think that students were greatly worried about their rights, about which a fair amount is heard these days.

And it must be added that I did not hear a loud clamour about obligations or even duties towards communities which had been so good as to lay the foundations for our future intellectual happiness.

We are, of course, faced with great problems now . . . some of which extend on a worldwide scale. The plethora of information may make it seem that we live in times far more difficult than any of those lived through by our predecessors. This is probably an illusion, nevertheless, everything . . . is being conducted on a great scale quite unknown by our forebears. This is largely due to the fact that the population of the world has increased and is increasing at a stupendous rate. It is people like you who will be called upon to make judgments whether certain activities are desirable and, to go even further, permissible. It is certainly true that day-to-day decisions are made by those who wield political power—but the outlook of those wielding political power is moulded to a considerable extent by those who have intellectual power and informed insight into the manifold activities of mankind . . .[17]

It was an event that marked the 21st year since the inception of the university, and the travel, the ritual and duties left him tired so that he limited his appointments and rested in the garden setting of his residence of privilege.

He sat there one day letting his mind roam back to the days when he was a child in the blazing summers before the Great War; when he was a boy and 'Sneaker' Thompson had fired his mind with the resolve to research; when he first heard the name of Pasteur from his sister's lips.

'The place I remember most was the house where we lived in the foothills, at Mitcham . . . it wasn't overbuilt then, and you could go walking over the hills and through the paddocks and nobody seemed to mind.'[18]

He flew down to Adelaide and, calling on Molly Bowen, walked up the hill for a last look at 'Coreega'; in the sub-divided estate,

one of his father's old pear trees, gnarled and awkward, was
dropping its fruit on the neat lawn of a brick and tile bungalow.
There was sadness in the visit and he said to Mrs Bowen,

'I have been away so long, yet people still remember me,
although I can't put a name to their faces. They are so very kind,
but I really don't know why they bother with an old man.'[19]

He flew from Sydney to Singapore on Sunday, 16th April and
then on to Bangkok where he stayed a brief while with a friend
before flying back to England.

He spent the month of May in preparation, and then, on 6th
June 1967, he and Dr Margaret Jennings, his collaborator and
special assistant for more than thirty years, were married. They
stood together and made their vows in the tiny room at the Oxford
Registry Office sandwiched in St Giles Street between the home
of the Quakers and the office of the University Appointments
Committee.

With the Registry staff, there were only two other witnesses—
Florey's life-long aide, James Kent, and Dr Jennings' housekeeper. Later, they called in a few members of the Dunn staff,
those who remained of the inner penicillin group, and there
were formal congratulations and drinks in the drawing-room at his
lodgings in Queen's College.

They began their brief idyll of eight months with a few days in
the sun in the Caribbean and a short visit to the Fulton home in
New Haven; then they returned, happy and comfortable with
each other, to face the coming winter in Oxford.

The new home of the Royal Society was opened several months
later, on 21st November in a setting of royal splendour. The white
marble of Nash's Carlton House Terrace gleamed in the light and
colour of the event as the Queen—the Royal Society's Patron—
performed the opening ceremony, accompanied by two Society
members, Lord Louis Mountbatten and the Duke of Edinburgh.

It was a night of triumph for Florey. As he stood with his wife
by his side, the new President, Lord Blackett, told the Queen that
Florey was 'the driving spirit, the architect of plans' who had
made the new home possible. He had begun his campaign a few

weeks after taking office, said Lord Blackett, when he decided to
settle a problem that had been looming for more than sixty years,
'Ma'am. To anyone not possessing the vision and perseverance
of Florey, our hopes seemed dashed at birth. He got the money.'

It was a chance for Florey to talk direct to his monarch, and he
took the occasion to repeat his concerns and worries over the role
of science in shaping the future, 'It could be that this new home of
the Royal Society will serve as a forum for examination of the
wider implications of what can be done with scientific manipula-
tions, particularly in biology, the possibilities of which are fraught
with far-reaching consequences for the human race.'

He went on, 'It is now essential for all of us to think about the
broad consequences of the increase in scientific knowledge which
is occurring at such a bewildering pace. The power of experiment
and observation is great and will increase—but, the very wide
implications in the modern world are only slowly being grasped.'[20]

His illness grew worse at Christmas, but still he struggled on
with his duties as Provost and attended to his laboratory interests
throughout January. He would entertain no discussion, no argument, that he should resign, and rest, and laze the days away.

On 15th February 1968, he asked Kent to prepare some mice
for an experiment in which he planned to use the electron microscope. It was their last experiment together. Kent did not see
Florey again until the following Tuesday when he noticed him
emerging from the conference room, where a symposium was in
progress.

He went out by the basement door and never came back.

When James Kent heard, on Wednesday 21st February that
Florey had died in the early evening, after a heart attack, he wept.

Florey's total estate, including his house and furniture, amounted
to £30 554. He left £100 and an old writing box from his desk
to James Kent, and a few similar gifts to other servants; £100
each to Queen's and Lincoln Colleges 'to buy a piece of plate, or
other similar object'; and the residue of his estate to various
relatives.

THE SIMPLICITY OF THE COMMEMORATION AT HIS PARISH church, in Marston; the tolling of the muffled bells, and the splendour and the music of the service in Westminster Abbey, were moving but insubstantial and fleeting memorials to Lord Florey.

There are more tangible memorials; portraits hang here and there—one of them above the oak staircase he climbed so often at the Sir William Dunn School, in Oxford; a building here and a laboratory somewhere else may bear his name; and there is a doctoral fellowship funded by public response to a joint appeal by the Royal Society and the Australian National University—a response far from overwhelming.

Across the whole Commonwealth of Nations littered with statues of sovereigns and soldiers waving stone swords, there is a single, insignificant bust to Florey, commissioned by the city fathers of his home town, Adelaide, in South Australia. It is an unimpressive thing, set upon a slim plinth, and it stands, half-covered with creeper, against a crumbling brick wall where it gains more attention from pigeons than from passers-by. In the complex of the modern university which he served to create, his name is located above a lecture-room in a dim corridor; but elsewhere in the mushrooming Australian capital, among the national collection of portraits and busts of politicians and vice-regal administrators, there is no sign, no vestige of Florey. It is as though he had never been there.

But he would not have had it otherwise. He was a realist, and he knew the public prized the stone sword above the petri dish. He gave no thought to memorials, nor to history, and he once growled in anger at a suggestion that a plaque should mark the laboratories in Oxford where the true discovery of therapeutic penicillin was made. Such things, he declared, belonged to royalty and politics, not to science.

His genius was in his grasp of the concept of antibiosis in the antagonism among microbes and his belief in the science of natural chemotherapy. His gift to the world came out of a single-minded resolution that did not allow him to be sidetracked by the sudden glory of the sulphonamides, that overcame the niggardly financial support, that ignored the threat to his own health. The ingredients that were needed to produce penicillin were the ingredients of Florey's character: courage, vision, leadership and learning on a broad scale. All these were needed to produce penicillin in time for the wounded in the Pacific jungles and on the Normandy beaches.

He was a realist and said penicillin did not come from a 'sudden flash of insight'. Yet it was his genius that saw the path and which took others along that way with him; he followed the road because it was basic to his nature and to the superb standard of his training.

His real memory rests not in churches, fellowships or buildings which bear his name, but in his service to humanity. It rests in the serried banks of multi-thousand-gallon fermenters in four continents, which produce the rivers of white crystalline penicillin—still the greatest of the antibiotics and which, once, was 1% of a teaspoonful of muddy-brown powder in Florey's laboratories.

His memorial is in the 200 million antibiotics prescriptions written each year across the earth, saving the lives of untold millions, and the centres of learning where scientists are given the stamp of quality which Florey gained from Sherrington.

Florey was totally averse and reluctant to wear a mantle of glory. He would have protested at the suggestion that his life's work reached more people than did the teachings of Jesus Christ. Yet, by the time he died, there was hardly a family on the face of the planet which had not been touched by what he did, and by what he set in motion.

That is his true memorial.

EARLY IN 1944, FLOREY WAS INFORMED THROUGH OFFICIAL channels that the Nazi propaganda machine was laying claim to the discovery of penicillin. To mark this great contribution to human welfare, he was told, Hitler had awarded an iron cross, first class, to the medical scientist responsible, none other than Hitler's personal physician, Dr Theodor Morell—a strange character who professional men in Germany regarded as a quack and who had taken a strange hold of Hitler. Albert Speer said of Morell, 'He is a screwball only interested in money.'

The announcement was as bogus as the claim to discovery and the man to whom the mythical award was made. In the *Militarhistorisches Bundesarchiv*, held in a complex at Freiburg, in the heart of the Black Forest, there is not a trace of a record on penicillin, not a single mention of the word.

Not one of the millions of German soldiers wounded in the slaughter on the Soviet front, in the battles in the west and in Italy, ever received the drug. Not one systemic injection was prepared for German use until the war was finished when criminals, both German and American, organized a blackmarket through which vicious and heartless frauds were perpetrated on sick and dying people. Even when penicillin became legally available to German hospitals and clinicians, it was material that had first passed through the bladders of American soldiers, reclaimed from the urine bought under contract from hospitals by the Berlin firm of Scherring. The irony of the origin of their first supplies escaped the German people at the time; only the healing power of the wonder drug mattered in that depressing era of total defeat.

The announcement of the Iron Cross award, despite its spurious character, revealed the Germans' awareness of the drug. Hitler was undoubtedly told of its strategic value and its effect on the public mind. Leading German scientists are now sure that Morell alerted him to the activities in which several of the big German pharmaceutical companies had been engaged, and of developments in Britain and America, and Morell was able to urge Hitler to give development of the drug his support. But support from the disintegrating German government in 1944 took only one form. Under the hammer-blows from the allied air armadas, and without essential supplies and equipment, only the use of words was left.

The German army medical authorities had expressed an interest in penicillin to the leading drug houses late in 1943, but it was not until after Hitler was informed of the drug that a meeting was called of medical scientists and biochemists in Berlin in October 1944; the meeting of talk and no outcome. There was no promise of government money, no directive and no decision possible in the chaotic conditions of life then facing each man and each organization.

Yet, there was then some penicillin in Germany. Tiny amounts had been won by the first German biochemist to attempt the identification of a penicillin-yielding mould and its extraction— Dr Heinz Öppinger working for the big drug firm of Hoechst. There were also three unexplained vials of yellow penicillin, made in England, which the German army medical sources claimed had been captured by the Afrika Corps in North Africa, but which, because of the incompatibility of dates and also the fact that no penicillin arrived in North Africa until after the defeat of Rommel's forces, aroused speculations which ranged between espionage agents obtaining the penicillin in England and the detection of the vials in food parcels sent to medical officers in prisoner-of-war camps. No documentary evidence exists in the fragmented filing systems left from the upheavals in post-war Germany—only the personal recollections from the men who used these tiny glass ampoules to compare with their own production of the drug.

When one of these ampoules came to Dr Öppinger, he had

been working on the penicillin problem for two years. He was a highly-trained biochemist and had worked as assistant to the Nobel Prize winner, Hans Fischer, in Munich; he was forty-two years old when he opened the penicillin work. This first German interest was triggered by intelligence reports from Sweden, early in 1942, which had translated details from the Oxford paper published in *Lancet* in August 1941.

'I became heavily engaged because it became clear to us that a lot of lives could be saved if we could be successful,' Dr Öppinger said later. As it was, he advanced faster and further than any other man in Germany, although other drug houses—Bayer at Leverkusen, and Scherring in Berlin, and various university groups— all took up the challenge later. Öppinger was a determined man; at the end of the war he was less than a year away from deep tank fermentation in volume that would have meant industrial production—but he had no Florey, no corn steep liquor and no Mouldy Mary.

Öppinger had to search for his own moulds. With his assistants, Dr Fussgienger, Dr Wegminn and Mr Dunzinger, he pored amongst wastebins, rotting fruit, kitchen waste and piles of leaves in the forest; they walked along gutters and through sewers, seeking the Penicillium moulds that might yield the drug.

'We had been interested in moulds for many years and we had a collection,' Öppinger remarked after the war. 'We knew about this antibacterial action before the war, and you must remember that we were working in this kind of field because it was here that we produced salvarsan.'[1]

They followed the Oxford lines, testing the mould juice against the same type of staphylococcus used by Florey's team, measuring the activity in the same way and getting, as Chain did, no more than a few units of activity in each millilitre. The hidden details of the British work, which had been banned or excluded from publication, were ineffectual in preventing the work in Germany. The standard of biochemistry in Germany was high; there were men as brilliant as Ernst Chain and who were quite capable of teasing the fragile molecules from the mould juice; and Öppinger was the first German scientist to do this.

'We were up against a nearly impossible task because we were getting only about two or three litres of broth from our cultures, and to pick the tiny amounts out from this was very difficult indeed,' said Öppinger. 'We got many bottles and started to enlarge our working area, and then, when the army heard of penicillin and expressed their interest, other firms and groups began working.'

'We got the first extract at the end of 1942 and this was just enough to test against cultures of bacteria. There was not enough for tests on animals at that time. We were not able to test penicillin on experimental animals until the middle of 1944, after the invasion of Europe had started. There was, then, only time enough left to make a few topical clinical tests at the hospital in Hoechst; but, while these were satisfactory, there was nothing dramatic. I saw the reports and they only dealt with organisms we knew were sensitive to penicillin. By that time it was too late to get enough for systemic trials of any kind. The bombing of railways, harbours and industry, closed it all down for us.'

Dr Öppinger went to the big penicillin meeting in Berlin, held under the chairmanship of Professor Rostock, of Munich, and there also were the senior army medical officers and the groups from the drug houses and the universities. A committee was formed, with Professor Konrad Bernhauer of Stuttgart as leader, to co-ordinate the activities of the various groups—but it was all a farce, with no prospect of advance.

'By the time of that meeting, we could get no yeast, no acids, no supplies or materials. It was all over. At the meeting in Berlin, there were many big words, and many plans, but they came to nothing. There were a lot of people there who knew nothing of penicillin and just used it for propaganda purposes, to show something other than the truth—that we could not make it for ourselves at that time. Our biggest task had been to breed the higher yielding strains of mould. I used to take out single spores of higher areas of yield with a micro-manipulator and we got up to about 20 units a millilitre; then came the idea that the rotating drum would be better than a surface bottle growth.'

But by the time Öppinger had built his rotating drum, the war was over. Öppinger then found his laboratory the object of

interest to a number of specialist officers from the allied armies.
One day, a broad, thick man stumped in and announced he was
from the Allied Commission and said he wanted an explanation
of what work had been done on penicillin during the war. The
visitor announced himself as Professor Harold Raistrick.
When he saw Öppinger's rotary drum, he asked how Öppinger
had obtained it. Öppinger remembered the incident clearly as he
recalled that Raistrick was brimming with suspicion. He told his
visitor that he had built it himself for submerged culture.
Raistrick was not satisfied, 'That was never built by a micro-
biologist, I am certain.' Öppinger replied, 'But I am not a micro-
biologist; I am a biochemist.' Raistrick looked at him for a
moment, and then said, 'Oh, well, then. In that case it is just
possible.'

Raistrick knew, as did Öppinger, that with the rotary machine
and the idea of deep fermentation, the German was close to his
breakthrough after three years of work. 'It was a natural step for
us and I had ordered the materials before the war ended. We had
made ascorbic acid this way and we had a lot of experience, and
then all we had to do was to find a suitable strain with a good
yield.'

With the aid of the American authorities, Öppinger obtained
some materials and enlarged his penicillin work, but could not
do much more than he had done during the war. Then it became
known in the community that he was working on producing
the new wonder drug which criminals had been selling on the
black market. Most of the penicillin in the possession of the
blackmarketeers had been stolen from American hospitals and
depots; but, when there was none, the worst criminals sometimes
used a mixture of flour and water and sold that for high prices.
Former SS officers and some Americans were caught, and in one
big trial more than forty people were found guilty and sentenced
for these crimes. Öppinger said he lived a life, at that time, with
the quality of a nightmare,

'Things were terrible here and life was hard to endure. I could
not come home from work at night but there were people waiting at my door, wringing their hands, on their knees, crying to
me, "Give some penicillin for my father," ... "My mother is

dying, help me," ... "Please, please, my son will die unless you give me penicillin." It was heart-breaking—terrible to endure. I had to move out of my house afterwards because American Air Force personnel wanted it for accommodation, and I got only a small sum; but people did not come pleading any more.'[2]

In 1946, according to Professor Auhagen of Bayer's, when the US army was responsible for health in the western sector of Berlin, problems of public health had grown to enormous proportions. Scherring obtained a contract with the American military hospitals to purchase all urine and, from that, production of penicillin, re-extracted from the urine, was started under licence from the occupying authority.

But all this re-extracted penicillin that went to the civilian hospitals was only a drop in a bucket. Then one day the American army authorities called together the men working in penicillin and said an aircraft would take them from Frankfurt to the United States where they would be taught the processes and techniques of penicillin production. They all duly turned up at Frankfurt; Bernhauer, Auhagen, Öppinger and others. But, just before the plane was due to leave, an American officer came running with an urgent order countermanding the action. The army had taken the initiative and not referred it to any other authority, and the sudden request for industrial co-operation alarmed leaders in the drug industry in America. The plans were cancelled and, later, agents arrived from America to negotiate with the German firms on licensing rights.

Öppinger's firm obtained a licence to produce penicillin from Merck's and this development led to a number of visitors in the subsequent years—among them Kenneth Raper, and the only member of the Oxford team Öppinger was to meet, Dr Ernst Chain, who called when he was on his way to Rome.

In general, most of the German work was never published, but towards the end of the war, Professor Bernhauer wrote an article on the mould and the methods of extraction and he sent it to the learned magazine *Naturwissenschaften,* but the controlling Nazi officials banned its publication.

Five years after the end of the war the German people got the penicillin for which Hitler gave his iron cross award to Morell; but it was obtained under American licences and produced in deep fermentation from the strains of the Peoria cantaloup.

When that stage was reached, the German government did issue the award of a cross—not an iron cross, but the *Bundesverdienstkreuz*, a four-bladed cross of red enamel which was a civil award recognizing the contributions made to medical science by Dr Heinz Öppinger for his work on penicillin.

'What happened about the iron cross to that odd man, Morell, I don't know. I never heard,' said Dr Öppinger. Nevertheless, Morell did earn a mention in the German annals of the war in relation to the penicillin question. On behalf of this writer, the official German military historian and archivist, Dr P. Zoske, found 'a hint of Dr Morell's activity'. In documents not at Freiburg but at Koblenz, he said, it was shown that late in 1943 Dr Morell had claimed, to the section of the army dealing with infectious diseases, that 'he had succeeded in isolating penicillin from the Penicillium mould'. This small amount, according to Zoske, had actually been produced at a chemical works in Olmutz and, at the army's request, had been handed to them for examination. Later, the Japanese authorities heard of this development and in June 1944, their military attaché in Berlin had formally sought information and material on which scientists in Japan could commence work.

He handed over two dried samples of the fungus—and there the record ends. Speculation on how the samples were shipped to Japan included a suggestion, afterwards given to Raistrick by the Germans, that it had been carried across the world by submarine, but no documentation—German or Japanese—substantiates the conjecture; neither was it important, for the secretive Japanese army had set up its own national penicillin committee six months before the Germans had instituted their search for moulds with antibacterial activity. By the time Morell's dried samples could have reached Japan in mid-1944—whether in a condition for revival or not—the first trial production of extract had been made there. This took place in August 1944. It was only after occupation that their penicillin industry began to take form under American tutelage and licence.

CHAPTER NOTES

Chapter 1
1 *Recordings. Australian National Library*, Canberra.
2 *South Australian Archives*, Adelaide.
3 *Ibid.*
4 DR ALLAN HOBBS. Personal communication. Adelaide 1970.

Chapter 2
1 DR WILLIAM GIBSON. University of British Columbia production.
2 *Recordings. Australian National Library.*
3 *Ibid.*
4 *Arctic*, 6, 212, 1953.
5 LORD FLOREY. Personal recollections. Canberra 1967.

Chapter 3
1 SIR ALAN DRURY. Personal communication. Cambridge 1970.
2 PROFESSOR ROBERT WEBB. Personal communication. Oxford 1970.
3 FLOREY AND GOLDSWORTHY. *Journal of Experimental Pathology.* UK 1929.
4 *Penicillin Review. British Medical Journal* 1944.
5 *Australian Medical Journal* 1944 and PROFESSOR DAVID GREY, personal communication. Melbourne University 1971.
6 *Antibiotics vol.* 2. Oxford Medical Publications.
7 SIR ALAN DRURY. Personal communication. Cambridge 1970.
8 *Ibid.*

Chapter 4
1 *Recordings. Australian National Library*, Canberra.
2 *Medical Research Council Annals.* London.
3 *Ibid.*
4 *Antibiotics* monograph Oxford 1949.
5 SIR RUDOLPH PETERS. *Caiian Magazine* of Gonville and Caius College, Cambridge.
6 *Ibid.*
7 SIR ERNST BORIS CHAIN. Lecture, *Search for Biodynamic Substances.*
8 PROFESSOR R. D. WRIGHT. Personal communication. Melbourne 1970.

Chapter 5

1 PROFESSOR SIR ERNST CHAIN. Personal communication. London 1970.
2 *Recordings. Pasteur Institute annexe*, Brussels.
3 SIR CHARLES KELLEWAY to a group of medical workers. Melbourne 1943.
4 H. W. FLOREY. *Lister Memorial Lecture 1945.*
5 SIR ERNST CHAIN. Personal communication. London 1970.
6 MRS JOHN MCMICHAEL (Florey's daughter). Edinburgh 1970.
7 PROFESSOR WRIGHT. Personal communication. Melbourne 1970.

Chapter 6

1 A. FLEMING. *Journal of Bacteriology.* London 1929.
2 SIR ERNST CHAIN. Recollections. London 1970.
3 *Records. British Medical Research Council.* London.
4 *Ibid.*
5 *Ibid.*
6 DR N. E. HEATLEY. Personal communication.
7 H. W. FLOREY. Personal recollections. Canberra 1967.
8 *Records of the Rockefeller Foundation*, New York.
9 *Ibid.* Letter from H. W. FLOREY.

Chapter 7

1 *Laboratory notes.* Sir William Dunn School, Oxford.
2 DR NORMAN HEATLEY. *Journal of Microbiology.* UK 1970.
3 SIR ERNST CHAIN. Personal communication. London 1970.
4 *Laboratory notes.* Sir William Dunn School, Oxford.
5 *Ibid.*
6 DR NORMAN HEATLEY. Personal communication.
7 DR NORMAN HEATLEY. *Journal of Microbiology.* UK 1970.

Chapter 8

1 *Records. Medical Research Council*, London.
2 *Royal Society of Arts Lecture.* 1944.
3 *First paper on therapeutic penicillin. Lancet.* 24 August 1940.
4 *Medical Research Council annals.* London.
5 FLOREY. Personal recollection, 1967. SIR ERNST CHAIN, 1970.
6 A. FLEMING. *Medical Research Club.* London 1940.
7 *Antibiotics.* Oxford 1949.

Chapter 9

1 MRS JOHN MCMICHAEL. Personal communication. Edinburgh 1970.
2 SIR HARRY WUNDERLIE. Personal recollection. Canberra 1970.
3 *Records. Medical Research Council.* UK.
4 DR C. M. FLETCHER. Personal communication. London 1970.
5 *Case notes.* Sir William Dunn School, Oxford.
6 *Penicillin Report. Lancet.* August 1941.
7 DR GLADYS HOBBY. Personal communication.

8   *Ibid.* Laboratory notes preserved from Presbyterian Hospital work, New York 1940–43.
9   MARTIN HENRY DAWSON. Letters left in personal papers.
10 DR GLADYS HOBBY. Personal communication.
11 *Ibid.*

Chapter 10
1   *Case notes. Penicillin Report. Lancet.* August 1941.
2   *Records. Medical Research Council.* UK.
3   PROFESSOR R. D. WRIGHT. Melbourne 1970.
4   *Records. Medical Research Council.* UK.
5   H. W. FLOREY *et al. Antibiotics.* Oxford 1949.

Chapter 11
1   DR NORMAN HEATLEY. Personal communication. Oxford 1970.
2   H. W. FLOREY. Personal communication. Canberra 1967.
3   *Records. N.R.R. Laboratories,* Peoria, Ill. USA 1941.
4   DR R. D. COGHILL. Personal communication. 1970.
5   H. W. FLOREY *et al. Antibiotics vol. 2.* Oxford 1949.
6   DR R. D. COGHILL (NRRL). *American Chemical Engineering Symposium,* Atlantic City, September. 1966.
7   *Records. NRRL.,* Peoria, Ill. USA.
8   PROFESSOR RONALD HARE. *The Birth of Penicillin.* George Allen and Unwin, London 1970.
9   OSGOOD NICHOLLS. Personal communication. 1971.

Chapter 12
1   *Antibiotics vol. 2.* 1949.
2   PROFESSOR BRIAN MAEGRAITH. Personal communication. 1970.
3   H. W. FLOREY. Letter to Dr Randolph Y. Major. Merck's, Rahway, USA.
4   H. W. AND M. E. FLOREY. *General and Local Administration of Penicillin. Lancet.* March 1941.
5   *Ibid.*
6   DR D. BODENHAM. Personal communication. Bristol 1970.
7   Personal appreciation in obituary. Published London 1966.
8   FLOREY AND FLOREY. *Case notes. Lancet.* March 1943.
9   FLOREY. Letter to Sir Charles Sherrington. Original in the Sherrington collection, University of British Columbia.
10 SIR HAROLD RAISTRICK. Personal communication. Felpham, Sussex 1970.
11 *Records. Medical Research Council.* London 1942.
12 *Government archives,* London.
13 *The Times.* London, 29–31 August 1942.
14 PROFESSOR ABRAHAM. Obituary note. London 1968.
15 DR NORMAN HEATLEY. Personal communication. Oxford 1970.

Chapter 13

1   By courtesy MRS LUCIA FULTON. Diaries. New Haven, Conn.
2   DR NORMAN HEATLEY. Diaries. Rahway 1942.
3   PROFESSOR FULTON. Diaries.
4   DR NORMAN HEATLEY. Diaries. Rahway 1942.
5   PROFESSOR FULTON. Diaries.
6   *New Haven Register.* Conn. March 1962.
7   DR WALLACE E. HERRELL. Personal communication.
8   *Ibid.*
9   DR JOHN EVANS. Personal communication. Kalamazoo 1970.
10 DR HINMAN. Personal communication. 1970.
11 DR R. D. COGHILL. *AICE symposium.* Atlantic City 1966.
12 *Archives. Surgeon-General's Office.* Washington DC.
13 DR R. D. COGHILL. Atlantic City 1966.
14 *Records 21st Army Group.* British Royal Army Medical College.
15 A. NEWTON RICHARDS. *Production of Penicillin in USA. Nature* February
       1964.
16 H. W. FLOREY *et al. Antibiotics.* Oxford 1949.

Chapter 14

1   MAJOR R. J. V. PULVERTAFT. *Lancet.* 18 September 1943.
2   *Ibid.*
3   *Ibid.* Personal communication. 1970.
4   *Records. Surgeon-General of the Army's Office.* Washington USA.
5   GENERAL SCHULLINGER. Personal records. Archives, Washington USA.
6   FLOREY AND CAIRNS. Special report. Royal Army Medical Records, London.
7   *Ibid.*
8   *Ibid.*
9   MAJOR W. H. D. PRIEST. Venereal Officer North Africa. Royal Army
       Medical Records, London.
10 LT-COL. E. BUTTON. Army Medical Reports, London.
11 FLOREY AND CAIRNS. Special report. Royal Army Records, London.
12 *Army Archives.* Washington USA.
13 *Ibid.*

Chapter 15

1   DR A. G. SANDERS. Personal communication. Oxford 1970.
2   *Ibid.*
3   *Ibid.*
4   DR COGHILL. Symposium. Atlantic City, 1966.
5   DR NORMAN HEATLEY. In Memoriam. Journal of General Microbiology.
       London 1970.
6   H. W. FLOREY. *Lister Memorial Lecture.* Royal College of Surgeons, London.
       11 October 1945.

7 DR WALLACE E. HERRELL. *History of Antibiotics.* Symposium, Philadelphia. May 1970.
8 H. W. FLOREY. *Royal Society of Arts Lecture,* November 1944.

Chapter 16
1 DR P. L. BAZELEY. Personal communication. San Diego 1970.
2 E. V. KEOGH. Personal communication. Melbourne 1969.
3 MISS LANGHAM. Personal communication. Queensland 1970.
4 JOHN LOWENTHAL et al. *Penicillin Clinical Trial Report.* Sydney 4 November 1944.
5 PROFESSOR JOHN LOWENTHAL. Personal communication. Sydney 1970.
6 *Adelaide Advertiser.* Report 1944.
7 E. H. PHILLIPS, FAULDINGS. Personal communication 1970.

Chapter 17
1 *Medical Research Council records.* London.
2 Personal communication. Peoria, Ill. USA.
3 PROFESSOR R. DOUGLAS WRIGHT. Melbourne 1970.
4 DR NORMAN HEATLEY. Biographical Memoir. US Philosophical Society 1968.
5 MRS JOHN MCMICHAEL. Personal communication. Edinburgh.
6 H. W. FLOREY. Lecture at Royal Society of Arts, London, 10 November 1944.
7 *The Oxford Magazine, vol. 64.* 29 November 1945.
8 DR C. M. FLETCHER. Personal communication.
9 *Medical Research Council records.* London.
10 Lecture at Royal Society of Arts. November 1944.
11 *Nobel Oration.* Stockholm, December 1945.
12 *Ibid.*

Chapter 18
1 PROFESSOR E. P. ABRAHAM. Personal communication. Oxford 1970.
2 H. W. FLOREY. Canadian Medical Association annual meeting. Quebec 1956.
3 H. W. FLOREY. *Antibiotic Products of a Versatile Fungus.* Annals of Internal Medicine, vol. 43, September 1955.
4 PROFESSOR E. P. ABRAHAM. Personal communication. Oxford 1970.
5 ROBERT W. NEWELL. *The Odyssey of the Cephalosporins.* Eli Lilly & Co. 1970.
6 *Ibid.*

Chapter 19
1 DR H. C. COOMBS. Personal communication. Sydney 1971.
2 *Memoriam. Journal of General Microbiology.* London 1970.
3 SIR MARCUS OLIPHANT. Personal communication. Canberra 1970.
4 *Ibid.*
5 SIR ROLAND WILSON. Personal communication. Sydney 1970.

6 SIR DOUGLAS COPLAND, Melbourne 1970. MRS MOLLY BOWEN, Adelaide 1970. Officials of Australian National University. Personal communication.
7 *Australian National Library. Recordings.*
8 Lectures at the Sir William Dunn School, Oxford.
9 H. W. FLOREY. *First Rivett Lecture.* Melbourne 1963.

Chapter 20
1 SIR RUDOLPH PETERS. *The Caiian.* Cambridge, November 1969.
2 MRS FULTON. Personal communication. New Haven.
3 *Proceedings of the Royal Society,* London.
4 *Ibid.*
5 *Ibid.*
6 *Ibid.*
7 *Australian National Library. Recordings.*
8 PROFESSOR H. H. HARRIS, Director, Sir William Dunn School, Oxford. Personal communication, 1970.
9 *Ibid.* Obituary.
10 *Proceedings of the Royal Society,* London.
11 *Australian National Library. Recordings.*
12 MRS E. BREBNER. Personal communication. Adelaide 1970.
13 PROFESSOR JOHN LOWENTHAL. Personal communication. Sydney University 1970.
14 PROFESSOR ROBERT WEBB. Personal communication. Sir William Dunn School, Oxford.
15 DR C. D. V. FLOREY. Personal communication. West Indies 1971.
16 *Public Address at National Press Club,* Canberra. August 1966.
17 *Conferring degrees. Australian National University* 1967.
18 *Recordings. Australian National Library.*
19 MRS MOLLY BOWEN. Personal communication. Adelaide 1970.
20 *Proceedings of the Royal Society,* London.

Appendix
1 DR ÖPPINGER. Personal communication. Hoechst, W. Germany 1970.
2 *Ibid.*

INDEX

Abingdon, 4–5
Abraham, Professor E. P., 56, 84, 87–8, 121–2, 136, 173, 208, 215, 221, 241, 250–1, 257–8
Actinomycetin, 62, 69; isolation of, 60
Adelaide, life in, 4–5
Adrian, Lord, xvi, xviii, 16, 44: tribute to Lord Florey by, xviii; tribute paid to Sir Charles Sherrington, 16; awarded Nobel Prize, 44
Akers, Mrs Elva, 120–1
Alexander, Constable Albert, 121–3, 130, 140, 173, 178–9
Alston, Aaron, 126
Ames, Charlotte, 5–6; death of, 6
Ames, William, 5
Antibiotic therapy, 156
Antibiotics, 58, 253–4; 'tailor-made', 217
Arendonk, Dr Arthur M. Van, 260
Arnold, Dr, 188, 190
Aspergilli mould, 144
Atkinson, Dr Nancy, 233
Australia: gains independent penicillin supply, 224; first penicillin patient, 227
Australian National University, 293
Ayrshire Society, 169

Bacillus brevis, 106n.
Bacillus pyocyaneus, 62, 76, 93
Baker, W., 216
Banks, Sir Joseph, 273
Banting, Sir Frederick, 30
Barnes, Dr J. M., 70, 92–3
Barry, Dr Hugh, 228
Bazeley, Dr Percival, 224–9, 231–3
Bernhauer, Professor Konrad, 298, 300
Best, Charles Herbert, 30
Binney, Sir George, 21–2
Blackett, Lord Patrick, 291–2
Blamey, General Sir Thomas, 223
Boaze, Professor, 215
Bodenham, Dr Dennis, 70, 163–5, 181, 197; acts as guinea-pig for determining penicillin injections, 164; produces cream for burns, 164
Bouin, Professor, 39
Bowen, Mrs Molly, 53, 232, 290–1
Boyd, Colonel J. S. K., 195
Brain, Lord, 284
3 O

Brebner, Mrs Emmeline, 284–5
Brevi compactum, 59
British Medical Association, 42
British Medical Journal, 58, 268
Brook, Dr Blyth, 256–7
'Broth', 36–7, 64, 81–4, 87, 107, 115, 125, 220, 242, 298
Brotzu, Professor Giuseppe, 255–8
Buchanan, Colonel, 228
Bumstead, Dr John, 176–7
Burnet, Dr F. M., 232
Burtt, Mr, 221
Bush, Dr Vannevar, 151, 153–4
Bushnell General Hospital, 182
Button, Lt-Col. Eardley, 202

Cairns, Professor Hugh, 14, 73, 119, 161, 195, 199–201, 203 ,208, 214
Cajal, Ramon y, 16, 39
Callow, Mr, 221
Callow, Ruth, 117
Campbell-Renton, Miss, 68
Carlson, A. J., 27
Carr, Dr, 170
Cephalosporin C, 258–60, 268, 273, 278; commercial production of, 259
Cephalosporium, power of, 255–9
Chain, Sir Ernst Boris, 37, 48, 51–2, 56, 59, 61–4, 67, 70, 73–7, 81–3, 87–94, 97–8, 106, 108–10, 116, 122, 126–7, 133–4, 146, 171, 208, 215–17, 220–1, 235–6, 244–5, 249–51, 255, 297, 300; joins Howard Florey as head of biochemical section, 49; his affinity with Florey, 56; experiments made by, 81–4; enthusiasm of, 82; injects mice with penicillin and success of experiment, 92–3
Chamberlain, Neville, 72, 94
Chambers, Robert, 27
Charles, J. H. V., 85
Chemotherapy, 31
Chifley, Ben, 262
Churchill, Sir Winston, 94, 169, 209, 211 and n., 219, 222, 226, 236, 243
Clampert, Molly, 8
Clark, Dr Mansfield, 154
Clostridium septique, 103
Clutterbuck, Dr P. W., 91
Cochran, Harold, 226

Telephone : Oxford 2273.
Telegrams: Pathology—Oxford.

SIR WILLIAM DUNN SCHOOL OF PATHOLOGY
UNIVERSITY OF OXFORD

Aug 2nd 1942

Dear Sir Charles,

Thank you very much indeed for sending me a copy of your lecture. It is most kind of you to have remembered me in this way. I was most disappointed that I did not see you when you were in Oxford but was delighted to hear that you were in the best of spirits.

We are all pretty busy here — we've had 48 weeks of teaching this year, finding through the medical students. A certain amount of research is going on but it is a matter of filling in large numbers of forms these days to keep anyone on the job.

The penicillin work is moving along & we now have a fairly substantial plant for making it here. It is most tantalising really, as there is, for me, no doubt

that we really have a most potent
weapon against all common sepsis.
My wife is doing the clinical work & getting
astonishing results — almost miraculous some of
them.   Our last case was a cavernous
Sinus thrombosis caused by a staphylococcus.
From the moment we gave the drug he started to
improve — he was comatose at one stage.
In a week he was peevish because he was
not allowed a newspaper.   I am afraid
the synthesis of the substance is rather distant
but if, say, the price of 2 bombers & some
energy was sunk into the project we could
really get enough to do a considerable amount.
We also have another lot of anti-bacterial
substances from moulds & plants under
investigation   & apart from the prospect of
some immediate use in the war there
substances are full of interest & open up
quite a vista.
       Our children are still with the Fultons.
They are growing apace & are being looked after
with great skill — there will be no holding them
when they come back.
my wife sends her warmest remembrances.
       with very best wishes
                                Yours sincerely
                                H. W. Florey.